D1433902

Lucan is the wild maverick among Latin epic poets: sneered at for over a century for failing to conform to humanist canons of taste and propriety, in recent years his work has been gaining in reputation. *Poetry and civil war in Lucan's 'Bellum Civile'* is a book founded on a genuine admiration for Lucan's unique, perverse and spellbinding masterpiece.

Above all, argues Dr Masters, the poem is obsessed with civil war, not only as the subject of the story it tells, but as a metaphor which determines the way that story is told. In these pages, he discusses in detail a number of selected episodes from the poem which illustrate this principle, and on this basis he offers a fresh and challenging perspective on most of the important issues in Lucanian studies – Lucan's political stance and his attitude to Caesar, his iconoclastic relation to Virgil and the epic tradition, his distortion of history and geography, his inconsistency, his self-destructive narrative technique and, finally, the apparent incompleteness of his poem.

This book is a major re-evaluation, provocative and persuasive, of a central figure in the history of Latin epic.

CAMBRIDGE CLASSICAL STUDIES

General Editors
M.F. BURNYEAT, M.K. HOPKINS, M.D. REEVE,
A.M. SNODGRASS

POETRY AND CIVIL WAR IN LUCAN'S *BELLUM CIVILE*

POETRY AND CIVIL WAR IN
LUCAN'S *BELLUM CIVILE*

JAMIE MASTERS

Research Fellow, Clare College
Cambridge

The right of the
University of Cambridge
to print and sell
all manner of books
was granted by
Henry VIII in 1534.
The University has printed
and published continuously
since 1584.

CAMBRIDGE UNIVERSITY PRESS

CAMBRIDGE

NEW YORK   PORT CHESTER

MELBOURNE   SYDNEY

CAMBRIDGE UNIVERSITY PRESS
Cambridge, New York, Melbourne, Madrid, Cape Town,
Singapore, São Paulo, Delhi, Tokyo, Mexico City

Cambridge University Press
The Edinburgh Building, Cambridge CB2 8RU, UK

Published in the United States of America by
Cambridge University Press, New York

www.cambridge.org
Information on this title: www.cambridge.org/9780521414609

First published 1994

A catalogue record for this publication is available from the British Library

Library of Congress cataloguing in publication data
Masters, Jamie.
Poetry and civil war in Lucan's Bellum civile / Jamie Masters,
p.   cm. - (Cambridge classical studies)
Revision of thesis (Ph. D.)
Includes bibliographical references and index.
ISBN 0 521 41460 1
1. Lucan, 39-65. Pharsalia. 2. Rome - History - Civil War, 49-48
B.C. - Literature and the war. 3. Caesar, Julius, in fiction, drama,
poetry, etc. I. Title. II. Series.
PA6480.M35 1992
873'.01-dc20   91-17707   CIP

ISBN 978-0-521-41460-9 Hardback
ISBN 978-0-521-04172-0 Paperback

for Annie
pars alia nostra

CONTENTS

ix

CONTENTS

MAPS

PREFACE

The appearance of Ahl's *Lucan: an introduction* in 1976 was momentous. His work, eloquent in its presentation, comprehensive in its aspirations, and motivated by a genuine interest in the poem, represented a consummation of all that was good in the critical tradition. At a stroke he made us a generation of post-Ahlians. His faults were many – in particular, his desire to smooth over the difficulties of Lucan's politics – and he will often be the principal target of my attack; but at his best he was admirable, and at his worst could not be ignored.

Johnson's *Momentary monsters* (1987) was about an attitude; rigidly refusing to be drawn into a close reading of the text, but having at his command powers of rhetoric that surpassed Ahl's – and even Lucan's – he brought to Lucanian studies a delirious enthusiasm which, if not quite rescuing the poet from the ranks of the second-rate, at least demanded that he be taken seriously on his own terms.

These two works are high points in Lucanian scholarship. There are others, as important but less obviously monumental. But their impact has only just begun to bring about a Lucanian revolution, and the mainstream of criticism still fails to treat the Bellum Civile with much more sympathy than the scholars of a century ago. The ghost of the 'courtisan brillant' (Pichon), the 'hot-headed Spaniard' (Rose), the 'marvellous boy' (Kenney), has stubbornly resisted exorcism.

The present work is motivated by a deep personal admiration for the poem, and by a desire to see Lucan treated with the same kind of respect and attention to detail that is characteristic of Virgilian criticism. As long as we believe Lucan to have been fallible, we will always find evidence for his fallibility. We confirm traditional literary history (which needs the silver age to protect the value of the golden), but we lose a great poet; and that is an exchange by which I cannot see we gain. I attempt here to reverse it.

xiii

In the course of writing this book, which is a revised version of my PhD dissertation, I have accumulated a fair number of debts. I particularly want to thank Denis Feeney, Stephen Hinds, Philip Hardie and Neil Wright, who have always read my work with great care, and have been unfailing in their encouragement. Alison Sharrock was my amateur mentor; the technical advice of Desmond Schmidt was invaluable at the word-processing stage. I should also like to thank my examiners, Michael Reeve and Don Fowler, whose keen and incisive observations formed the basis for the revision of my dissertation; and similarly Charles Martindale, who read through the dissertation a short time after my examination; I may not always have acted upon their advice, but I have certainly profited from it.

Finally, three special debts: John Henderson (who supervised me), Jaś Elsner, and Emily Gowers. My friends, my anxiety of influence.

1

CAESAR AT THE RUBICON

When Caesar finally appears as an actor, after Lucan's extensive introduction at the beginning of book 1 (1–182), he crosses a number of boundaries. First is the Alps, whose crossing immediately conjures up reminiscences of Hannibal (picked up a little later by Caesar himself in 1.303–5).[1] But that is a limit casually transgressed;[2] now he comes to the river Rubicon. The tiny stream (*parvi Rubiconis*, 185) is puny in comparison with the hugeness of the enterprise (*ingentis ... motus*, 184), but the huge apparition of Roma (*ingens ... patriae trepidantis imago*, 186)[3] steps in as if to reinforce it, and in her appeal to Caesar to go no further, re-emphasises the sanctity of the Rubicon as a limit which no army may legally transgress:[4]

---

[1] The motif of Hannibal's invasion is played on extensively in the *Bellum Civile*: the civil war is worse than Hannibal's invasion (or Pyrrhus'), 1.30–1; Caesar recrosses the Alps backwards in 3.299; Pompey illogically chooses not to go to Spain because he does not want to cross the Alps (even though he is travelling by sea) – presumably he does not want to be a Hannibal like Caesar, 2.630; Caesar attacking Massilia like Hannibal attacking Saguntum, 3.350; Curio fighting in Libya has many Hannibalian (and Jugurthan) overtones – see Ahl 1976 chapter 3; Goebel 1981 p. 87 notes a parallel with Livy's Hannibal in the second half of Caesar's speech before Pharsalus; Caesar is worse than Hannibal in not burying his fallen enemies, 7.799–801; Pompey mistrusts the Mauri because they remember Hannibal, 8.284; more general references to Carthage and Libya abound, e.g. 3.157, 2.91, 8.269. Just as Caesar often plays the part of Hannibal, so Pompey is characterized by *delay*, as was Fabius.

[2] Lebek 1976 p. 116: 'Die Einleitung passt zu Lucans Konzeption von Caesars blitzartigem Handeln'.

[3] On *ingens* and *parvus* here, see Narducci 1980 p. 175 n. 3.

[4] Many models are suggested for the apparition. Thompson and Bruère 1968 p. 6: Ascanius and Apollo in *Aen.* 9.638ff, the ghost of Hector in *Aen.* 2.270ff, and of Creusa in 2.772–4; Grimal 1970 p. 56: Cicero's prosopopoeia in *Cat.* 1.17ff; Lausberg 1985 p. 1589: Achilles prevented by

1

'quo tenditis ultra?
quo fertis mea signa, viri? si iure venitis,
si cives, huc usque licet.' (190–2)

Caesar is struck with terror, and stops right on the verge of crossing ('languor *in extrema* tenuit vestigia *ripa*', 194), but none the less attempts to argue the point; and excusing himself to Roma in a grandiose address (195–203) makes his fatal decision, and crosses:

inde moras solvit belli tumidumque per amnem
signa tulit propere. (204–5)

The river, we notice, has suddenly become *tumidum*, a last-ditch attempt to oppose the *ingentis motus* where the *ingens imago* had failed. But apparently to no avail. Caesar's crossing is celebrated with the simile of the Libyan lion who, having brooded and stalked long enough, suddenly attacks and bursts through a group of hunters (205–12).[5]

No, that is not quite right. In spite of the 'undoing of delay', the perfect in 'tulit' and the adverb 'propere', Caesar has not crossed the river yet; or if he has, he must do it again.[6] For with line 213 we are back to where we started.

fonte cadit modico parvisque inpellitur undis
puniceus Rubicon... (213–14)

Athena from drawing his sword (*Il.* 1.194ff); *ibid.* p. 1606: Achilles and the Scamander (*Il.* 21.211ff). On the historical sources and parallels, see Narducci 1980.

[5] Getty 1940 ad loc. says this simile comes from *Aeneid* 12.4–8 and from *Iliad* 20.164–74; and compares Sen. *Oed.* 919–20. Thompson and Bruère 1968 p. 8 add *Aeneid* 10.726–8 of Mezentius as an aggressive lion. See also Lebek 1976 pp. 120–1, Ahl 1976 pp. 105–6, and Lausberg 1985 p. 1584. All the commentators have missed the obvious point that Lucan's lion, inasmuch as he runs himself through by leaping at the hunters' spears, is pointing up Caesar's *suicide*; the effects of the civil war are that Caesar obscurely destroys himself: so also the ambiguity of 'in sua templa furit' 1.155, going back to the proem 'in sua victrici conversum viscera dextra' (1.3). Albrecht (1970 p. 287) at least sees the lion's death as a premonition of Caesar's assassination.

[6] The repetition of the river-crossing is noticed by Goerler 1976, who argues that repetition allows Lucan to depict the same event from two different points of view (Caesar's, and the soldiers').

This introduces seven lines of ecphrasis on the river (213–19) which pick up the earlier *parvi Rubiconis ad undas*, and explain why the river is – has been all along – swollen (as in 204); here too the notion of the Rubicon as a boundary is given due emphasis ('Gallica certus / limes ab Ausoniis disterminat arva colonis', 215–16). And now, finally, the crossing, given to us for a second time – but it is not Caesar who crosses: *primus*, which we expect to agree with Caesar, in fact agrees with *sonipes* (conveniently singular for plural); then the whole army crosses *en masse*; then ... Caesar is already across (*superato gurgite*, 223): *his* crossing has been passed over.

It is quite an extraordinary opening sequence: of course Lucan is making a deliberate play of the contradiction between Caesar's urgency and his own expansive, repetitive narrative. *Mora* itself is a boundary that Caesar is trying to break through: Lucan's account sets up a series of narrative devices that obstruct Caesar's progress, that impose boundaries he must cross. Indeed, that the Rubicon crossing is a 'scene' at all implies a stopping of the narrative before it has really got started, all the more so if we remember that Caesar's *Commentary* had ignored the Rubicon, and made the capture of Ariminum immediately afterwards the first of Caesar's actions in the civil war.

But more boundaries follow. In his eagerness to prosecute the war with all speed, Caesar breaks with normal Roman military practice and marches by night[7] (swift as an arrow or a shot from a sling, 229–30), and arrives at Ariminum, which is the *Latii claustra*, the gateway of Latium (1.253). It is daybreak: a boundary of time that marks the very first day of the war:

> ... vicinumque minax invadit Ariminum, et ignes
> solis Lucifero fugiebant astra relicto.
> iamque dies primos belli visura tumultus
> exoritur. (231–4)

This sunrise is the first of two that Lucan gives us for this single day,[8] a repetition which, if not as illogical as the repeti-

---

[7] Thompson and Bruère 1968 p. 7.   [8] Syndikus 1958 p. 15.

3

tion of the river-crossing, none the less serves a similar purpose: to multiply the boundaries, and trip up the narrative.
The second sunrise is ironically accompanied by protestations
of urgency:

> noctis gelidas lux solverat umbras.
> ecce, faces belli dubiaeque in proelia menti
> urguentes addunt stimulos cunctasque pudoris
> *rumpunt fata moras.* (261–4)

Having captured Ariminum, Caesar is faced with the problem of justifying himself to his troops. That this is another
mora and another boundary for Caesar to cross is clear from
the simile of the race-horse straining to cross the starting-line:[9]

> ... accenditque ducem, quantum clamore iuvatur
> Eleus sonipes, quamvis iam carcere clauso
> immineat foribus pronusque repagula laxet. (293–5)

Eventually, after Caesar has confused his troops with pseudo-
Aenean rhetoric,[10] Laelius manages to bring them round, and
they shout approval. But Caesar must now call up his forces
from Gaul, which are enumerated in a long, delaying, catalogue;[11] and typically, ironically, the delay is coupled with the
insistence on *no* delay:

> [Caesar] nequo languore moretur
> fortunam, sparsas per Gallica rura cohortes
> evocat... (393–5)

And finally, with his forces assembled and ready to go, he
moves on. But then Lucan switches to an account of the panic
at Rome that lasts until half-way through book 2; Caesar is
left stranded by Lucan's capriciously changing narrative. If we

---

[9] Note the 'imagery of cosmic dissolution' in *repagula laxet*; for which see
Lapidge 1979 p. 349 on the Stoic terms εἰρμός and ἀναλύω, and pp. 363ff
on Lucan's application of such terms as metaphors in the action of the
poem.

[10] For Caesar's pose as a new Aeneas, see Ahl 1976 p. 202 and 209ff, and
Martindale 1984 p. 69.

[11] See Mendell 1942 esp. p. 5 for the delaying effect of geographical catalogues in Velleius Polybius and Curtius. Note too Ovid's catalogue of
dogs in *Met*. 3, 'quosque referre mora est' (3.225). On delay in Lucan's
catalogues, see chapter 3 pp. 54–5.

wish to extend this thesis further, as I think we should, we may note that the whole of the introductory portion of the book, so far as we know unique in narrative epic inasmuch as in its 182 lines it contains no action, just general reflection on Lucan's part (as well as an invocation of Nero), is a device to delay the Rubicon scene.[12]

So far so good; but what is the point? What does Lucan gain by this delay and this emphasis on boundaries and their transgression? In the first place, it gives substance to Lucan's starting-point; with the crossing of the Rubicon, the story begins, and Caesar crosses out of the mist of history into the action of the poem. As a second explanation, we might follow the line taken by Thompson and Bruère, and say that these transgressions emphasise Caesar's impiety, especially since the Rubicon-limit is sanctified by the apparition of Roma herself, and since the heavily Virgilian feeling of Caesar's reply to Roma lays bare, by its allusions to the piety of Aeneas and Ascanius, Caesar's hypocrisy.[13]

This is fair enough, but we can do more. Lucan is always on the sidelines, so to speak; often entering into the poem in his own person, he shouts encouragement or cries out in dismay.[14] But, powerless as Lucan may be to prevent the final catastrophe, he has at least the power, as poet, of delaying it within his poem; we can conclude, then, that Lucan is anxious

---

[12] Hence, perhaps, some irony in the introductory discussion of Crassus who was a *mora* for civil war (1.100) – the discussion itself is a *mora*. Dr P.R. Hardie (*per litteras*) has suggested another humorous point: 'iam' in 183 implies that, during the overextended prologue, Caesar has had time to cross the Alps! (Though of course it plays on an epic cliché: see Lebek 1976 p. 116 and n. 12.) On the baroque expansion of the prologue, see Albrecht 1970 pp. 284–5.

[13] Thompson and Bruère 1968 p. 7 on the Virgilian parallels in this speech. Their general thesis that Virgilian allusions point up by contrast Caesar's hypocritical impiety is too simple to be all-embracing, and does Lucan's ingenuity little credit; but that is only a small blemish in an otherwise useful article.

[14] See esp. Syndikus 1958 pp. 39–43; also Albrecht 1970 p. 273; Ahl 1976 p. 151; Williams 1978 p. 234; Mayer 1981 ad 8.827; Johnson 1987 p. 7; and Lausberg 1985 p. 1571 for a cautionary note on the extent of Lucan's innovativeness in this respect.

to display his reluctance to allow the action to proceed, and he achieves this by erecting barriers that are at once literary and artificial. But again there is more. Although Lucan is reluctant, he does yet continue the action; and in writing the poem he is allowing the civil war to be re-enacted, he *is* re-enacting the war.

Cairns[15] notes the standard convention whereby the author of a poem can describe himself as doing what he is writing about; this convention is fully explored by Lieberg,[16] who traces its use from before Virgil till well into Late Latin literature, and indeed detects its influence in some modern European literature. Lieberg restricts himself to examining those passages where poetry itself is explicitly the subject of discussion, places where, for instance, the bucolic poet is represented as a shepherd or the elegist as a lover, where the poet of an Iliad is seen as acting out himself the role of Achilles. From this convention Lieberg goes on to deduce the possibility that ancient poets regarded language – their poetry – as somehow constitutive of reality. Crucially for our discussion, Lieberg shows us that time and time again the poet of *war* is represented as a military commander, a *dux*;[17] more generally, since the poet is as often represented as a warrior,[18] we might say that the epic poet is strongly identified with his protagonists, be they generals or warriors; and the same applies to the other genres, in which the dramatic poet identifies with his actors, and the bucolic poet with his shepherds.

Lieberg does not make the final step (although he comes very close to doing so) of assuming that the convention of the poet as protagonist extends, beyond the context of explicit discussions of poetry within a poem, to exert its influence even on passages where no specific 'literary' point is immediately discernible, that is to say, on the structure, subject and treatment of the poem as a whole. But the step is a natural one, and

---

[15] 1972 p. 163 and n. 6.

[16] 1982 passim; chapter 1 (on Virgil) however summarises the main points of the rest of the book.

[17] *Ibid.* p. 88, 94; so also the historian Pollio, p. 75.

[18] *Ibid.* pp. 56ff, as Achilles; pp. 69–70; p. 89; p. 90; pp. 99–100, as Jason; p. 103.

it will become central to my position that Lucan, in spite of the comparative scarcity of *explicit* literary self-reference in his poem, identifies strongly with his two main protagonists (and with many of the lesser figures); so strongly that, to some extent, the poem is its own commentary: the actions performed within it (the subject-matter), and the struggles of its creator to narrate those actions (the 'composition-myth'),[19] run in symbolic parallel.

For Caesar to wage war is, in Lucan's terms, for the poet to compose epic. But we may press Lieberg's conclusions still further. If the poet's composition is constitutive of reality, if the poet, like Amphion,[20] magically 'creates' a reality through song, then in the same sense Lucan is 'creating' the civil war, he is actually 'waging a war', a war which, as we are told right at the beginning, is a *nefas*; surely too the poetic re-enactment of the war can be censured as being a cognate *nefas*. If the war is as evil as Lucan tells us it is, then the blame must rub off on the poet as much as it is attributable to his protagonists. Lucan has the choice: he need not write this poem; but he does, and it is at the Rubicon, the start of the action proper, that he makes his decision, and thus becomes a counterpart of the Caesar that he is portraying.

Seen from this point of view, the apparition of Roma takes on the quality of a literary *revocatio*, where, standardly, an authority figure appears (usually in a dream, hence the dream vocabulary *visa ... imago*, 186) to deter the poet from writing the poem he has started on.[21] Roma confronts Caesar and tells him to turn back; so Roma metaphorically confronts

---

[19] On this concept, see chapter 4, p. 139.

[20] Lieberg 1982 pp. 37–9 discusses the implications of the figure of Amphion, who built the walls of Thebes by singing.

[21] The *revocatio* was so overworked in the Augustan age that it is hardly surprising if Lucan feels no need to signal it – particularly since it had, by his time, reached such a height of sophistication that almost any authority figure could be substituted for the original Apollo. Examples are: Virg. *Ecl.* 6.3ff (Apollo); Hor. *Sat.* 1.10.31ff (Quirinus); *Sat.* 2.6.13ff (Horace himself); *Odes* 4.15 (Apollo); Prop. 3.3.13ff (Apollo); 4.1 (Horos); Ov. *Am.* 1.1 (Cupid); *Ars* 2.493ff (Apollo); liminal cases are Hor. *Sat.* 2.1 (Trebatius) and *Epist.* 1.1.7–9 (unnamed). The original *revocatio* is in the prologue to Callimachus' *Aetia*. See Wimmel 1960 pp. 135–42.

Lucan and tells him to desist from writing the *Bellum Civile*; and Lucan, as Caesar, unlike almost all the other poets who included *revocationes* in their works, refuses to comply. The identification of the Roma apparition passage as a *revocatio* is confirmed by an unmistakable allusion to Propertius 4.1. Here Propertius, who is about to write a grand poem on the ancient greatness of Rome, is confronted by Horos, who cries out 'quo ruis imprudens, vage, dicere fata, Properti?' (4.1.71), possibly parallel to Roma's 'quo tenditis ultra? / quo fertis mea signa, viri?' (1.190–1) – and advises him to write elegy instead. But just before Horos interrupts, Propertius, referring to his projected poem, addresses Roma in the following words:

> *Roma, fave*, tibi surgit opus, date candida cives
> omina, et *inceptis* dextera cantet avis! (4.1.67–8)

which is clearly alluded to in Lucan's 'Roma, fave coeptis' (1.200).[22] So Lucan, in ignoring this *revocatio*, is disobeying the sacred command of a divine figure, and is hence as impious as Caesar; and it is through Caesar that he enacts his own impiety. In spite of delay and hesitation, Lucan allows the action to continue; for being, in a sense, himself Caesar, he is as anxious as Caesar to move on.

But there are two sides (only two?) to any struggle. Lucan may be Caesarian in his ambition to recount, and thus recreate, the horrors of civil war, but none the less there *is* reluc-

---

[22] On *coeptum* as 'poetic endeavour' see Sharrock 1988 ad Ov. *Ars* 2.38. Statistically speaking, in the thirty-odd examples of *coeptum* as a substantive in Ovid, Virgil, Pseudo-Virgil, Lucretius, and Manilius (it does not appear in Horace, Propertius or Tibullus), fourteen explicitly refer to the matter or making of poetry: Ov. *Met.* 1.2, *Fast.* 4.784, 6.652, 6.798, *Ars* 1.30, 3.671, *Rem.* 704, *Pont.* 2.5.30, *Trist.* 2.555; [Virg.] *Culex* 25, 41; Virg. *Georg.* 1.40; Lucretius 1.418; Manilius 3.36. A further four seem to me to be eminently arguable cases of the type I am now discussing: Ov. *Met.* 7.194–5 (Medea's potions), Ov. *Met.* 8.200 and *Ars* 2.38 (Daedalus and Icarus), and Virg. *Aen.* 9.625 (Ascanius). *Coeptus* as an adjective qualifying a word like *labor* often bears the same explicit sense (e.g. Ov. *Ars* 1.771) but the statistics are not so compelling; so too with the substantival *inceptum*, of which the explicit examples are Prop. 4.1.68 and Hor. *A.P.* 14; and the adjectival 'inceptum ... laborem' at Virg. *Georg.* 2.39.

8

tance, there *is* 'mora', the narrative *does* make the gesture of tying itself in knots in order to obstruct the progress of its demonic protagonist. And in this weak, plaintive resistance to the evil of reenacting evil, we see another part of the schizophrenic poetic persona; another Lucan who has more in common with the figure of Pompey. For delay is Pompey's character-note: as Fabius to Caesar's Hannibal (see note 1), he wages his war above all by avoiding conflict, by escaping first from Rome, then from Italy altogether; he cannot bring himself to crush Caesar at Dyrrachium,[23] and must be bullied by his supporters into committing himself to battle at Pharsalus.[24] His desire to defer the end and prolong the now comes across very clearly, too, in his parting from Cornelia at the end of book 5.[25]

In the struggle between Caesar and Pompey, then, lies the paradigm of Lucan's narrative technique: the conflict between the will to tell the story and the horror which shies from telling it, between arrogant confidence in the triumph of evil, and a weak timidity that perforce identifies itself with piety, virtue, *fas*. The parallel can be developed further. Pompey represents the past: as an old oak that is honoured because of its antiquity, honoured simply because it has always been honoured, Pompey, the shadow of a great name, is a once-great general who now rests on his laurels. Caesar, by contrast, is powerful *now*, a bolt of lightning that will (we suppose) blast this past glory. Pompey is practically an old man (1.129–30); Caesar, by implication (though not in fact), practically a youth. Young opposes old; novelty opposes tradition; and in this dualism we see the conflict at the heart of Lucan's relation to the epic genre. To write epic at all involves some allegiance to the tradition, and for that reason Pompey, the symbolic embodiment of Lucan's poetic heritage (one thinks of Virgil in particular),[26] is what Lucan would like to be. But in this admiration

---

[23] 6.299ff.   [24] 7.51–123.

[25] 5.722–815; see esp. 732–3, 'blandaeque iuvat ventura trahentem / indulgere morae et tempus subducere fatis'.

[26] Interestingly, Quintilian used the Pompeian image of the dead but sacred tree to describe the poet Ennius (*Inst. Or.* 10.1.88).

there is always an 'anxiety of influence';[27] and to use Bloom's terms, the 'strong' poet, the 'ephebe', must represent the past as corrupt, dead, tottering – must, indeed, destroy it, in order to earn the honour that the past will not relinquish; the new poet standing at the end of a tradition must be a Caesar.

The poem is a civil war. Lucan is Caesarian in his ambition, but Pompeian in his remorse; the Pompeian in him condemns Caesar, but the Caesarian in him condemns – kills – Pompey. This paradox, this internal discord which aligns the poet with each party and with both simultaneously and with neither, is one of the fundamental premises of the poem's violent logic, and will be the basis for much of what I will have to say in the ensuing chapters.

[27] The title of an influential work by Bloom (1973).

2

MASSILIAN COMPILATION

Lucan's description of the naval engagement at Massilia is the earliest extant full treatment of a sea battle in Latin poetry; which is not to say that no Roman poet had treated sea battles before him. Roman sea-power had been important since the first Punic war, and no doubt Naevius' *Punica* had dealt with one or more of the significant sea battles; Ennius certainly treated naval affairs in his *Annals*: we possess some fragments that may come from descriptions of sea battles, and others dealing with training and fitting of fleets.[1] One phrase at least from Ennius, 'pectora pellite tonsis' (fr. 218 Skutsch), seems to find its place in Lucan, 'remis pectora pulsant' (3.543), suggesting, if not that Lucan is here alluding to Ennius, then that he is writing within a tradition of sea-battle episodes in epic, a tradition to which Ennius had contributed.[2] But the details of this tradition must remain largely a matter of guesswork; and consequently we are not able to do for sea battles what, for instance, Morford (1967, pp. 205–58) has done with storms; so our analysis of the episode must be approached from other angles.

Perhaps the most obvious paradigm for Massilia would be Actium, inasmuch as both battles were fought during a civil war. No treatment of Actium on the scale of Lucan's treatment of Massilia survives,[3] but it is worth while making a broad comparison with Virgil's rather brief description of the

---

[1] See Skutsch 1985 ad *Ann.* 217–9, 238, 294–6, 375–80.

[2] Conte 1970 p. 135 sees an allusion; Pichon 1912 pp. 217–8 (and afterwards Skutsch 1985 ad *Ann.* 218) denies one. On the general issue of Ennian influence, see Conte 1970 and Albrecht 1970 pp. 277–80.

[3] A few lines of a *Bellum Actiacum* were recovered from the ruins of Herculaneum, date and author unknown, but obviously composed between the time of Actium and the eruption of Vesuvius. None of these fragments deal with the battle itself. See Benario 1983.

battle and Augustus' ensuing triumph as pictured on Aeneas' shield in *Aen.* 8.675–728. As for the battle itself, Virgil has little in common with Lucan, taking only seven lines to describe the clash of ships, the exchange of weapons and the bloodying of the sea (689–95), and concentrating instead on visual portraits of the protagonists, and the intervention of the gods (the latter, of course, inadmissible in Lucan's epic).[4] But the notion that Antony has behind him the combined forces of the East (685–88), and the – admittedly very scanty – lists of foreign peoples defeated (705–6) and paraded in Augustus's triple triumph (724–8), provide an unmistakable parallel with Pompey's catalogue which immediately precedes the Massilia episode, and show that the whole narrative from Caesar's entry into Rome to the end of book 3 forms a complex which responds to this climax of Virgil's shield description. In Virgil, Augustus enters Rome triumphant, to the joyful adulation of the people, after Actium (*Aen.* 8.714ff); in Lucan, Caesar enters Rome *before* Massilia without any triumph (*BC* 3.73–9) and *without* the joyful adulation of the people (3.80–2), and where Virgil's Octavian had donated his spoils to the temple of Phoebus (*Aen.* 8.720–1), Lucan's Caesar plunders the temple of Saturn of spoils won in earlier wars (*BC* 3.154–68). Instead of Augustus' triumphal parade of conquered eastern peoples (*Aen.* 8.722–8), Lucan presents us with a verbal parade of Pompey's forces which consist precisely in his 'triumphs' (so 2.644 'omnes redeant in castra triumphi'), peoples of varied tongues and dress:

> tam variae cultu gentes, tam dissona volgi
> ora   (*BC* 3.289–90)

with which compare Virgil's

> quam variae linguis, habitu tam vestis et armis   (*Aen.* 8.723)

---

[4] On Lucan's omission of 'divine machinery', see e.g. Schönberger 1961 pp. 108ff, Albrecht 1970 p. 270, Le Bonniec 1970 pp. 166ff, Lausberg 1985 pp. 1608–11.

The difference between the two 'parades' is that Pompey's is not so much a triumph as a preemptive funeral procession;[5] Pompey's eastern peoples have not yet been defeated (though they soon will be): we have not yet had an Actium.

Sources

Cassius Dio offers us two paragraphs (41.19; 41.25; and a passing mention at 41.21) which frame his treatment of the Ilerda campaign; Florus has a paragraph (2.13.23) – in fact, proportionately very expansive treatment considering the extreme brevity of his whole history; but he was much influenced by Lucan,[6] and may have taken his cue from him here. From Appian we learn that Caesar was at Massilia when he heard of the mutiny at Placentia, but that is all (*BCiv* 2.47). Plutarch mentions the heroism of one Acilius who fought in the Massilian sea battle (Plut. *Caes.* 16)[7] as an exemplum of the loyalty Caesar inspired; but in his chronological treatment of Caesar's civil war campaign, Massilia is never mentioned. No doubt this is partly because Caesar himself was not present for most of it – he initiated it, and then went off to Spain; but the overall tone of our sources suggests that Massilia is little more than a detour, an annoying obstacle on the way to the important events at Ilerda. So Suetonius: 'et quamquam *obsidione Massiliae*, quae sibi *in itinere* portas clauserat, summaque frumentariae rei penuria *retardante* brevi tamen omnia [sc. in Spain] subegit' (Suet. *Jul.* 34.2); so too Florus: 'sed ad Hispanienses Pompei exercitus *transeunti* per eam [sc. Galliam] duci portas claudere ausa Massilia est' (Flor. 2.13.23). It is paradoxical that if Massilia is to be compared with Actium, of all the campaigns in the civil war it would appear to be one of the least significant.

---

[5] So 3.290–2, 'tot immensae comites missura ruinae / excivit populos et dignas funere Magni / exequias Fortuna dedit'.

[6] Pichon (1912 pp. 70ff) characteristically denied such influence, claiming that apparent coincidences were mediated through Livy; but see Westerburg 1882, Jal 1965 p. 360, and Lintott 1971 pp. 493–4.

[7] See note 29.

Lucan's Massilians themselves plead their unimportance to Caesar:

> vel, cum tanta vocent discrimina Martis Hiberi,
> quid rapidum deflectis iter? non pondera rerum
> nec momenta sumus ...   (3.336–8)

a plea that Caesar dismisses contemptuously in his reply[8]

> vana movet Graios nostri fiducia cursus.
> quamvis Hesperium mundi properemus ad axem
> Massiliam delere vacat.   (3.358–60)

but, as it turns out, Caesar cannot brook the delay, and dashes off to Spain before battle actually begins, leaving his subordinates to continue where he has left off:

> dux tamen inpatiens haesuri ad moenia Martis
> versus ad Hispanas acies extremaque mundi
> iussit bella geri   (3.453–5)

But in spite of this, Lucan's Massilian episode is weighty and extended far beyond its apparent unimportance.[9]

Caesar's commentary contains the only treatment of the Massilian campaign that comes anywhere near to being as full as Lucan's account. We may notice in his version the tendency to make Massilia important in its own right: he arrives in Gaul – no indication that he is only 'passing through' (Caes. *BCiv* 1.33.4) – and hears that Domitius has been sent to Massilia, and that the Massilians are preparing for a siege, so he attempts to negotiate with them (Caes. *BCiv* 1.34–5). Eventually he leaves, having seen to it that his subordinates have everything they need for a successful operation. As the Spanish campaign progresses, we hear more news from Massilia (Caes. *BCiv* 1.56–8), and then after the Spanish campaign is concluded, book 2 opens with a full account of the remainder of the Massilian operation (Caes. *BCiv* 2.1–16). Clearly Caesar's lengthy and detailed commentary offered more scope for a full treatment of this relatively small episode, but that does not

---

[8] Note that *vana fiducia* is a Caesarian sneer at the Massilians' *fides*; on which see Opelt 1957 p. 445 and Rowland 1969 p. 205.

[9] Syndikus 1958 p. 18.

alter the fact that it becomes in Caesar's hands quite a *big* episode, and one which occupies an emphatic place at the beginning of a book.

Such considerations might lead us to conclude that Caesar was Lucan's principal source for the episode; but things are not so simple. Livy too recounted the siege of Massilia, like Caesar (and indeed Dio) using it to frame the story of the Spanish campaign – so much we can tell from the Livian periocha (for book 110). While of course it is impossible to know exactly how Livy treated the episode, we may guess that he did so with detail at least comparable to Caesar's: that Massilia is mentioned at all in the periocha implies more than a passing mention in Livy's lost book; and the phrase *longam obsidionem* (*Periocha* 110.11 Rossbach) might suggest that the siege received lengthy treatment. So it is quite possible that Livy's treatment of the episode was on a scale at least approaching Caesar's; and our next question must be, which of the two was more important to Lucan?

Lacking Livy, of course we cannot say. We can only fall back on a more general issue: how likely is it that Lucan used Livy (or Caesar) as a source for the poem as a whole? The question seemed to have been answered once and for all by Pichon in 1912: Caesar is irrelevant; Lucan consulted only Livy. The influence of Pichon's position was immense; his conclusions were regarded as definitive, and rapidly acquired the status of a *communis opinio*; and so, largely, they remain today. However, the last thirty years have seen some degree of dissatisfaction with the simplicity of Pichon's claims; and while no one would deny that Livy was an important influence on Lucan – the evidence available to us makes that conclusion, at least, inevitable – none the less a succession of commentators have shown in their various ways that the total exclusion of Caesar from the list of influences is as unnecessary as it is unjust.[10]

---

[10] See Griset 1954 pp. 109ff; Haffter 1957 (whose article I will discuss at length in chapter 7); Rambaud 1960; Lintott 1971 pp. 488–9 n. 6 and passim; Ahl 1976 pp. 190–1. Bachofen's dissertation of 1972 undertakes

Pichon's argumentation, in any case, was suspect. In the first place he accepted, with some reservation (though hardly enough), the questionable rule of the 'unity of source' originally formulated by Nissen; so that he was able to maintain that, by and large, ancient historians were faithful to a single secondary source, and had recourse to other sources only in exceptional circumstances. This single source was the one which 'inspired in them the most confidence'; once it was chosen, they felt no need to trace backwards to a more distant, primary source. In sum, Pichon wished to draw a distinction between two historiographical methodologies: the ancient, with its ethic of loyalty (and ultimately of partisanship); and the modern, with its ethic of precision, scientificity, scholarship.[11]

Such a position has its difficulties, some of which even Pichon recognised. The law is not absolute; it cannot be proved; and there are exceptions. Lest we should be tempted to see Lucan as one of the exceptions, Pichon introduced the second stage of his argument. Historians, being casual about the truth, relied on the simplest and most convenient means of deriving their facts; so much the less should Lucan have taken pains to consult more than one main historical source, dilettante that he was:

Rien ne nous permet de croire qu'il fût plus épris d'investigations minutieuses et pénibles qu'on ne l'était communément alors. Son éducation avait été celle de tous les jeunes gens distingués de cette époque, ce qui veut dire que la rhétorique y avait tenu plus de place que l'érudition. Sa vie était celle, non d'un fureteur voué à la compilation savante mais d'un homme du monde, d'un courtisan brillant et spirituel, faisant des vers sur toute espèce de sujets, avec une abondance qui exclut l'idée de lentes recherches ... (p. 53)

to compare at length the material in Caesar and Lucan, but draws no conclusions; the dissertation was supervised by Haffter, and we can only guess that it was intended to support Haffter's position. Syndikus 1958 pp. 1–11 attempts to preserve Pichon's position by relaxing its constraints and admitting the influence of other sources – Caesar excluded. But his discussion is sometimes impossibly circular, as, for instance, when his only evidence for the Livian account is Caesar and Lucan.

[11] Pichon 1912 pp. 52–3.

The jibes are cheap; and unhelpful.[12] But the passage is revealing. Where Pichon fails is in his assumption that *only* the painstaking scholar, devoted to minute research, would care to consult more than one source. The root assumption behind this is that the only motive for using additional sources is to find the truth – what really happened, what can be pieced together from conflicting reports; and this is the aim of scholarship. But truth is not the issue here; for truth is, as we shall come to see, the last thing that Lucan is interested in displaying for us. In those terms, certainly, Lucan is no scholar. But what should be obvious is that even the conscious decision to lie, distort and misrepresent does not preclude the exploitation of more than one source; that the ends of conscious distortion may indeed be *served* by such exploitation.

Viewed from this perspective, the notion of 'source' needs some redefinition. We are moving away from Pichon's narrow sense of source as an author one consults in order to derive information for use in the new work; and towards a concept of source more akin to a literary 'model'. Knowing what we do about the techniques of *imitatio*, we are in a better position to see that Lucan may have chosen his model not as a 'source' for facts – with which, in any case, he was probably largely familiar[13] – but as *a point of departure*. It is in these terms, I believe, that we should view the relationship between Lucan and Caesar. Lucan need not have relied on Caesar for his facts; but I wish here to sustain the hypothesis, advanced first by Griset, Haffter and Rambaud, that Lucan's *Bellum Civile* is a deliberate counterpoise to Caesar's commentary of the same

---

[12] Pichon's view of Lucan's dilettantism is a fantasy that is typical of his time. Since then a growing body of scholarship has demonstrated Lucan's detailed allusion to a remarkable range of other works, implying just the sort of erudition Pichon wanted here (as elsewhere) to deny. For a defence of Lucan's claims as a *doctus poeta*, see chapter 5.

[13] So Lintott 1971 pp. 488–9 n. 6: 'Lucan must have learnt the basic story of the civil war and particular topics for declamation in childhood. He could have written much of the work out of his own head and only needed to refer to a historical work to get material for detailed descriptions. He need not always have referred to the same work.'

name; that, in short, just as Lucan opposes and confronts Virgil in the domain of literary epic, so does he oppose and confront Caesar in the domain of history.

Pichon did not take account of this possibility, and consequently his objections to Caesar as a source do not amount to much. In the first place, he dismissed Caesar's commentary on the grounds that it was not highly regarded (and hence not widely read?) in antiquity. The evidence, however, is thin;[14] and Caesar's works need not have been highly regarded in antiquity for Lucan to have been interested in using them. Secondly, Caesar's account of the civil war was 'inégal ou irregulier', and so did not provide the required 'tableau complet et sûr';[15] but since we are not supposing that Lucan was using Caesar as his sole source for the facts, Caesar's failure to present the full picture does not disqualify him. And finally, Pichon maintains that Caesar's partiality would have been plain to the pro-Pompeian Lucan, and would have made him an unacceptable source.[16] By contrast, Livy's history, if not exactly anti-Caesarian, was at least written with a certain benevolent objectivity.[17] But in the first place it is not possible to derive from Lucan's poem any consistent political stance; I have already had something to say about Lucan's divided 'allegiance' to both Caesar and Pompey, and will have more to say (particularly against Lucan's 'Pompeianism') in later chapters. To call him a Pompeian is largely to miss the point. But in any case neither a purely Pompeian Lucan nor a Lucan with mixed allegiances requires an unbiased source, if the poem is set up to confront that source, and reverse or otherwise distort the biases.

Ultimately the whole question is complicated by the loss of the relevant books of Livy's history. As Pichon points out, any

---

[14] Pichon 1912 pp. 54–5: Cicero and Hirtius do praise Caesar's works, but in Pichon's view can be disregarded because they had a vested interest in so doing. However, Pichon's only evidence for antiquity's low opinion of Caesar as a historian is negative: he is not mentioned by Quintilian except as an orator. That is remarkable; but hardly conclusive.

[15] *Ibid.* p. 55.   [16] *Ibid.* p. 55.   [17] *Ibid.* pp. 58–9.

apparent coincidence between Lucan's and Caesar's accounts can be ascribed to the mediation of Livy, who used Caesar as his source.[18] But it has not been shown that there is any need to suppose such mediation; and there are positive reasons for guessing that Lucan would have consulted Caesar. Caesar is, of course, one of the two main protagonists of Lucan's poem, and it is a poem which has the ostensible aim of doing Caesar down, of retelling the story of the civil war in such a way as to show Caesar in a bad light. This being so, it is hardly conceivable that Lucan would have had no interest in what his evil protagonist had to say for himself in his own account of the war; particularly in view of the strong identification between poet and protagonist which we investigated in the first chapter. Furthermore, and crucially, Lucan's poem deals with the very same period as Caesar's commentary, a period stretching from the crossing of the Rubicon (or, in Caesar's case, a few days earlier) to the beginning of the Alexandrian war. This coincidence of scope, which certainly was not mediated by Livy (whose own disposition of material within books is charted by the periocha), provides strong, positive evidence of the relevance of Caesar's work to Lucan's, and particularly of Lucan's wish to rival Caesar's account.[19]

Because of these general considerations, we can be reasonably confident that, although Lucan may have consulted Livy for the composition of his Massilian episode (we cannot know), Caesar on his own is a significant enough model to merit a detailed comparison. Some preliminary work by Opelt, and by Oliver,[20] has shown how Lucan's account is a recognisable yet profound distortion of what we know from the historiographers, Caesar among them. Since in fact the other sources do not differ from Caesar in any way (apart from a small detail in Cassius Dio), we need feel no misgivings about

[18] *Ibid.* pp. 59ff.

[19] This is Haffter's main contribution to the argument, and it of course entails the assumption that the poem is complete; a position which I defend at length in chapter 7.

[20] Opelt 1957 pp. 435ff; Oliver 1972 pp. 326–9.

taking our cue from Bachofen,[21] and analysing Lucan's deformation of history by a comparison with Caesar's (equally distorted) account, without reference to Livy.

Caesar's and Lucan's Massilia

Sequence of events in:

Caesar	Lucan
(1) Caesar's petition to Massilians (1.35.1–2)	
(2) Massilians' reply (1.35.3–5)	(1) Massilians' petition to Caesar (303–56)
	(2) Caesar's reply (356–72)
(3) Domitius arrives to organise defence of Massilia (1.36.1–3)	(3) Caesar perceives Massilian resistance (373–4)
(4) Therefore Caesar builds ships and siege engines for an attack ... (1.36.4)	(4) Caesar builds a rampart (375–87)
(5) ... involving some timber-cutting (1.36.5)	(5) Deforestation for the rampart (394–8)
	(6) Desecration of the sacred grove (399–452)
(6) Caesar departs (1.36.5)	(7) Caesar departs (453–5)
(*) [Account of the Spanish campaign (1.37–55)]	
(7) First sea battle [at the Stoechades]: Massilians defeated (1.56–8)	[See number 15]
(*) [Account of the Spanish campaign (1.59–87)]	
(8) Trebonius builds siege walls, requiring much timber (2.1)	
	(8) Advance of two towers along the newly constructed rampart (455–62)
(9) Superiority of Massilian artillery (2.2.1-2)	(9) Superiority of Massilian artillery (463–73)

---

[21] Bachofen 1972; specifically on Caesar's and Lucan's Massilian episode, see pp. 11–16 and 101–14.

(10) ... against the advance of the *testudo* (a kind of siege engine) (2.2.3f)	(10) ... against the advance of the *testudo* (a military formation) (474–86)
(11) Arrival of Nasidius with a fleet (2.3)	
(12) Massilians repair their old ships and recruit sailors from young and old (2.4)	[See number 14]
(13) Second sea battle [at Taurois]: Massilians again defeated (2.5–7)	[See number 15]
(14) Caesarians build a tower close to the walls of Massilia... (2.8–10)	
(15) ... from which they undermine and breach the wall in spite of Massilian resistance (2.11.3–4)	(11) Caesarians attempt to undermine the walls but are successfully driven off by the Massilians (487–96)
(16) The Massilians plead for a truce, which is granted (2.12–13)	
(17) The Massilians treacherously break the truce, break out of the city, and burn the siege works (2.14.1–4)	(12) The Massilians break out of the city and set fire to the rampart (497–508)
(18) Trebonius rebuilds the siege wall (2.15)	
(19) The Massilians surrender again (2.16)	
	(13) The Caesarians have recourse to the sea, and arrive at the Stoechades (509–16)
	(14) Massilians recruit sailors from young and old and bring out old ships (516–20)
	(15) Sea battle: Massilians defeated (521–762)

Lucan's account is not, as Rambaud would have it, a case of setting the record straight, by including real events that Caesar had suppressed. [22] Rather, we receive the impression of a contrived, consistent and wilful distortion of the events that Caesar relates; and in the one place where Caesar can be shown to differ from the other historiographical accounts (on the breaking of the truce), Lucan has differed still further.[23] In other words, where Caesar is subtle in his distortions, Lucan is wild and blatant: he utterly out-Caesars Caesar. He has avoided any mention of Domitius or Nasidius, and has reversed the roles of Caesar and the Massilians as aggrieved and aggressor.[24] In Caesar's own account, Caesar was the one who first approached the Massilians for a parley; in Lucan, the Massilians approach Caesar, who arrogantly thrusts them away. Further, in Caesar's account, he claimed that his decision to attack was merely a response to the aggression of Domitius, who had begun to fortify Massilia against him (even while the Massilians were protesting their neutrality). In Lucan, of course, there is no Domitius; the Massilians resist, on their own account, only because they do not wish to be involved in civil war.[25] But motivation is not the only thing that Lucan

[22] Rambaud 1960 p. 162 (the general principle), p. 159 (the inclusion of the grove episode).

[23] Cassius Dio (41.25) has it that it was Caesar's soldiers, rather than the Massilians, who broke the truce; and the siege works were burned in retaliation. Since it is clear that Caesar's version of events is more favourable to his propagandistic purpose, we may well suspect that he is not telling the truth. None the less, it remains the case that Lucan makes no mention at all of the truce, so that the Massilians' sally from the city is an exuberant follow-up to their success so far. See Oliver 1972 p. 326 n. 12.

[24] So Bachofen 1972 p. 103 .

[25] Indeed, Lucan has deprived the episode of any 'serious' motivation. Caesar fights because he is the sort of person who *would* (Bachofen 1972 p. 104, 'Caesars ira ist der Kriegsanlass' – ira being Caesar's character-note); the first major battle of the civil war is fought on the issue of whether or not the Massilians are to be involved in the civil war at all; the disappearance of Domitius from Lucan's account ensures that Caesar has no good reason to attack, and that the battle is one purely between Greeks and Romans – not a civil-war battle at all.

This is typical. Lucan deprives history of its logic; deliberately sets about substituting arbitrariness ('Massiliam delere vacat' 3.360) for military or political necessity in his interpretation of motive; similarly his

has changed; the order of events is also victim to a distortion which we will find absolutely typical of Lucan's dealings with historical material.[26] He has melded two sea battles into one, two sets of land battle into one, and two sets of siege-work building into one;[27] he has made the sea battle into the culmination of the campaign, instead of the breaching of the wall, as in Caesar (and indeed Livy); and has ignored the capitulation of the Massilians. To cap it all, he has expanded his treatment by including the surely fictitious episode of the desecration of the Massilian grove,[28] and by giving us an account of the sea battle replete with grotesque *Einzelszenen* whose historical veracity no one now would think of defending.[29]

An important part of Lucan's deformation of Caesar consists in his refusal to treat the Massilian and Spanish campaigns as simultaneous, jumping back and forth from one to the other, as Caesar does; rather he treats first Massilia as a whole, and then Ilerda as a whole in the next book. For Rambaud this kind of practice is evidence of Lucan's allegiance to the Sallustian monograph style of historical writing, which Lucan chose as a deliberate counterpoise to Caesar's annalistic style; so the primary aim of his writing is to present a series of self-sufficient episodes, rather than an account that

accounts of battles give us no information about tactics, strategy, battle-array; things happen apparently for no better reason than that they happen. On the general issue, see Syndikus 1958 esp. pp. 17–20, and on Massilia, ibid. p. 31 and Opelt 1957 p. 443.

[26] See Fantham 1985 on the Caesarian mutiny in book 5, where elements of two historical mutinies are combined; and on the general issue of historical distortion, Lintott 1971. It is quite evident that Lucan's distortions proceed from a very accurate conception of what really happened, as defences of Lucan's historicity repeatedly show (see e.g. Grimal 1970).

[27] Also two sets of wood chopping. Caesar barely mentions the deforestation the first time round; as Phillips (1968, p. 296) rightly points out, the closest parallel to Lucan's deforestation is enacted by Trebonius much later in the episode.

[28] For the fictitious nature of the grove episode, see Phillips 1968 p. 299.

[29] Opelt 1957 p. 437, 442–3. Only one of the individual scenes (the Massiliote twins, 3.603ff) has its roots in a historical anecdote (the story of the Roman Acilius, as told in Suet. *Jul.* 68.4; Val. Max. 3.2.22; Plut. *Caes.* 16). See Esposito 1988 pp. 97–103.

attempts to maintain an illusion of chronological ordering.[30]
Sallustian influence in general is certainly a major factor in
Lucan's poem,[31] but here there is more to it than that. Caesar's account of events at Ilerda starts when Caesar himself
leaves Massilia for Spain; in other words, the narrative goes
where Caesar goes (as it does always, naturally enough, in
Plutarch's *Life*), and if Massilian events are reported in the
midst of events in Spain in such a way as to suggest the impartiality of the annalistic style, yet the narrative sees to it that
Caesar is never displaced from his central position; the first
Massilian sea battle becomes the turning-point for Caesar's
campaign in Spain – 'hoc proelium Caesari ad Ilerdam nun-
tiatur; simul perfecto ponte celeriter fortuna mutatur' (1.59.1)
– as if success at Massilia was no more than a portent for
Caesar's success elsewhere. Lucan, by refusing to follow Caesar
to Spain before the Massilia story is complete, is challenging
the Caesar-centrism of Caesar's narrative; and also imposing a
delay on Caesar's speedy successes.

Before proceeding any further, it will be useful to consoli-
date the results of my analysis so far. What Lucan has in common with Caesar is that both authors have, as far as Massilia
is concerned, made a mountain out of a molehill: an episode of
really very little importance has been worked up by Caesar
into a mammoth carpentry lesson, and by Lucan into a cosmic
conflict to rival Actium – one would hardly have guessed
that in the first sea battle Brutus had only twelve ships to
the Massilians' seventeen[32] (compare the 900 warships at
Actium). So while Lucan's Massilians may have been right in
historical terms to underrate their own importance, none the
less as far as the *Bellum Civile* is concerned they *are* 'pondera
rerum' and 'momenta', as indeed their name, MASS-ilienses,
implies.

Secondly, in the transition from Caesar's account to
Lucan's, the historical material has undergone a process of

[30] Rambaud 1960 p. 157; cf. Syndikus 1958 p. 77.
[31] Gagliardi 1974; Ahl 1976 p. 120 n. 2; Esposito 1988 pp. 36ff.
[32] Caes. *BCiv* 1.36.4, 1.56.1. In the second sea battle Brutus added six captured Massilian vessels to his fleet bringing his total to eighteen (2.5.1).

considerable *exaggeration*, at the same time as an almost paradoxical *compression*.[33] That is to say: on the one hand Lucan
has removed the intervening blocks of narrative concerned
with the Spanish campaign, and has melded together all events
of a similar nature, so that we are presented with *one* set of
negotiations, *one* siege by land, *one* sea battle, and so on. But
on the other, those single, compressed events (and particularly
the sea battle) are filled out with huge masses of invented
material.

And thirdly, Lucan's treatment of Caesarian material is a
deformation, involving chopping and changing; it is an act of
defiance, an act of rivalry and aggression, perhaps even of
desecration.

The images that I have tried to present as an analysis of
what Lucan is doing with his historical source – mountain,
pondus and *momentum*, mass, exaggeration, compression,
blocks, material, chopping, desecration – are, it is true, my
own interpretative interpolations. None the less, most, if not
all, can be justified as legitimate Latin metaliterary vocabulary; and my reasons for insisting on this set of metaphors will
be obvious: for it will be my claim that the events narrated in
Lucan's text themselves symbolise the process of creating that
text.

The desecration of the grove

The episode, as Phillips rightly argues, is patterned after an
episode in Ovid's *Metamorphoses* where Erysichthon dese-
crates a grove sacred to Ceres (Ov. *Met.* 8.741–76).[34] Lucan's
version itself is something of a desecration, if not specifically
of Ceres' grove, then certainly of Ovidian groves in general:
instead of a *locus amoenus* we are given a *locus foedus*, so to
speak, a vile and eerie forest where the cliché of protection
from the sun is a shadowy threat; where nymphs and demi-

---

[33] So Bachofen 1972 p. 94. On the compression, and the corresponding
paralysis of the narrative, see Syndikus 1958 pp. 55–6.

[34] Phillips 1968 pp. 298–9. Dyson's (1970) suggestion, that Lucan may also
have been inspired by a real event which took place in AD 60 (as related
in Tac. *Ann.* 14.30) is more of biographical than of literary interest.

gods are specifically excluded; where the absence of birds, wild beasts, wind and lightning is not a symptom of Arcadian bliss, but of supernatural terror, where fall (*cadit* 412) black springs instead of cool clear ones. A typically Lucanian twist to an old topos, and, in this sense at least, programmatic; which is to say, the easiest and most blatant way of demonstrating poetic style is to manipulate a poetic commonplace in an individual way; and this kind of interest in the eerie, the grotesque, the darkly supernatural coming from the black wellsprings of inspiration, is a well-known characteristic of the Lucanian manner. With the cutting down of the grove we witness the resurrection of another old topos, whose roots reach back, through Virgil, as far as Homer:

> *procumbunt* orni, nodosa inpellitur *ilex*
> silvaque Dodones et fluctibus aptior alnus ...   (*BC* 3.440–1)

which alludes unmistakably to Virgil's

> *procumbunt* piceae, sonat icta securibus *ilex*
> fraxineaeque trabes cuneis et fissile robur
> scinditur, advolvunt ingentis montibus ornos.   (*Aen.* 6.180–2)

a topos which appears in a different form at *Aen.* 11.135ff; Macrobius (*Sat.* 6.2.27) was the first to point out its predecessor in Ennius (*Ann.* fr. 175–9 Skutsch); it began with Homer (*Iliad* 23.114–22).[35] It should be pointed out at this stage that in Homer, Ennius and Virgil the wood that is thus collected is to be used for funeral pyres: Lucan appears to be unique in using this topos for the collection of material to build a rampart. But in fact, Lucan is definitely playing on these funerary connotations: for the pile of wood making up the rampart *does* eventually burn, and becomes one of a succession of ersatz funeral celebrations which anticipate the grand funeral Pompey will never have; and with the words '*maiorque* iacens apparuit agger' (508) we are surely reminded of Pompeius

---

[35] The parallel is noted by Austin 1977 ad *Aen.* 6.179ff; see also Silius 10.527ff (funeral pyres after Cannae) and Stat. *Theb.* 6.90ff (an expiatory pyre); and on the topos generally, Williams 1968 pp. 263ff.

Magnus,[36] who achieves his true greatness through defeat and death.[37] Now, what makes this topos special is that it enacts itself symbolically. Topos – locus – lucus[38] is one avenue; but, more importantly, *silva*, like Greek ὕλη, is often used as a metaphor with the sense 'material, subject-matter'.[39] Thus deforestation becomes a metaphor for the plundering of poetic material from another source, and inasmuch as this example of deforestation is itself continually a topos that comes from another source, we see that it enacts on the plane of epic action what it represents on the plane of literary activity.

Of the grove episode as a whole, then, we see that this act of desecration, this hewing and carting of wood as material for a huge structure, is an analogue for Lucan's treatment of his predecessors' material in his own poem. Moreover, the theme of forests, woods, trees and deforestation is widespread throughout the whole of the poem: we have already seen, for instance, the rather less expansive description of the cutting down of trees to make a barricade at Brundisium:

> tunc placuit caesis innectere vincula silvis
> roboraque inmensis late religare catenis   (2.670–1)

and Caesar's hypocritical complaint that against him 'in classem cadit omne nemus' (1.306). One reason for Lucan's insistence on this particular metaphor of literary plundering is that it ties into a nexus of tree / grove imagery whose centre is Pompey, as he is described in the famous oak simile of book 1. Indeed, so strong is the parallel between that simile and this desecration, that many critics have rightly seen the latter as a literalisation of the former: when Caesar cuts down the first oak, this is symbolic of his victory over Pompey.[40] The grove

---

[36] For *maior* as a constant pun on Pompey's nickname, see Mayer 1981 ad 8.78.

[37] See Feeney 1986(A) p. 243.

[38] See Hinds 1987 pp. 36–42 for the constant play in ecphraseis on locus/lucus/lacus.

[39] *OLD* s.v. silva 5(b).

[40] Rosner-Siegel 1983 pp. 175–6; Ahl 1976 p. 156 n. 18, p. 199; Rowland 1969 pp. 206–7.

is old and has been untouched for years ('longo numquam violatus ab aevo' 3.399; 'belloque intacta priore' 3.427) as Pompey's oak is old (that is, dead (1.138ff) and decorated with ancient offerings (1.137)) revealing Pompey's status as representative of tradition and the past;[41] and further, the resurrection of old things long untouched has been a recurrent theme in the poem so far: first, when the men of Ariminum bring out their old and decayed weapons ('deripuit sacris adfixa penatibus arma / quae pax longa dabat' 1.240–1); then when Caesar plunders the treasury ('eruitur templo multis non tactus ab annis / Romani census populi' 3.156–7). Soon the Massilians are to reach back into their resources in order to build up their naval power:

> ... omne suum fatis voluit committere robur
> *grandaevosque senes* mixtis armavit ephebis.
> accepit non sola viros, quae stabat in undis,
> classis: et *emeritas repetunt navalibus alnos* (3.517–20)

The topos in general can be taken to symbolise the resurrection of epic style and epic subject-matter; so here, when what is being brought into use is quite literally *material* (*silva*), the self-referential metaphor is particularly strong.[42] Moreover, the grove itself is literally a place of resurrection:

> iam fama ferebat ...
> ... procumbentis *iterum consurgere* taxos (3.417–9)

which is a vague reminiscence of the Roman matron's vision:

> *consurgunt* partes *iterum*, totumque per orbem
> rursus eo (1.692–3)

The grove is, in this sense, a model of the civil war, where what falls rises again;[43] and, given the basic identity of the civil war with the poem itself, we may wish to see that Lucan, in his grove episode, has given expression to the notion that the poem too is a repetition, a resurrection of other poems through this very process of 'deforestation'; and in the future it will

---

[41] See chapter 1 p. 9.   [42] See also chapter 4 p. 138.

[43] For the repetitiveness of civil war see also Grimal 1970 pp. 88–9 (repetition of Sulla and Marius).

itself be subject to the same process. So the civil war will go on for ever, as will the practice of writing through rewriting; it has already happened: Caesar is cutting down in order to make rise again (in his huge siege wall) a grove which has already fallen and risen again; so Lucan is re-using material that has already been used and re-used.[44] Always this process of cutting and re-using will be a criminal act, a desecration, since it is a despoliation of what is sacred and revered in the literature of the past: all poetic writing, in Lucan's vision, is an impious war. If Caesar's soldiers are afraid to strike these trees because

> in sua credebant reditura membra securis   (3.431)

it is not merely a case, as Phillips suggests,[45] of a universal belief from antiquity to the present day that sacred trees would harm those who chopped them; it is rather the case that the soldiers 'realise' that this deforestation is civil war, and to chop down these trees would be a suicide of the type that we see in the poem's prologue:

> in sua victrici conversum viscera dextra   (1.3)

and it is only Caesar who has the audacity to go through with this sacrifice which is also a self-sacrifice.

The barricade at Brundisium

I have been interested so far in the images of material, chopping and desecration. There remain the more positive images

---

[44] So also within the grove already exists an artistic deformation of a number of trees:

> simulacraque maesta deorum
> arte carent caesisque extant informia truncis   (3.412–13)

These are rough-hewn statues of the gods of the grove: but if one glosses 'simulacra' as 'umbrae' it becomes clear that this is the grove's version of the Pompeian oak (on the *trunci* here, Rosner-Siegel 1983 p. 176). But these *trunci* are already *caesi* (cf. 450 'caesi nemoris' – 'caesi', as always, plays on the name 'Caesar'); in other words these Pompeian trunks have already been 'Caesarified': the grove contains objects that have already been subjected to the process of destruction and re-use.

[45] 1968 p. 297.

of poetic construction, centering around the building of Caesar's *agger*. Lucan has already given us an example of *agger*-
construction in his description of the barricade at Brundisium
in book 2; and some remarks on this earlier episode are in
order before we proceed.

Brundisium is the place to which the Pompeian forces have
retreated when Caesar has shown himself able to overrun the
whole of Italy. Caesar soon arrives on the scene, and attempts
to blockade the harbour in two ways. His first plan is to build a
solid barrier by casting huge rocks into the sea; but (according
to Lucan) the rocks are so heavy that the sea-bed cannot bear
their weight, and all of them are swallowed into the sand
(2.661–9).[46] So Caesar has recourse to a second plan: to construct a floating bridge across the harbour, made out of tree-
trunks bound together with chains, built up into a huge *agger*
on which are placed tall towers (670–9). Pompey realises that
he is in danger of being trapped, and makes his escape by night
through a narrow gap in the barricade, losing only two ships
which become ensnared in it (680ff).

To get an idea of the individual bent of Lucan's account, it
is worth thinking about the other historiographical versions,
among which Caesar, again, is the fullest we have.[47] In the
first place, Lucan distorts the strategic considerations which
motivate both the siege and the escape: Pompey retreats to
Brundisium apparently with every intention of staying there to
recoup his forces,[48] and escapes only because he is threatened

---

[46] In Lucan's version, the whole of the solid earthwork disappears. According to Caesar (*BCiv* 1.25.5–10), the parts built most closely to the shore
stand firm, whilst the parts built in deeper water break up; the firm part
of the earthwork is used as a base from which the floating barricade
extends.

[47] The Livian periocha gives us even less to go on than it did for Massilia:
'[Caesar] Cn. Pompeium ceterosque partium eius Italia expulit'.

[48] Two things make this clear: first, Pompey's retreat to Brundisium is compared to the retreat of a defeated bull to a place where it can build up its
strength for a triumphant return (2.601–9); Brundisium is the refuge,
when all the rest of Italy has been taken by Caesar:

> sic viribus inpar
> tradidit Hesperiam *profugus*que per Apula rura
> Brundisii *tutas* concessit Magnus *in arces*. (2.607–9)

by Caesar's blockade (2.680–2). Caesar cannot bear that Pompey should share even the edge of Italy with him, but also does not want to let him escape (2.658–661), and it is because of this that he constructs the barricade. The picture we get from the sources is more complicated, and there are some important details that Lucan has left out. Why does Pompey stay in Brundisium, and why does he leave? Cassius Dio and Appian are clear on this point: he is doing his best to leave, but there are not sufficient ships for all;[49] the flight to Brundisium is preparatory to a retreat from Italy altogether. Caesar's commentary is more uncertain, and cannot guess whether Pompey intended to stay and use Brundisium as a base from which to control the Adriatic, or was waiting for ships to take him away. Acting on the former possibility, Caesar builds the barricade in order to neutralise Brundisium's effectiveness as a port, and to force Pompey to withdraw (*BCiv* 1.25.3–4). In any case, ships do arrive for Pompey before the barricade is completed, and Pompey escapes, perhaps because of the threat of the barricade, or perhaps because he has intended to do so all along (*BCiv* 1.27.2).

No shortage of ships in Lucan, then; and no new ships come at the last minute to rescue Pompey. This means that in Lucan's version Pompey *could* leave whenever he wants to; when he does leave it is because he is threatened by the barricade; and this throws weight onto the barricade as the be-all-and-end-all of the operation. Another remarkable feature of Lucan's account will confirm this impression. Although he treats Caesar's engineering works in heavily exaggerated rhetorical detail, the earthworks that *Pompey* prepared are not so much as hinted at. This is all the more surprising because in all the sources other than Caesar the only earthworks considered worthy of recording were those of Pompey: the trenches and stakes used to block the roads leading to the harbour.[50] In

And secondly, Pompey sends his son Gnaeus to raise forces in the East, giving no indication of any intention to join them outside Italy (2.628–49).

[49] Dio 41.12.1; App. *BCiv* 2.40.

[50] See App. *BCiv* 2.40, Dio 41.12.3, Plut. *Pomp.* 62.3. They ignore Caesar's barricade probably because it was never completed.

Caesar's commentary, it is true, the Caesarian barricade receives more emphasis than Pompey's earthworks (which are represented as a hurried, last-minute ploy before final evacuation, Caes. *BCiv* 1.27.3–4); but Lucan has gone one step further than Caesar, in not allowing the Pompeian defences to appear at all: Lucan wants only major, massy earthworks on the scene, and he wants those earthworks to be Caesar's. Concomitantly, while Caesar says (*BCiv* 1.28.4) that as Pompey's fleet escaped his own troops gave chase in little boats, Lucan has it that far from chasing in little boats, Caesar's soldiers were waiting in ambush on the barricade itself (2.711–12).

In sum, while three of the historiographers ignore Caesar's barricade, Caesar's own account gives it a good deal of prominence; but of all the versions, Lucan's is the one which most emphatically makes the barricade the focal point of the conflict. The exaggeration in his account is also distinctive: the rocks cast into the sea to make the unsuccessful solid barrier are mountains (2.664; and compared to mountains, 2.665ff);[51] the floating barricade is compared to that archetype of *audacia*, Xerxes' bridge across the Hellespont (2.672–7); Caesar has said nothing in his own account to justify Lucan's *aggere multo* (2.678), and the trembling *longae ... turres* (679) imply something much taller than the two-storey towers placed at intervals along the barricade (Caes. *BCiv* 1.25.10); later, the two wings of the barricade coming together at the centre will be compared to the Symplegades (2.715–9). Everything in Lucan's account, even futility (663), is *immense*.[52] At the most basic level, this immensity is programmatic, if only because it is paradigmatic: there is an emphasis on massive constructions in the poem as a whole because that is the sort of poem it is – a massive, epic poem; one of the genre that declares itself alone to have room for heavy weights and huge sizes.

The metaphor of the poem as a temple seems to reach back as far as Pindar (*Ol.* 6.1–3); Richard Thomas has recently

---

[51] Bachofen 1972 p. 89, on Lucan's stressing of the gigantic here.
[52] Bachofen 1972 p. 91, 'Lucan steigert die Errichtung der Blockade zu einem ungeheuren Unternehmen ...'

argued for the existence of a Callimachean temple metaphor,[53] which provides the model for the *locus classicus* in Virgil *Georg.* 3.13. Horace claims that in the first collection of Odes he has constructed a funerary monument (*Od.* 3.30.1ff);[54] Manilius sees the progress of his poem as parallel to the building of a city (Man. 2.772ff). Clearly the image of the poem as a building of some kind (not necessarily a temple) was well established, both as simile and metaphor – explicit and implicit. One index of the extent to which the analogy was regarded as a commonplace is the recurrence of the phrase *surgit opus*, applied exclusively to the composition of a poem,[55] but obviously to be understood in terms of the building metaphor. It is the phrase used by Propertius in 4.1.67 (the poem to which Lucan alluded in the Rubicon scene);[56] Manilius (another author who was certainly an important influence on Lucan)[57] used it twice (1.113, 2.782 'consurgit opus'). In Ovid the phrase appears twice in this standard sense (Ov. *Fast.* 5.111 'surgat opus'; *Trist.* 2.559–60 'surgens ... opus'), and once punningly.[58]

And so to Lucan. We have seen that the Brundisium episode makes quite a meal of Caesar's barricade, and that the immensity of this barricade is at least symptomatic of the character of the poem as a whole. A barricade is not a temple, a monument, or a city, but it is a construction of a sort, and, as constructions go, it is the one most appropriate for the context of a martial

---

[53] Thomas 1983 esp. pp. 96–99.

[54] Cf. Ovid's imitation in *Met.* 15.871–2.

[55] The single exception is Ov. *Fast.* 4.830 ('surgat opus'), of the foundation of Rome; where, however, the context suggests strongly an allusion to Propertius 4.1.67, and hence an equation of the building of the city with the writing of the *Fasti*. In other words, Ovid provides an early example of the conceit I attribute to Lucan here (see infra).

[56] See chapter 1 p. 8.

[57] Pichon 1912 pp. 235–40 is, typically, not convinced; but the case is argued for in more detail by Schwemmler 1916; and reaffirmed by Lapidge 1979 p. 358 etc.

[58] *Am.* 1.1.27: 'sex mihi *surgat opus* numeris, in quinque residat'; the pun is between the notion of the poem rising grandly like a building, and the elegiac couplet rising and falling from hexameter to pentameter.

epic. Already it has been suggested that Lucan sees his own activity as a poet as closely analogous to Caesar's activity as a wager of war; we now need only make a final step to see that Caesar's construction of the floating *agger* parallels Lucan's composition of the poem, in accordance with the metaphor of poem-as-building. The only difficulty consists in the fact that the poet obstinately refuses to tell us, explicitly, that this is what he is doing. But otherwise he has made it as clear as he can:

> tunc aggere multo
> *surgit opus* longaeque tremunt super aequora turres.   (2.678–9)

Lucan's main contribution to the poem-as-building topos, then, is to apply it to military earthworks.[59] Now, the metaphorical significance of the *agger* is very rare in poetry; but in rhetoric, in the form *exaggero* and its cognates, it is to all intents and purposes a technical term, with the sense 'exaggerate'.[60] The barricade then represents that very kind of blustering, over-the-top, exaggerated and heavily rhetorical poetry for which Lucan has so often been censured; and which now, even with disgust, he advertises as the style he has chosen to champion.

Trees, ramparts, ships

And so back to Massilia. Here, indeed, the language is much the same: as the barricade was a floating bridge from one side of the harbour to another, so Caesar's *agger* at Massilia is a kind of bridge from a high mound to the city itself. The mound is as high as the city, and it is on this that Caesar places his camp: and the image of Caesar on one height and Massilia on another will recall for instance the civil-war imagery of the twin-peaked Parnassus (3.173): two heights which are *pares* (so 380 'par tumulo').[61] Furthermore, by building his *agger*,

---

[59] In addition, though I do not have space to discuss it here, he has melded the poem-as-building topos with the poem-as-sea-voyage topos (this earthwork floats); on which, see my discussion of the ships at Massilia below.

[60] *TLL* 'exaggero', 1148.72ff.

[61] On Parnassus, see further chapter 4 pp. 108–14.

Caesar will, so to speak, pit this gladiatorial pair one against the other:

> tunc res inmenso placuit statura labore,
> aggere *diversos* vasto *committere colles* (3.381–2)

The language of civil-war literature recommends ceaselessly the paradox of unified disunity or disunified unity – *concordia discors* – a paradox that is present in the language of the gladiatorial show, where *pares* who are not in fact 'equal'[62] are 'put together' in a parody of harmony. A civil war is both *divisive* and *conjunctive*, and we will see especially in the sea battle a preponderance of *con-* and *dis-* compounds.[63] Thus Caesar's act of joining two disjoined hills is an act that symbolises his participation in (or even his instigation of) the civil war. Hence it also symbolises the act of writing the poem which is identical to the war, the poem whose prologue itself is an *inmensum opus* (1.68), as this grand plan of joining the opposing heights is a *res inmenso statura labore* (3.381). It is indeed a conception so huge that it does not get built until a little later; in the meantime (385) Caesar constructs a *longum opus* (dare we say, not quite as long as an *immensum opus*?) to blockade Massilia by land as he had blockaded Brundisium by sea.

It is the hill-joining *agger*, rather than the lesser blockade, into which the masses of truncated forest are piled. It is in the building of this larger siege work that we find the imagery of exaggeration with compression. The metaphorical sense of *agger* (especially in the compound *exaggerare*) we have already seen in my discussion of the Brundisium blockade; here,

---

[62] Since they are standardly of different races, using different weapons: see Ahl 1976 p. 88 and n. 12.

[63] Cf. the Massilian petition: 'concurrunt ... contagia ... coactis ... cunctis (*root* 'coniunctus') ... committat ... conspecto ... diversi ... committitis' (3.321–8 – one in each line). The examples in the sea battle are less densely packed, but note the parody of brotherly love in

> saevus conplectitur hostem
> hostis et inplicitis gaudent subsidere membris
> mergentesque mori. (3.694–6)

(the conceit is anticipated by Virgil, *Aen.* 11.743–4).

out of hewn wood Caesar creates with great effort an enormous structure – so Lucan, using the material of his literary
predecessors (and here Caesar's commentary in particular) has
created an elaborate and exaggeratedly enormous episode.
But in spite of its sheer physical bulk, the structure of the
siege work is made firm through compression:

> tunc omnia late
> procumbunt nemora et spoliantur robore silvae,
> ut, cum terra levis mediam virgultaque molem
> suspendant, *structa laterum compage ligatam*
> *artet humum*, pressus ne cedat turribus agger.   (3.394–8)

compression which imitates the compression that the literary
material has undergone in Lucan's poem.

The wood from the deforestation is also used to make ships:

> ... rudis et qualis procumbit montibus arbor
> conseritur, stabilis navalibus area bellis.   (3.512–13)

The Roman ships are further described in 527ff: they are tall
(*sublimes* 528, applying in fact to the ships of both sides); they
include four-banked ships – Lucan's language here recalling
his descriptions of earthworks:

> quasque quater *surgens extructi* remigis ordo   (3.530)

– and ships with more banks of oars (531–2). Now, with four-
banked and five-banked ships Lucan has already gone beyond
usual patterns of naval construction: Casson's work on ancient seafaring has shown that even the largest ships were
probably no more than glorified triremes – ships, that is, with
three banks of oars but with more than one oarsman at each
oar.[64] So when in Lucan we come to Brutus' ship, which is not
merely a *hexeres* (a trireme with two men to an oar?) but undoubtedly a ship with six separate banks of oars, we are being
asked to imagine something truly immense:

> celsior at cunctis Bruti praetoria puppis
> verberibus senis agitur molemque profundo
> invehit et summis longe petit aequora remis.   (3.535–7)

---

[64] Casson 1971 pp. 99–103; similarly, Morrison and Coates 1986 p. 47.

... not only immense, but extremely implausible: something as near as possible to a floating mountain. *Liburnae* in the previous line (534) gives us the clue; it is well known that a number of these lighter craft took part in the battle of Actium, and in Horace *Epode* 1.1 the single word *Liburnis* is enough to tell the readers that they are reading an Actium poem. So, given the Actian connotations of this word appearing in Lucan, without a doubt these huge and massive ships with four, five and six banks of oars allude to Virgil's description of Actium in *Aeneid* 8:

> alta petunt; pelago credas innare revulsas
> Cycladas aut montis concurrere montibus altos,
> tanta mole viri turritis puppibus instant.   (*Aen* 8.691–3)

... floating land-masses and floating islands. By creating these impossible ships, Lucan has tried to literalise Virgil's exaggerated imagery.

Just as the *agger* was an exaggeration which was made firm through compression, we will find that these exaggerated ships find success through another kind of compression. The Massilian ships are lighter and more agile – true, as it happens, according to Caesar[65] – and Brutus recommends that his ships try to cramp up the sea so as to afford no room for the Massilians to manoeuvre. Brutus' words 'iam consere bellum' (560), recalling the construction of the ships themselves (*conseritur* 513), suggest also what is happening on the literary plane, the melding of two sea battles into one; everything is joined and mashed together:

> tum quaecumque ratis temptavit robora Bruti
> ictu victa suo percussae capta cohaesit;
> ast alias manicaeque ligant teretesque catenae,
> seque tenent remis: tecto stetit aequore bellum.   (3.563–6)

These lines point to the suicidal nature of Brutus' tactics, which involve the proffering of the ships' weakest points to the

---

[65] The first sea battle, Caes. *BCiv* 1.58; but in Caesar's version, Brutus' tactics are not so explicitly suicidal – the Romans use grappling hooks in order to impede the enemy.

prows of the enemy[66] (3.561) so that paradoxically the Massilians destroy themselves ('ictu victa suo'); it is a suicide that is obviously analogous to the suicide of civil war. And the result of this suicidal, civil-war tactic is the heaping up of corpses and the coagulation of blood, two more images of exaggeration with compression ('concreto sanguine' 573; 'conferta[67] cadavera' 575).

But the imagery (as always) is overdetermined. To write a poem is often, in the metaliterary imagery of Roman Callimacheanism, to go on a journey. This can be a journey on land; but more interesting in the present context is the journey by sea. The small boat ventures onto the immensity of the sea, for instance, as the fragile talent ventures on a major poetic endeavour (from which the poet is dissuaded).[68] I have shown that Lucan has a taste for introducing such metaliterary conceits into the action of his poem, where the part they play is no longer explicitly programmatic, but where their programmatic flavour is none the less striking. It is quite like Lucan not to leave these topoi in their received form, and to develop them by specialisation in context, and by combination with other topoi; and so here. The Roman ships are not the small boats of Augustan imagery; they are half ship, half *agger*, huge mountainous things that happen to float on the water. They are not going anywhere: like the barricade at Brundisium, they are stuck pretty much where they are, particularly because of Brutus' tactics, fighting it out bloodily, suicidally, randomly. To literalise the intense concentration of metaphor which manifests itself on the plane of action as the Massilian sea battle is almost to betray it. But we can gain glimpses. Huge mountainous warships, a vast and overblown martial epic; a vast and overblown *talent* which does not shrink from the

---

[66] Compare for instance Scaeva's 'confringite tela / pectoris inpulsu iugulisque retundite ferrum' (6.160–1).

[67] MSS *conferta* or *conserta*: the latter would of course mesh more nicely with my argument, but Housman is probably right to opt for *conferta*.

[68] For the ship image in general, see Kenney 1958 pp. 205–6; for the small boat and epic overreaching, compare Prop. 3.3.22–4, 3.9.3–4; Hor. *Odes*. 4.15.3–4, and see Wimmel 1960 p. 231.

dangers of the sea. Two sizes of ship are in conflict (the lighter Massilian ships, and the heavier Roman ones); a reflection, it seems, of two kinds of poetic vision in conflict, audacity battling with monstrosity. A poem that collides in on itself; a poem, finally, that goes nowhere, is always jammed, obstructed, static.

Civil war

Virgil's image of clashing mountains at Actium seems to suggest, among other things (for instance, the Symplegades), the gigantomachy,[69] in which giants hurled land masses as weapons. Lucan's use of gigantomachic imagery is widespread throughout the poem,[70] but it is noticeably dense in his Massilia episode. From the start, in the Massilian petition to Caesar, the theme is conjured as an exemplum of the war from which the Massilians would like to withdraw (3.315–20), and their notion of a Jupiter who wields thunderbolts and is the sole ruler of the sky is a clear analogue of Caesar, who is *like* a thunderbolt and is aiming at sole *regnum* of the Roman state. The building of *aggeres*, and especially the placing of towers on the *agger* which equal the height of the Massilian walls, has obvious connotations of piling Pelion on Ossa to reach the heights of Olympus[71]:

> stellatis axibus agger
> erigitur geminasque aequantis moenia turris
> accipit   (3.455–7)

Stellatis axibus is a phrase that has caused some confusion; it must mean something like 'with planks arranged in a star-like pattern', or as Duff translates 'with planks arranged latticewise', but the expression is surely meant to connote the starry axis of the skies at which these giant-like builders are aiming. The towers which tremble and wave make the Massilians believe that there is some geological disruption afoot (459–61); but we will be reminded of the mythological explanation for

---

[69] Hardie 1986 pp. 100–101.   [70] See Mayer 1981 ad 8.551.

[71] Cf. *Aetna* 48–9: '*construitur* magnis ad proelia montibus *agger*, / Pelion Ossa premit, summus premit Ossan Olympus'.

such disruption: giants struggling beneath mountains. Further-more, the Greek artillery which crashes down on the Romans is surely intended to suggest the weapons of gigantomachy: 'tenso ballistae turbine rapta' (465), the crushing weight of rocks, fire.

If the Massilian campaign is an earthly gigantomachy, there is a problem. Caesar, as we have seen, is Jupiter. But if he is Jupiter, why is he piling Ossa on Pelion? Why are the Massilians using thunderbolt-like weapons against his army? There is throughout the episode a fundamental confusion about which side is which, who represents what.

Because Lucan has carefully avoided mentioning either Domitius or Nasidius, the Massilians are pure Massilians. Moreover, Lucan is insistent on their Phocaean origins, so this is a battle between Greeks and Romans. How, then, is this a civil-war battle? The commander of the Roman forces is Brutus – which Brutus? Pompey's Brutus (Junius), or Caesar's Brutus (Decimus)? Historically, we know the answer, but Lucan is determined to suppress it: for him even Pompey seems to be on the Roman side. But Caesarian fire and speed seem to be on the side of the Massilians:[72]

> telum flamma fuit, rapiensque incendia ventus
> per Romana tulit celeri munimina cursu.   (3.501–2)

... while the huge *agger* which is burnt by this fire – an agger built by the Caesarians – is an image of Pompey's downfall, as I have suggested. Things are confused even more by the un-deniable fact that the Massilians are themselves a paradigm of Rome[73]; and like Rome, Massilia is founded by exiles from the East (339–42), their *fides* recalling the *pietas* of Aeneas. Since Rome was founded by exiles from Troy, is the Massilian campaign a replay of the Trojan war, Trojans versus Greeks? Or does the east-versus-west theme recall the battle of Sala-mis? Things are so confused that you do not know if the man you strike is Greek, Trojan, Persian or Roman. From this mass of undirected animosity we can deduce at least one thing:

[72] So Rowland 1969 p. 207.
[73] See Rowland's sensitive discussion, 1969 passim.

the Romans are destroying themselves: both sides are represented on both sides. It is, finally, important that Caesar's side is constantly referred to as 'Romans': the poet has involved his Roman readers in the act of civil war by eliciting their sympathies for the Greek side, and making Rome the enemy.[74]

To conclude with a few minor points concerning the sea battle. Caesar's destruction of the forests not only symbolises his destruction of Pompey, but in a more specific sense mirrors the coming sea battle. Lucan has seen to it that the men involved in the battle are made to look like trees and trunks.[75] Hence the overuse of the word *robur*, in the sense of 'wood' (395, 414, 421, 444, 494, 510, 570, 664), then in the sense 'strength, firmness' (still, however, referring to wooden objects, 457, 532, 563); then, a line which refers to both the strength of ships and the strength of men (as the context shows):

omne suum fatis voluit committere robur ... (517)

and finally, in the sense of bodily or military strength (584, 625, 729). The image of men as trees is reinforced by Lucan's use of *truncus* to denote injured bodies (615, 642, 669, 760) and *procumbere* for a man falling dead (616, 725) – a word that has been used repeatedly for the falling of trees (419, 426, 440, 512). Another repeated theme, which has connections with trees and trunks, is *pondus*: we will remember that Pompey's oak was 'pondere fixa suo' (1.139). The Massilians claim that they are not 'pondera rerum', but in both sea and land battles they both are and use *pondus*.[76]

Weight, congestion, splitting apart, broken fragments, sui-

---

[74] See Opelt 1957 p. 438, who believes that Lucan's patriotic sympathy here temporarily overcomes his anti-Caesarianism; which is to view the same effect from a different perspective.

[75] For the trees-as-people image in general, see the excellent discussion by Nisbet 1987.

[76] 581 (weight of weapons); 626 (a Massilian uses his own weight as a weapon to damage an enemy ship); 649 (sailors capsize a ship by their weight); 725 (Argus falls, and is impaled by spears that have stuck to him, thus 'helping them by his weight').

cide: these themes and many more are crushed into the sea-battle description. Every pattern of death imitates in some way Lucan's civil-war imagery,[77] from the crew which wages *impia bella* against its own members who have fallen overboard and who try to climb back again (663ff); to the individuals pierced by double weapons (587ff) or crushed between two prows (652ff) or torn apart from two sides, by friends and enemies (635ff); to the suicidal dives (622ff) or self-injuring falls (725); to the sailors who tear apart their own ships to use as weapons (670ff). The whole battle repeatedly enunciates the single fact of civil war, a state of being which has invaded every level of things, from the cosmos, to the individual, to the poet and his language.

[77] For some of these, see Rowland 1969 pp. 207–8.

ILERDA

While a hugely insignificant and pointlessly bloody war has been waged about Massilia, the real fighting has been taking place on the edge of the world. Instead of slaughter without importance,[1] Lucan promises us that the Ilerda campaign will have all of the importance with hardly any of the slaughter (4.1–3) – and therefore, incidentally, whatever slaughter does take place during the campaign (e.g. at 243ff) will automatically be classed as 'non multa', even if there is actually a lot of it ('Caesar . . . spoliatus milite multo' 254), for it is implicitly to be contrasted with a future slaughter that *will* be classifiable as 'multa'. It is a typically Lucanian technique, a simple enough device which serves the poet's long-term aim of building up an almost infinitely slow climax: before Pharsalus every battle must somehow not count, either because it is a digression (Massilia) or because it is bloodless (Ariminum, Corfinium) or because it is indecisive (Brundisium, Dyrrachium). The Ilerda campaign fails to count on other scores too: because it is fought on the edge of the world, and because Pompey is not present. It is only at Pharsalus that we will witness a decisive battle overwhelmed with slaughter at the centre of the world at which everyone is present (even some characters who we know were historically not present: Cicero, Sextus). Only then will a battle count (and only then will the poet lose his voice).

Reading the civil war

Pitted against Caesar, and representing the Pompeian side, are Afranius and Petreius.

> iure pari rector castris Afranius illis
> ac Petreius erat; concordia duxit in aequas

---

[1] See chapter 2 pp. 13–14.

imperium commune vices, tutelaque valli
pervigil alterno paret custodia signo   (4.4–7)

'Afranius . . . ac Petreius', plural, are melded into the singular 'rector . . . erat', which presides over a linguistically plural camp ('castris . . . illis'). The potentially pejorative sense of *pari* ('in conflict as a gladiatorial pair'),[2] which will be echoed in PAR-*et*, is neutralized by Lucan's glosses 'concordia . . . aequas . . . commune . . . alterno'. These two generals are set up as an ameliorative version of the pairs-in-conflict we have seen throughout the poem up till now; for instead of the dangerous situation of two rulers (Caesar and Pompey) of a single state, leading to civil war, Lucan depicts Afranius and Petreius as if they were consuls, the legitimate paired rulers of Rome, harmonised in their *par potestas* and mimicking the conventional alternation (by month) of consular rule.

Let me say that again.

'rector . . . erat', singular, is fractured by the plural 'Afranius . . . ac Petreius' and further put into question by the linguistic plurality of the Pompeian camp ('castris illis'). The pejorative sense of *pari* ('in conflict as a gladiatorial pair'), which will finally be picked up in PAR-*et*, must ultimately undermine any attempt to see this fracturing as innocuous; Lucan's glosses 'concordia . . . aequas . . . commune . . . alterno' are no guarantee in a poem which persists in showing equality and togetherness as aspects of conflict and divisiveness; and which will not allow us to trust euphemism, since 'sceleri nefando / nomen erit virtus' (1.667–8). In a civil-war situation this *par potestas* which is enacted by alternate periods of command cannot be anything other than a gross parody of the consulate whose conventions it mimics. Indeed, by blurring the distinction between the twinned power of the consuls and the twin powers of Caesar and Pompey, it undermines even the possibility of a return to the norm of republican government: the civil war is a logical extension of the consular system.

Which of these two opposed interpretations are we to choose? The one, standard, unexceptional, inert, and almost

---

[2] See Conte 1974 ad 6.191, Ahl 1976 pp. 86–7.

certainly 'true'; the other, opportunistic, manipulative, and perverse (but which is which?). My attempt to split the interpretation of these four unremarkable lines will appear in itself perverse or artificial, because the norms of reading demand a partial non-reading; which is to say, any interpretation (no matter how liberal and multivocal) involves the suppression of another (other) interpretation(s). In this instance we have in fact three choices: accept one reading, accept the other, or try to be impartial and accept that no one reading does justice to the text – but even this last choice is a choice that suppresses the possibility of a univocal reading. There is no justice.

The split is a civil war enacted by the reader through the text. The text is the Roman state; and two sides which are the same (two readings of the same text) militate against each other. How are we to decide in favour of one reading over another? 'Quis iustius induit arma / scire nefas' (1.126–7). And yet, how are we not to decide? To be impartial, to be non-partisan, is impossible, or at least only possible if we stop reading the text (a Stoic withdrawal of the kind that Cato rejects?). To read is to be involved in the *nefas* of partisanship, or in the *nefas* of non-partisanship (do we not have to reject Lucan's partisanship in order to be impartial?).

As a partisan of Caesar, I shall take the view that Afranius and Petreius stand as a fracturing of the figure of Pompey.

The topography of Ilerda

We have so far posited and acted upon the principle that Lucan does not necessarily describe an event simply on the grounds that it happened, but makes a selection from the facts that are true, and adds some which are his own invention in order to produce an account which is a recognisable distortion of what we would accept as a historically accurate account, and which serves his artistic and polemic purposes more effectively than that accurate account could. This is not an unusual principle; we can see it reflected in almost all Lucanian scholarship to date.

The facts that are 'true' are broadly defined as those which appear in the other sources and which do not conflict with

45

each other; where there is conflict, common sense developed into historical acumen comes into play. For the campaign at Ilerda we have a breezy summary in Plutarch (*Caes.* 36), and Florus (2.13.26–8), passing mentions in Suetonius (*Jul.* 34.2, 75.2), a couple of sentences in Orosius (6.15.6), some full paragraphs in Appian (*BCiv* 2.42–3), a fairly detailed account in Cassius Dio (41.20–23), and an extremely full account in Caesar (*BCiv* 1.37–55; 59–87). Livy was, we presume from the periocha, similarly full; but, as for Massilia, we will proceed from the assumption that Caesar's account is worthy of independent scrutiny.[3]

A reconstruction of the topography of Ilerda has already been undertaken by, among others, Kromayer and Veith,[4] using Appian, Cassius Dio and Caesar as sources. If I choose to go over the same ground again, it is to fill in details which seem to me obscure, to present precisely the source of each fragment of information, and to emphasise certain points of particular importance for the study of Lucan's account.

None of the sources cited by Kromayer and Veith (the other sources are too brief to give any topographical details) provide us with anything like Lucan's topographical ecphrasis; what we need to find out must be gleaned from passing remarks scattered through their accounts, taken in conjunction with what we know from present-day geography.[5] So, to begin with, Ilerda (modern Lérida) is situated on the western bank of the river Sicoris (Segre). Further west flows the Cinga (Cinca); the two rivers merge further south, and together join the Hiberus (Ebro) flowing east towards the sea (see Map 1).

Afranius and Petreius are encamped on a hill adjacent to Ilerda (see Map 2),[6] and in the town itself they have collected

---

[3] On Lucan's and Caesar's Ilerda, see Bachofen 1972 pp. 17–22 and 116–132.

[4] 1924, sheet 19 (with the accompanying notes). See also Kraner and Hofmann 1906, map 3; and CAH Vol. IX pp. 649–50.

[5] Since the ancient geographers tell us nothing about, e.g., the river Cinga; the name is only found in Caesar and Lucan.

[6] 'erat inter oppidum Ilerdam et proximum collem, ubi castra Petreius atque Afranius habebant ...' (Caes. *BCiv* 1.43.1); cf. Dio 41.20.4.

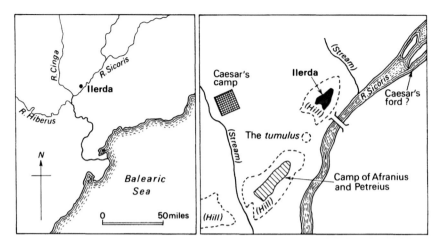

Map 1. The area around Ilerda   Map 2. The battlefield of Ilerda

their supplies.[7] The town overlooks a bridge which, naturally, the Pompeians control.[8] Caesar has sent on ahead his *legatus* Fabius, who has encamped north of Ilerda on the western bank of the Sicoris – that is, on the same side as the town[9] – and who has built two bridges four miles apart,[10] presumably also to the north of the town. Caesar arrives; and after attempting to engage the Pompeians, he makes camp on the plain which stretches to the west of Ilerda.[11] He then attempts,

---

[7] 'commeatu omni quem in oppidum contulerant . . .' (Caes. *BCiv* 1.43.2).

[8] '.. celeriter suo ponte Afranius, quem oppido castrisque coniunctum habebat, legiones IIII equitatumque traiecit' (Caes. *BCiv* 1.40.4).

[9] Fabius' men cross the river (and are cut off by the sudden destruction of their bridge), Caes. *BCiv* 1.40.3; the Pompeians cross the river in order to attack them (see previous note). Therefore, Fabius' men must be regularly stationed on the same side of the river as the Pompeians.

[10] Caes. *BCiv* 1.40.1.

[11] Caes. *BCiv* 1.48.3 shows that his camp was between the Cinga and the Sicoris. That he encamped 400 paces away 'ab infimis radicibus montis' (Caes. *BCiv* 1.41.3) implies that he did not ascend a hill, and certainly the strategy whereby he kept his fortifications a secret makes it clear that he must have been on the plain (Caes. *BCiv* 1.41.4–5). According to Appian (*BCiv* 2.42), Caesar did encamp on high ground – ἐπὶ κρημνῶν – but other curious distortions in this paragraph undermine our confidence in

47

unsuccessfully, to seize the hillock which lies between Ilerda and the Pompeians' camp.[12] How does this square with Lucan's account? As we might expect, his description is recognisably similar while differing from the sources in a number of details. 'Correctly' he has it that Ilerda is on a hill (4.11–13), on the banks of the Sicoris (13–14). The bridge is there (15–16), and although the sources tell us nothing about its construction we have no reason not to believe that it is made of stone as Lucan says. Correctly too he has placed the Pompeian camp on an adjacent hill (16–17), and the hillock in between the camp and the town (32–3). But when we come to Caesar's camp we run into problems. According to Lucan, Caesar pitches his camp on a rival hill on the other side of a river (17–18) which must be the Sicoris. Now, as we have seen, Caesar does not encamp on any hill, and neither does he encamp on the eastern bank of the Sicoris. And the problem goes deeper than that: at this stage in the campaign, before the *prima dies belli* (24) and Caesar's secret fortification of the plain (described in 28–31), Caesar had not yet arrived at Ilerda and therefore had no camp at all. We must suppose that Lucan is referring to Fabius' camp;[13] but, again as we have seen, Fabius' camp, which may or may not have been on a hill, is assuredly not on the eastern bank of the river, and is in any case many miles north of the Pompeian camp – hardly, as Lucan implies, right opposite it. Finally, although Lucan is perfectly right to claim that the Cinga runs some way off on the edge of the area, and that it joins the Hiberus, it is none the less strange that he does not mention its confluence with the

his accuracy: he attributes to Caesar's troops a disaster which actually befell Fabius' troops before Caesar arrived, and distorts the chronology accordingly. Even so, it is not impossible that Lucan has taken his cue from the tradition that Appian represents, inasmuch as he too has no mention of Fabius and, as I show below, agrees with Appian on the detail of the placing of the camp.

[12] Caes. *BCiv* 1.43.

[13] Fabius is not mentioned, for the good reason that Lucan wants to contrast the oneness of Caesar with the plurality of the Pompeians.

Sicoris, as if he wanted to pretend that only the Cinga, and not the Sicoris, lost its name in the Hiberus (20–23).

What has Lucan to gain by distorting things in this way? The manner of his distortion, I would propose, is surreptitious, rather than blatant; so whereas it was reasonable to suppose that Lucan's rewriting, compression and exaggeration of the Massilian episode would be obvious to a Roman who had any familiarity with Caesar's commentary, the alterations of detail in the topography of the Ilerda campaign are so subtle and so 'unimportant' that it seems impossible that Lucan should have been expecting his readers to recognise the difference. That he differed is axiomatic; precisely where and how is obscure. On the face of it, then, we should not expect to find any despoliated forests or compressed *aggeres* (and in fact we do not), nor any other symbolic commentary on the construction of the ecphrasis out of source material, such as featured in the account of Massilia.

The usefulness of our inquiry into the 'real' topography of Ilerda consists in this: that where Lucan agrees with his sources, we may suspect (wrongly, I think) that the information is there because it is true, and for no other reason; it is dead wood, it does little beyond assisting an illusion of realism; but where Lucan disagrees with his sources, we have no choice but to assign to him a transcendent purpose. In the case of Ilerda, then, what is this purpose?

The topography of Ilerda plays on the kind of 'civil war' topography that Lucan presented to us in his account of Massilia. As Lucan has engineered things so that the Pompeians and Caesar occupy rival hills of equal size, just so in book 3 Caesar occupied a hill equal in height to the hill on which Massilia stood (3.379–80),[14] which provided, as we saw, a typically civil-war image of parity in conflict, with connotations of the gigantomachy (so Ilerda too is piled on a mountain-top, 4.11–13). At Ilerda, however, things are not so simple: for although the Pompeians' hill is clearly opposed to

---

[14] See chapter 2 p. 34.

Caesar's hill, it is also opposed to Ilerda on another hill next
to it:

> colle tumet modico lenique excrevit in altum
> pingue solum tumulo; super hunc fundata vetusta
> surgit Ilerda manu ...
>   ... *at proxima rupes*
> signa tenet Magni, nec Caesar colle minore
> castra levat. (4.11–18)

the opposition of Magnus' camp to Ilerda recalling the opposition of the Massilian hill to Caesar's hill:

> *proxima pars* urbis celsam consurgit in arcem
> par tumulo [sc. Caesaris] (3.379–80)

and just as the river divides the camps of Pompey and
Caesar ...

> *medius dirimit* tentoria gurges (4.18)

so too a hill divides the Pompeian camp from the city of Ilerda,
as we discover a little later:

> collem ...
> qui *medius* tutam castris *dirimebat* Ilerdam (4.32–3)

and the phrase is earlier used of the split between Asia and
Europe ('mediae dirimens confinia terrae', 3.275), and it seems
to be something of a civil-war motif.[15] Haskins (ad loc.) takes
castris as referring to Caesar's camp, so that the hillock protects Ilerda from Caesar, as it should; Caesar's object, we sur-
mise, is to overcome an obstacle that prevents him from taking
the town. But is this really what Caesar needs to do? It is the
Pompeian camp that he should be attacking. Furthermore, the
'real' topography shows that the hillock stood between Ilerda
and the *Pompeian* camp (see above); and Caesar wished to

---

[15] Cf. the split between Italy and Sicily (2.435ff and 3.60–3); and 1.100–3,
where instead of water dividing land, we find a thin strip of land dividing
water at the isthmus of Corinth, there explicitly made a symbol of events
on the historical plane (Crassus keeps Pompey and Caesar from colliding
in civil war). The symbol is double-edged: for while it appears to denote
uneasy stability, it already connotes the divisiveness of civil war (Pompey
and Caesar *should* be unified).

seize it in order to cut off the Pompeians from the town (where they had gathered all their supplies). To be fair, Lucan's *castris* are unnamed, and context lends as much credibility to one interpretation as the historical sources do to the other (since in Lucan the last camp named was Caesar's); perhaps we should compromise and allow a literal force to the 'plural' in *castris* – so the hillock protects Ilerda from both Caesar's and the Pompeians' camp.

The Pompeian camp, then, is split off from the town to which it should be joined, mirroring its internal fracturing which I discussed above. It now looks as though Ilerda is the object of a Roman siege, except that the besiegers (Caesar plus the Pompeians) are at war with each other.

Ilerda is a primeval town:

> super hunc fundata vetusta
> surgit Ilerda manu   (4.12–13)

which recalls a phrase from Virgil:[16]

> saxo incolitur fundata vetusto
> urbis Agyllinae sedes   (*Aen.* 8.478–9)

describing a town in pre-Trojan Italy. The link with this Virgilian world has been prepared for by the fact that the Celtae participate in the foundation-by-exiles topos that is characteristic of the Roman / Trojan race:

> profugique a gente vetusta
> Gallorum Celtae miscentes nomen Hiberis   (4.9–10)

(just so were the Trojans mixed with the Latins, *Aen.* 12.823–8). The double appearance of the word *vetusta* in the same metrical position within four lines accentuates the primeval nature of Ilerda, which is comparable to that of the Italy into which Aeneas brings his discord. Save that whereas the Italian / Trojan war was like a civil war because the Trojans were

---

[16] So Thompson and Bruère 1970 p. 152, who use this and similar evidence to support their theory that 'Lucan employs [Virgilian reminiscence] to demonstrate that the Spanish episode was similar to, but more monstrous than, its Virgilian prototype, the bloodshed of which led to lasting peace' (p. 158).

fighting against those who were one day to be their compa-
triots, in Lucan the split is *within* the 'Trojan' camp, as well as
outside it, inasmuch as Pompey and Caesar are fighting each
other as well as, apparently, the Spaniards.[17]

And what of the rivers? First of all we should make the
obvious point that the course of the Cinga appears to parallel
(it does not do so without difference) the history of the Celtic
race.[18] The river:

> nam gurgite *mixto*
> qui praestat terris aufert tibi *nomen Hiberus*   (4.22–3)

and the Celts:

> profugique a gente vetusta
> Gallorum Celtae *miscentes nomen Hiberis*   (4.9–10)

And in addition, where the Cinga is *rapax* (4.21), the Asturians are *impiger* (4.8). So, as often, Lucan has given us a
symbolic river – in fact, a pair of symbolic rivers, the Cinga
and the Sicoris. Now by this point in the epic, Lucan has made
us familiar with two topoi describing paired rivers: first, that
one river is slow (characteristically Pompeian), and the other
river is fast (characteristically Caesarian); and second, that the
one river flows into the other and thereby loses its name.[19]
These two topoi often appear together, but not invariably so.
What is unusual about this instance is that while the slowness

---

[17] By whom I mean, of course, only the inhabitants of Ilerda. As for the
Spaniards fighting on the Pompeians' side (4.8–10; cf Caes. *BCiv* 1.38–
39), it is significant that Lucan says nothing of those *Gauls* who fought
for Caesar (Caes. *BCiv* 1.39.2); clearly he wants Caesar to appear as all
Roman, while the Pompeians are subject to the internal discord of having
foreign auxiliaries – the kind of discord that we saw in Pompey's catalogue, esp. 3.288–90 'coiere nec umquam / tam variae cultu gentes, tam
dissona volgi / ora'.

[18] Henderson 1988 pp. 138–9.

[19] Topos of fast versus slow: 3.207–8 (Marsyas and Maeander); 5.461–7
(Genusus and Hapsus). Topos of losing name: 3.256–63 (Tigris and
Euphrates); 1.399–401 (Isara and the unnamed Rhône); 6.371ff (rivers
that run into the Peneus). On the symbolism of the fast-slow contrast
(as signifying Caesar/Pompey) see Schönberger 1960 p. 87 and 1961
pp. 50–1. See also Gassner 1972 p. 162f, and my chapter 5 pp. 169–172.

of the Sicoris ('placidis praelabitur undis' 13) as against the violence of the Cinga ('rapax' 21) suggests a Sicoris / Cinga pairing, the river into which the Cinga flows and loses its name is not the Sicoris but the Hiberus, suggesting a Hiberus / Cinga pairing. A third river has intervened to upset the neat opposition of the other two.

Just so the neat interpretation of the symbolism of the rivers is made impossible. We expect (do we not?) the Sicoris to stand for the Pompeians, the Cinga for Caesar – on the grounds of the slow / fast contrast. But the rushing Cinga is, as I have indicated, aligned with the Asturians and the Celts, tribes which are fighting on the Pompeian side. So both rivers, the fast and the slow, have their Pompeian aspect, even though they are opposed to each other; it is a third river that, Caesar-like, will dominate.

What I hope I have shown is that Lucan's topography is symbolic of an internal split within the Pompeian camp: first through its uncertain pairing of hill against hill (which of the three hills is opposed to which?) and second through its uncertain pairing of river against river. In the case of the rivers (and less clearly in the case of the hills), it is arguable that the symbolism portends a Caesarian element in the Pompeian camp – that is, the split creates a Pompeian half and a Caesarian half of the Pompeian camp – inasmuch as the Cinga, naturally a Caesarian river, now symbolises (partly) the Pompeians.

The battle for the hillock

prima dies belli cessavit Marte cruento ...   (4.24)

This is the first day of the war, how many more 'first days' are there going to be? Perhaps the question is rhetorical; but if the first day of the civil war was the day after the crossing of the Rubicon:

iamque dies primos belli visura tumultus
exoritur   (1.233–4)

then it is remarkable that Lucan should present the first day of the Ilerda campaign in language that suggests it was the first day of the civil war as a whole. A further point along these

lines emerges from a comparison with Caesar's account. On
the day after his arrival at Fabius' camp, Caesar

omnibus copiis triplici instructa acie ad Ilerdam proficiscitur et sub castris
Afrani constitit et ibi paulisper sub armis moratus facit aequo loco pugnandi
potestatem. potestate facta Afranius copias educit et in medio colle sub
castris constituit. Caesar ubi cognovit per Afranium stare quo minus proelio
dimicaretur . . . castra facere constituit.   (Caes. *BCiv* 1.41.2–3)

Caesar offers battle by approaching the Pompeian camp, is
refused, and departs. Now Lucan:

> prima dies belli cessavit Marte cruento
> spectandasque ducum vires numerosaque signa
> exposuit. piguit sceleris; pudor arma furentum
> continuit, patriaeque et ruptis legibus unum
> donavere diem   (4.24–8)

Lucan has given over a whole day to an exposition of the
troops which in Caesar's account takes hardly any time at all
('paulisper . . . moratus'); consequently in Lucan's account the
fortification of Caesar's camp must take place towards night-
fall (4.28–9), whereas in fact by evening the fortifications were
already completed.[20] Why has Lucan expanded this little episode to fill a whole day? Because for him this exposition of
troops on both sides is a stillborn 'catalogue of forces'; it contains, that is, the *threat* of a catalogue (and we will see in the
next section how that threat is realised); and as such it effectively marks this 'first day of the war' as a beginning which
reenacts the beginnings of those other epic wars which began
with catalogues – the *Iliad* (a good example of a pseudo-begin-
ning), the second half of the *Aeneid*, and of course the *Bellum
Civile* itself.

The threat of a catalogue is the threat of more delay; here
above all we see that a catalogue (or, on the level of the action,
a parade of troops) is a response to the desire not to continue
with the poem (not to continue with the war); it is a response

---

[20] 'sub vesperum Caesar intra hanc fossam legiones reducit' (Caes. *BCiv*
1.41.6). Caesar's ditch took some hours to dig; Lucan's Caesar's ditch is
subita (4.29).

to *pudor* and to *pietas* not only on the part of the troops who do not fight, but on the part of the poet who so obviously sympathises with them and who in any case has invented the whole situation. The Ilerda campaign, which from the very start was characterised as something preliminary (and hence as something delaying the really important battle), is itself subject to delay (and will be again shortly, with the arrival of the storm clouds). And behind this multiplication of delays – which exhibits itself throughout the *whole* poem – is the 'virtuous' Lucan who must contend at every stage with his 'nefarious' counterpart. *But* this delay does not in fact exist; it remains only a threat; there is no catalogue; the one-day deferral is dealt with summarily in five lines. It will be objected that we have already been given two extended troop catalogues, and even Lucan had more taste than to subject us to another; but while I recognise the justice of that opinion, I none the less insist that the lack of a full-blown catalogue here is significant. Lucan is a poet who above all composes by bulk; by which I mean (and without any pejorative undertones) that Lucan, who has made it his job to attack the Callimachean principle of *mega biblion mega kakon*, perversely and deliberately uses sheer bulk as one of his poetic devices – in a way which seems utterly unique in Latin poetry. If a catalogue has been omitted, Lucan may be ceding to taste (and maybe the composition of catalogues is unrewarding for the poet himself), but he is killing two birds with one stone; the absence of a catalogue is a victory for Caesar and for the 'nefarious' Lucan, who can proceed with their civil war without any hindrance.

The second day of the war ('luce nova' 32) is slaughterless and inconsequential. The fight that takes place for the possession of the hillock is recognisably similar to the account we read in Caesar, but is subject to the usual Lucanian distortions. Broadly speaking, Lucan melds together two skirmishes that follow one after the other;[21] first, according to Caesar,[22] the Caesarians make for the hillock, but are beaten to it by the Pompeians; there is some fighting, and then the Pompeians

---

[21] Lintott 1971 p. 490 and n. 2.   [22] Caes. *BCiv* 1.43.

are reinforced and the Caesarians retire. Second,[23] the ninth legion (Caesarians) find themselves in difficulties at the foot of the hill on which Ilerda stands (this is *not* the hillock); after some heroic fighting they drive back the Pompeians and escape with the assistance of the cavalry. At the end of the day both sides claim the advantage.

One reason for Lucan's compression of the two battles into one, and his suppressing of any mention of a fight about Ilerda, we have already seen: he wants to avoid showing that Ilerda is on the side of the Pompeians (in Caesar's version the Pompeians are forced to retreat inside the walls);[24] this battle is (not obviously, but suggestively) a battle within the besieging camp, a battle for control of a point from which the city may be attacked. And a second reason: this characteristic *compression* of two events,[25] which finds its analogue in the pitting of two sides against each other ('*com*mittere'), results in an episode that is uncharacteristically brief (contrast the sea battle at Massilia). Once again, the 'nefarious' poet is seeing to it that the action is not delayed.

For jaded palates: a battle fought perpendicularly. The little hillock has grown into a steep mountain ('rupes ... in altas' 37; 'adverso ... in monte' 38); up a vertical cliff-face the soldiers ascend, and (like walking up a wall) their bodies are parallel to the ground ('acies ... supina' 38), supported only by the shields of those below them (who are in turn supported ... and so on, 39–40). This comic image is then succeeded by a picture of rock climbers using their spears as pegs and cutting footholds with their swords (41–3). Into this vertical plain the cavalry impossibly arrive to interpose themselves between the climbers and those at the summit (44–5). The climbers are saved; the victors hang suspended ('pependit' 47) over the field they have uselessly ('inritus' 47)[26] conquered. There is, so far as the reader is able to tell, no actual fighting (4.40); what

---

[23] Caes. *BCiv* 1.45–6.   [24] Caes. *BCiv* 1.46.2.   [25] See chapter 2 p. 25.
[26] 'inritus ... victor' seems to nod in the direction of Caesar's judgement that the battle was indeterminate (Caes. *BCiv* 1.47); but surely it is possible to detect in the words a notion of the futility of winning a vertical field.

fighting there is is directed against the problems of gravity; so Lucan uses 'normal battle' topoi to describe things that have nothing to do with battle. 'hoste relicto / caedunt ense viam' (42–3), the cutting of footholds, clearly and pointedly plays on the Lucanian cliché (which finds a precedent in Virgil)[27] of cutting one's way through the enemy, of always taking the bloodiest possible route. And the principal danger for the soldiers on the cliff-face is the danger of *falling* ('casura' 39; 'lapsura ruina' 43), mimicking the potential 'fall' in death of soldiers on a normal battlefield.[28] Indeed, the notion that the soldiers on the verge of falling are supported by other soldiers on the verge of falling plays on a conceit that we have seen twice already, one of a mass of executed Romans, compressed into so small a space that there is scarcely room for them to fall:[29]

> densi vix agmina volgi
> inter et exangues inmissa morte catervas
> victores movere manus; vix caede peracta
> procumbunt, dubiaque labant cervice. (2.201–4)

---

[27] *Aen.* 10.372–3 'ferro rumpenda per hostis / est via'; see Thompson and Bruère 1970 p. 153; Conte 1974 ad 6.124. Examples in Lucan are 1.150, 2.439–40, 6.124.

[28] For *cado* as 'die', see *OLD* 'cado' 9.

[29] Or for the victors to move their hands. That weapons cannot be wielded in the crush is a topos that is closely connected with the 'sustinuit se cadens' topos, and indeed it seems to me that 4.40 'nulli telum vibrare vacavit' is a gesture towards it. Two other examples are relevant to my discussion, one from Curio's African war later in the book, the other from the battle of Pharsalus:

> densaturque globus, quantum pede prima relato
> constrinxit gyros acies. non arma movendi
> iam locus est pressis, stipataque membra teruntur;
> frangitur armatum conliso pectore pectus.
> ... fluvios non ille cruoris
> membrorumque videt lapsum et ferientia terram
> corpora: conpressum turba stetit omne cadaver. (4.780–7)

> Pompei densis acies stipata catervis
> iunxerat in seriem nexis umbonibus arma
> vixque habitura locum dextras ac tela movendi
> constiterat gladiosque suos conpressa timebat. (7.492–5)

57

and secondly, describing a similar phenomenon when a forest is cut down (in a context where there is a strong link between trees and men):

> propulsaque robore denso
> sustinuit se silva cadens   (3.444–5)

In any case the mutual support of the soldiers on the hill imitates close formation in a normal battle: compare

> [sc. acies] in tergum casura umbone sequentis erigitur.   (4.39–40)

with these lines from the siege of Massilia:

> ut tamen hostiles densa testudine muros
> tecta subit virtus, armisque innexa priores
> arma ferunt, galeamque extensus protegit umbo   (3.474–6)

Finally, we must suppose that given Lucan's refusal to mention a single death,[30] a single javelin thrown, or a single sword thrust, given, that is, that this battle is not so much a battle as a mountaineering expedition, Lucan's final words on the episode must be a joke:

> hactenus armorum discrimina   (4.48)

The storm and the flood

Two days later, says Caesar, the flood. Let us be precise about this: the flood that Caesar describes is nothing like Lucan's deluge. A uniquely heavy fall of rain causes the Sicoris to burst its banks, and as a result both of the bridges built by Fabius are destroyed.[31] Therefore Caesar's troops are cut off in the peninsula formed by the Sicoris and the Cinga; on that peninsula supplies are scarce.[32] This is the sole difficulty that Caesar faces. There is no flood that overwhelms the fields, the camp, the hills; Caesar is stranded on dry land. Ahl's comment on the flood is amazing: 'In [Lucan's] account of the floods in Spain ... *his narrative almost exactly corresponds to that of Caesar in the Bellum Civile, dwelling on the meteorological and geographi-*

---

[30] Contrast in Caesar's account, the list of casualties, *BCiv* 1.46.4–5.
[31] Caes. *BCiv* 1.48.1–2.
[32] Caes. *BCiv* 1.48.3–1.49; see Bachofen 1972 p. 122.

cal causes of the disaster. But then, unlike Caesar, he comments ruefully that the impiety of civil war merited another great flood to inundate the whole of Spain' (1976 p. 280; my emphasis). The extent to which Caesar comments on the causes is to say that there was an enormous storm and that the mountain snows were melted;[33] it is hard to see how that can be construed as 'dwelling'. As for the 'almost exact correspondence', I suggest that only the sequence of events in the campaign can compel us to believe that Lucan is describing the same phenomenon as Caesar.

It is well known that behind Lucan's description of the catastrophic deluge lies Ovid's account of Deucalion's flood in *Met.* 1.262ff.[34] It is not part of my self-imposed brief to investigate in any detail the correspondences between Lucan and Ovid here; let us take it as read that they exist and see what we can deduce from them. One model that we are offered for their comprehension is *emulation*:[35] Lucan seizes on this chance mention of something like a flood in the sources in order to outdo his predecessor, he has distorted the facts of history in order to create an episode which is comparable by its similarity to a specific episode which he wishes to rival; one might almost say, he has created common ground, a battlefield on which to fight out the claims of poetic superiority[36]. This model is of course supremely important inasmuch as this war

---

[33] Caes. *BCiv* 1.48.1–2.

[34] See Morford 1967 pp. 44; and add Thompson and Bruère 1970 p. 153, Linn 1971 pp. 12–59.

[35] This is implicit in the tone of Thompson and Bruère (see note 34) and emerges explicitly in their remarks on Virgil's influence on the passage: 'the similarities ... are sufficiently marked to justify the assumption that Lucan wished his audience to recognise his model, and that he was confident he would not suffer by comparison' (p. 154). See also Linn 1971 pp. 12–59.

[36] Longinus 13.4 speaks of imitation as strife: 'I do not think there would have been so fine a bloom on Plato's doctrines ... had he not been striving heart and soul with Homer for first place, like a young contestant entering the ring with a long-admired champion, perhaps showing too keen a spirit of emulation in his desire to break a lance with him ...' (translation by Dorsch).

between two poets is analogous to the historical war between Caesar and Pompey, but as a strategy for reading it does not take us very far: we note the correspondence, we note the ways in which Lucan has surpassed or failed to surpass his rival (usually on questionable aesthetic grounds), we make our judgement and give sentence. What else is there to say? A second model for comprehension – and one not unrelated to the first – has no obvious name, but we may call it *pointed allusion*. Under this strategy we are not specifically interested in poetics; we see the comparability of the two passages as a means of signifying, say, that the Spanish floods were somehow *like* the primeval deluge; initially we will restrict ourselves to investigating only those likenesses that manifest themselves as verbal correspondences in the text; later we will see the allusion as an invitation to make broader comparisons (as well as, obviously, contrasts). Any reading strategy may be subject to abuse, and it seems to me that Lucanian criticism has failed to find a use for the information that such and such an event is (un)like another event in a previous poem. To take an example: Thompson and Bruère, who are interested in the first storm in the *Aeneid* as a model for Lucan here, conclude that 'by echoing [*Aeneid* 1.90] Lucan indicates that his Spanish cloudburst dwarfs the storm that swept Aeneas to Africa' (1970 p. 153). What, precisely, does this tell us? Merely that Lucan wanted his storm to appear very big indeed. The urgent question is *why*; and why specifically the *Aeneid* storm? Other favourite conclusions deriving from this reading strategy are that the comparisons emphasise the pathos of a scene, or underline Caesar's *nefas*. All we ever learn is all we ever knew: Caesar is wicked, and the *Bellum Civile* is bombastic and full of (misfired) attempts at inducing pathos. Useless and reductive as these conclusions are, it seems to me that the approach itself is not at fault; the problem is, how to use it.

The storm and the ensuing flood are a kind of battle:

> hactenus armorum discrimina: cetera bello
> fata dedit variis incertus motibus aer   (4.48–9)

The lines signal a delay (so much for battle; now weather interfered), but they also suggest that the weather is simply an alternative version of warfare, replacing the *motus* of war[37] with the *motus* of winds – and we have already seen winds as an image for conflicting loyalties (2.454–60), a battle at sea (3.549–52) and Caesar's violence (3.362–5).[38] So much for arms, then; now the winds take over the war. The scales are turned

> atque iterum aequatis ad iustae pondera Librae
> temporibus vicere dies   (4.58–9)

in an astronomical parody of the image presented to us at the beginning of the book:[39]

> Martem . . . non multa caede nocentem,
> maxima sed fati ducibus momenta daturum.   (4.1–2)

and from the lands of the East one wind, the Eurus, collects every cloud it can find (4.62–70) to thrust them into the western corner of the sky. The wind is like a general gathering his troops (clouds) for war, and here Lucan leans on the fact that Ovid had personified his wind, the Notus (*Met.* 1.264–9); that is to say, while Lucan's demythologising trend forbids him to talk of the east wind as having wings, a face, a beard, hair and hands (and so too his rainbow – 4.79–82 – is precisely *not* Iris, as it is in Ovid, *Met.* 1.270–1), he is none the less at liberty to use the Ovidian reminiscence to make his wind seem like a person.[40] Further, Lucan has changed Ovid's south wind into an east wind, a change which offers us a clear example of poetic overdetermination. On the one hand, it is the natural wind to have chosen for the job of driving clouds into the West

---

[37] For *motus* as a term denoting civil upheaval, see Nisbet and Hubbard 1978 ad Hor. *Odes* 2.1.1.

[38] Winds and storms as an image for martial conflict are extremely common in epic similes: see e.g. Hom. *Il.* 11.297–8; 305–8; 16.765–9; Ennius fr. 432–4 (Skutsch); Virg. *Aen.* 10.356–9.

[39] Duff brings out the rather shadowy image in his translation 'war not guilty of much bloodshed, but destined to turn decisively the scales of fate for the rival leaders'; cf. the gloss in Commenta Bernensia, 'inclinationem ad se ducibus daturum'. Of course the words play equally on the *momenta* of the Massilians (3.338).

[40] On Lucan's demythologising, see Albrecht 1970 pp. 273–4 and 281, and Martindale 1981 p. 75.

– it is pointed in the right direction;[41] and on the other, it is obviously Pompey's wind; Pompey is always associated with eastern lands, by virtue of his eastern triumphs, much as Caesar is often associated with the North. Next, the gathering of the winds is an ersatz catalogue to replace the one we were denied in 25–6. Specifically it is a miniature replay of the massive catalogue of Pompey's eastern troops in book 3; the repeated relative pronouns, *quascumque ... et quas ... et quas ... quidquid ... quidquid ... quidquid ...* (4.62–7), parallel the similar accumulation of relative pronouns in the earlier catalogue, e.g. *qua ... qua ... qua ... quaque* (3.271–7).[42] Finally, into the West these assembled Pompeian clouds rush under the impulse of a Pompey-like wind to put a stop to the strife of arms. They do so by flooding Caesar's camp (hence, contrary to logic, the Pompeian camp appears to be unaffected, in spite of the fact that the flood overwhelms hills [4.98]):

> iam naufraga campo
> Caesaris arma natant, inpulsaque gurgite multo
> castra labant   (4.87–9)

Floods too have military connotations: in book 6 Pompey's success at Dyrrachium will be compared to the flooding of the river Po (6.272–8),[43] but the notion of an advancing army as a wave (on land or sea) is as old as Homer.[44] The flood besieges the soldiers just like a military force:

> nulloque obsessus ab hoste
> miles eget   (494–5)

[41] However, it is perhaps not the right wind to have chosen for *spring*, if we pay any mind to Virgil: 'ver magnus agebat / orbis et hibernis parcebant flatibus Euri' (*Georg.* 2.338–9).

[42] Of course Caesar's catalogue also uses the same technique; but what makes the cloud catalogue specifically Pompeian is that all the clouds are gathered from eastern lands, like Pompey's troops.

[43] Cf. Virg. *Aen.* 2.496–99. Lucan's language there puns on the link between action and simile: Pompey is given 'mutandae ... licentia terrae' 6.271 ('the freedom to change position'); and a flood entails a different kind of *mutandae terrae* – changing the land into sea. There is a similar play between 6.44 ('castra ... mutat') and 6.60 ('in melius mutare locum').

[44] Hom. *Il.* 4.422–6; cf. Aeschylus' adaptation in *Pers.* 86–90. Compare also the destruction of the wall by flood (paralleling in some way the Trojan war) in *Il.* 12.3–33.

But in spite of these obvious successes, in spite of the hugeness of the flood, it is not enough. In the end it is just *parvo ... pavore* (121), and Fortune steps in to see that the bad weather retreats.

Lapidge[45] has rightly seen in the flood-description language that evokes what he calls the 'imagery of cosmic dissolution'; he cites the 'tension' of a 'pressure on boundaries whose collapse is imminent' in 4.72–5, and sees the 'huge watery abyss' as analogous to the Stoic ecpyrosis. In another place (p. 361) he notes that a Lucanian phrase which alludes to Stoic cosmology ('antiquum chaos' 1.74) in fact derives from Ovid, but adds 'and yet there is no reason to assume that Ovid, here or elsewhere, was following Stoic doctrine', and indeed this appears to be the *communis opinio* about Ovid's philosophical leanings.[46] It is strange, then, that in the flood-description, this most Stoic of passages, Lucan should be drawing on the un-Stoic Ovid – often, indeed, those lines which are most Stoic are precisely the most Ovidian.[47] I do not wish to challenge the prevailing view that Ovid was not particularly Stoic; what I do want to say is that Lucan's flood is not a purely Stoic phenomenon: it plays on Stoic language, suggests a Stoic catastrophe, but equally plays on Ovidian flood-language which in turn plays on the Ovidian description of chaos; and all of this is subsumed into a wider artistic purpose, which can be examined outside of a Stoic framework.[48]

We are in danger of becoming bogged down. Therefore let us summarise and expand. We know that in Lucan the civil

---

[45] 1979 pp. 364–5. Cf. Morford 1967 pp. 44–7.

[46] Galinsky 1975 p. 47 remarks on Ovid's distinction between long-lasting character and fleeting corporeal existence as having affinities with some principles of the Stoic Posidonius, but posits that Pythagoras is an intermediary. Spoerri 1959 pp. 43–4 emphasises the differences between Ovid's account of the creation and that of the Stoics.

[47] Lapidge cites as 'Stoic' 4.98–101; cf. Ov. *Met.* 1.309–10, 292, 286–7.

[48] Lapidge, I think, would not disagree: although he sees Stoic imagery as 'central to the meaning of the poem' he concludes that 'Its use in the Pharsalia does not demonstrate that Lucan was a doctrinaire Stoic, but it suggests at least that he was the inheritor of a rich tradition of Stoic cosmological vocabulary ... and that in the application of this Stoic vocabulary, he displayed striking originality' (1979 p. 370).

war is comparable to the final catastrophe, the end of the world.[49] We know that Lucan's flood is a watery ecpyrosis (see above), so it is a smaller version of the end of the world. We know that Lucan's flood is like Ovid's flood. Ovid's flood is a premature return to the chaos which precedes it by some 200 lines. Therefore Lucan's flood looks forward to the end of the world, but through Ovid's flood it looks back to the beginning of the world. This is appropriate, since Lucan's ecpyrosis is 'antiquum repetens iterum chaos' (1.74): as the world returns to its own destruction, so too civil war retraces itself (1.692–3).

Chaos is formlessness and lack of definition (Ov. *Met.* 1.6–9), as is Ovid's flood (*Met.* 1.291–2), and Lucan's flood (4.99, 104–5; cf. 4.130, rivers regaining their definition after the flood). But is the same true of civil war? It is certainly the case that the *transgression* of boundaries is one of the most insistent themes in the poem, and there is a case to be made for saying that a definition transgressed is a definition destroyed. But civil war creates as many boundaries as it destroys: its keynote is *division*, and it is itself a *discrimen*.[50] The evil of civil war does not consist in a resulting formlessness, an absence of definition, so much as in *re-definition* – of *ius*, of *libertas*, on the political plane; of land in opposition to sea, and wall in opposition to wall on the geological plane.[51] If formless chaos is sometimes invoked as being 'like' civil war, it is clear that in many ways it is crucially 'unlike' civil war. We cannot be too hasty, then, in our reading of Lucan's 'sic' (1.72), especially

[49] See Lapidge 1979 p. 360 on 1.72–80.

[50] *Discrimen* is a key word in the *Bellum Civile*, often literally in the sense of a dividing line or a distinction between things (9.401, 9.493, 10.91, and here at 4.104), but often of the crisis of battle, the crisis of civil war, events of critical importance (2.599, 3.336, 4.48, 4.192, 4.770, 5.194, 5.249, 5.557, 5.723, 6.415, 7.242, 8.389, 10.532); in these cases, the *discrimen* is the thing that will 'make a difference', will distinguish between losing and winning, will decide between the republic and the domination of Caesar; the original sense of 'division' is never absent, and indeed takes its colour from the motif of division (i.e. the Roman state divided) that is part of the fabric of civil-war discourse.

[51] On walls see Saylor 1978 p. 247; on land and sea see Schönberger 1960.

since it becomes clear as the poem progresses that universal catastrophe is represented not as *parallel* to, but as an alternative *preferable* to civil war. So the astrologer Nigidius Figulus hypothesises about the ecpyrosis and the cataclysm that might be portended if the stars were in certain positions; but the climax, what the stars actually do portend, is civil war, the worst of all possibilities (1.651ff, cataclysm; 1.655ff, ecpyrosis; 1.658ff, civil war). And here most blatantly, in the description of the flood, Lucan calls for a cataclysm to wipe out civil war (as Jupiter used a flood to destroy the evil of the human race);[52] rather than have re-definition he would prefer no definition at all.

But it is obvious that the alternatives are not clear-cut opposites; it remains true that civil war has close parallels with cataclysm and a return to chaos. We noted the same problem at the beginning of the flood passage, where it was arguable either that the *motus* of wind and cloud was an alternative to the strife of arms, or that it was a meteorological re-enactment of the strife of arms. The doubt is appropriate, for in Lucan's epic the alternatives are always the same: Pompey is not so different from Caesar, as Sulla was barely distinguishable from Marius. Duality merges into unity at the same time as splitting into triplicity. Everything folds in on itself, twofold, threefold, and it is a chaos that never achieves the repose of formlessness; it is a paradoxical chaos of definition and re-definition, always changing, and, in a parody of the Stoic ecpyrosis, always spawning rebirth.

Crossing the river

A cataclysm, an ecpyrosis, a return to chaos: all these bring about a new beginning.[53] Ovid's *Metamorphoses* began with chaos, the poem like the world emerging out of formlessness into order, and his flood was so closely linked to this beginning that the whole of the passage from chaos to the end of the

---

[52] Note the way in which Lucan's prayer that the cataclysm may come is modelled on Jupiter's instructions to Neptune in *Met.* 1.277–80.

[53] Sandbach 1975 pp. 78–9.

flood can be regarded as a prologue to the rest of the poem.[54] The introductory episode of the *Aeneid* – the storm – has been shown by Hardie to play on a return to chaos.[55] There is, therefore, already in Lucan's flood-description an element of the introductory, or, since we are well into the poem by now, an element of the re-introductory. New beginnings have been plaguing us since the beginning of the book (*prima dies belli*, the catalogue); and if we are to believe the Vacca *Life*, book 4 was historically a 'new beginning' because the first three books were published in advance of the rest:[56] with book 4 we are moving into unpublished territory.

A new beginning, and a new Rubicon. The strategic reasons for constructing coracles, building a bridge, digging trenches and swimming across the Sicoris, indeed the reasons for having to cross the river in the first place, are completely eliminated in Lucan's account:[57] Caesar appears to cross the river simply as a demonstration of his power, and it is enough to frighten the Pompeians into retreat:

> postquam omnia fatis
> Caesaris ire videt, celsam Petreius Ilerdam
> deserit... (4.143–5)

and since the logic of the situation has been ignored,[58] the scene appears as an arbitrary exhibition of a variety of river-

---

[54] Galinsky 1975 p. 85, 'after the Introduction (the Creation and the Deluge) the poem falls into three parts of about equal length ...'

[55] Hardie 1986 pp. 190–1.

[56] In Hosius' edition (1905) p. 335.25; see, however, chapter 7 n. 19.

[57] Caesar's explanation runs as follows: the river must be crossed first of all in order to link up with Caesar's supply train (*BCiv* 1.54.5). Fabius' bridges have been destroyed; Caesar needs the coracles to send men across in order to build a new bridge from both banks (*BCiv* 1.54.3–4). The Sicoris is diverted into a multiplicity of canals in order to make it fordable (*BCiv* 1.61.1); thus he avoids having to send his cavalry up to the bridge, which is too far away, and makes them more mobile against the Pompeian foragers whom they are in the habit of harassing. Finally, all of Caesar's men swim across the still deep and swiftly-flowing ford, to save time in their pursuit of the retreating Pompeians (*BCiv* 1.64.2–7).

[58] Syndikus 1958 p. 18 (on why the Pompeians retreat); cf. Bachofen 1972 p. 124.

crossing methods, starting small and building up in audacity. First, Caesar uncharacteristically weaves little boats out of twigs and cowhide – the littleness of the boats (*parvam* ... *puppem* 131–2) explicitly contrasted with the overgrown size of the river (*tumidum* ... *amnem* 133). A small start, but a start at least (*primum*, 131); in Egypt these coracles are the first sign of order in the chaotic flooding of the Nile;[59] and as a first stage in the rebirth of the war, the poem, it is probably appropriate that Lucan alludes to Virgil's Bugonia – the rebirth of bees (and hence, one supposes, of poetry).[60]

This stage poses no problems: the boats shoot across the river like lightning ('super emicat' 133), and the next stage begins immediately. A huge bridge is constructed out of felled trees, recalling the by now instantly recognisable theme of deforestation;[61] the bridge, which stretches far out into the fields on either side (140; n.b. 'DIS-tendit'), is larger than absolutely necessary for the purpose in hand: it is built in *fear* of a further swelling of the already swollen river, it is a defence against the river's incursion. Third stage: not a defence, but an attack. Caesar will ensure that it is impossible for the river to increase

[59] 'sic, cum tenet omnia Nilus / conseritur bibula Memphitis cumba papyro' (135–6). *Nilus*, in juxtaposition to *omnia*, of course plays on *nil* (see Ahl 1985 pp. 121–2), giving the punning sense 'when nothing holds everything' – a glimpse of chaos. *Conseritur* suggests the weaving metaphors of the Stoics describing the fabric of the (ordered) universe; see Lapidge 1979 p. 349 (συμπλοκή) and p. 354 (the Roman equivalents, *nexus, contextus*).

[60] The allusion to *Georg.* 4.284 ('caesis ... iuvencis'; cf Lucan 4.132 'caeso ... iuvenco') is noted by Thompson and Bruère 1970 p. 154 as 'curious'; as for Virgil's Egyptian coracles a few lines later (*Georg.* 4.289; cf. Lucan 4.134–6), they suggest poetic rivalry as a motive: Lucan is more precise than Virgil, and names three places where coracles are used, as against Virgil's one. Of course, British coracles are a natural thing for Lucan to mention, since Caesar mentions them in his account ('imperat militibus Caesar ut navis faciant cuius generis eum superioribus annis usus Britanniae docuerat', *BCiv* 1.54.1); it is precisely significant that Lucan should speak of Egyptian coracles at all, that he should bother to allude so gratuitously to Virgil's Bugonia. On bees as a symbol of poetry, see Wimmel 1960 p. 175 n. 3.

[61] See chapter 2 pp. 25–9.

(141), by dividing it into rivulets; irrationally[62] this is conceived as a punishment (143), a Xerxes-like imposition of human will on natural elements.[63] Divide and conquer – this is how he will win the civil war. And finally, the fourth stage: the Caesarians cast all caution to the winds, and throw themselves bodily into the current (148ff). This fourth stage, exposing oneself gratuitously to immense personal risk, is always Caesar's trump card, and it is the height of his audacity: he will do it again at the mutiny of Placentia, and again when he sails the Adriatic alone in book 5. So at last Caesar's troops come out safely on the opposite shore, and the story gets going again.

Rivers are poetically loaded symbols, as we have seen often enough in Lucan so far, and of course they had been since the time of Callimachus. Now while it is obviously plausible that the Sicoris, after the deluge, should be swollen (whereas the swelling of the Rubicon was less plausible), we need not deny the possibility that the tumidity of the river is neatly overdetermined, and that we should read this river-crossing scene, like the Rubicon episode, as programmatic in significance. So: the crossing of the river in coracles plays implicitly on the nexus of Callimachean metaliterary imagery. The boats are small, and woven (*texitur* 132) out of twigs – twigs which are like the papyrus from which are woven (*conseritur* 136) Egyptian boats. The papyrus is a kind of reed, and undoubtedly we are to see an allusion to the topos of weaving things (e.g. baskets) out of reeds.[64] These therefore 'slender' boats, which are so suggestive of the 'slender' style of composition, bear up against the weight of their occupants ('vectoris patiens' 133); compare Prop 3.3.22, 'non est ingenii cumba gravanda tui', and perhaps the image of the huge hero Aeneas born up by Charon's 'cumba' in the underworld (*Aen.* 6.412–6). The river

---

[62] For it is here that Lucan departs most capriciously from the motivation attested by Caesar.

[63] Saylor 1978 p. 247.

[64] Virg. *Ecl.* 10.71, 'dum sedet et gracili fiscellam texit hibisco'; see Wimmel 1960 pp. 67–8. It is interesting that the papyrus has as much of a literary connotation as *harundo* ('reed', 'pen'), since, of course, paper was made out of it.

itself is tumid, and finds its parallel in the Ocean on which British coracles journey. Hence, by a bit of clever manipulation, Lucan has provided us with a variation on the 'small boat on a big sea' topos, which is used as a symbol of the great enterprise to be undertaken by a small and fragile *ingenium* – or by an *ingenium* that prefers the slender style[65] – and he has innovated, it appears, in melding the small boat topos with the weaving topos.

We know by now that Lucan has long since passed the point at which he can represent himself as journeying in a *small* boat: the floating land-masses at Brundisium and Massilia were his exaggerated response to that old topos. In fact this river-crossing scene is an elaborate joke: it shows Caesar acting out the role of a Callimachus, or an Apollo, and mimicking a Callimachean concern with slenderness, but in a way that is none the less typically Caesarian and askew. His little boats proclaim a slender *ingenium*; but his troops cross the tumid and Ocean-like river anyway,[66] quickly (*festinat* 137), casually, and with no interference from an Apollo figure (such as we would expect after the *revocatio* at the Rubicon). 'Fluviique ferocis / incrementa timens' (138–9) attests a Callimachean disdain of swollen rivers, and by building his bridge far from the banks he ensures that the current will not sweep anything away;[67] but this technique involves cutting down a *nemus* (138), and the resulting bridge is enormous. Finally, rather than abandoning the Sicoris and finding a slender Callimachean fount, he splits the swollen river into rivulets to bring it down to the required size. The river is suitably chastened for its excessive largeness; but Caesar's attitude of arrogant mastery in performing this typically civil-war act is at odds with Callimachus' emphasis on the holiness of his foun-

---

[65] Chapter 2 p. 38.

[66] Cf Ovid's Pythagoras, who admits that he has ventured into the middle of the sea: 'et quoniam magno feror aequore plenaque ventis / vela dedi ...' (Ov. *Met.* 15.176–7).

[67] Cf. Hor. *Sat.* 1.1.56–8 which plays implicitly on this topos: 'eo fit / plenior ut siquos delectet copia iusto, / cum ripa simul avolsos ferat Aufidus acer'.

tain,[68] and his obedience to the dictates of Apollo. One may in fact detect a process of reversal in this passage: starting from a slender *ingenium* confronting a swollen river, and ending with an attenuated river confronted by a swollen ego.

But in the end it is a purposeless show. What does Caesar care for the Callimachean programme? The enemy is escaping: Caesar and his troops do not bother to use either the bridge or the newly created ford (149–50), and coracleless they plunge into battle through the swollen waters (151). After all, this is an epic. Slenderness is out of place.

Universal love

The Pompeians escape towards Octogesa. Once again, Lucan spends some few lines describing the topography of the coming battle, and it is a topography that is strangely familiar. On the one hand, as Thompson and Bruère point out, there is an allusion to the site of Turnus' ambush in *Aen.* 11.522–7;[69] Turnus' ambush was a diversion away from the main field of battle; and for Petreius, who is fleeing towards the very edge of the world ('tendit in ultima mundi' 4.147) in a campaign which is already conceived as being on the edge of the world ('at procul extremis terrarum Caesar in oris / Martem saevus agit' 4.1–2), the reminiscence is not inappropriate, marking the Spanish campaign as a diversion away from the coming conflict with Pompey in Greece. And on the other hand, Lucan's ecphrasis recalls the series of ecphraseis (of which Ilerda was the last example) that play on the lie of the land as a geographical reflection of the military situation. As we must expect, the gorge through which the Pompeians are passing[70] is hemmed

---

[68] See Wimmel 1960 pp. 223f.

[69] Thompson and Bruère 1970 p. 155.

[70] 'Are passing', rather than 'are to pass'; Duff's translation of 160–2, 'Caesar saw that *if* the enemy reached that gorge, the war *would* slip from his hands ...', is surely inaccurate, since to read the relative clause as conditional depends on reading *emitti* as a future infinitive. Only by reading it as a present infinitive do we feel the full force of the absurdity in 167, 'dixit et ad montis tendentem praevenit hostem': Caesar overtakes the Pompeians so quickly that he reaches the mountains first even though they seem to have already arrived; 'hoste potito' is replaced by 'hostem tendentem' as if we had moved a step backwards in time. That's fast!

in by two opposed rocks, one on either side (157). Until now we have been willing to assume that if, out of context, Caesar possesses one hill and the Pompeians another (let us call this the inert, 'classic' form of the motif), then this symbolises the conflict that is civil war. But we have seen that this classic form is rarely allowed to remain inert; my discussion of the topography at Ilerda showed that the two-hill motif could be activised by the upsetting addition of an extra hill. Now in the gorge of Octogesa Lucan gives us a different kind of surprise: neither of the opposed crags is occupied, and the camps will both be sited in the valley in between. They occupy, in other words, precisely that line of definition that ought to separate them: a boundary is on the verge of being transgressed, and there is little to distinguish the two camps:

> illic exiguo paulum distantia vallo
> castra locant   (4.168–9)

Topographical proximity becomes an index of familial proximity (so *propinquum* 177)[71] and the little that separates the two armies spatially suggests that they are no longer to be opposed. The scene is well set, then, for the exhibition of love that follows; and in fact it is the nearness of the two armies which precipitates their fraternisation, as brother recognises brother across the short distance, and friend recognises friend.

Lapidge (1979, pp. 366–7) is quick to pick up on the cosmological overtones of the fraternisation scene, but as before his determination to find a simple correspondence between cosmic dissolution and civil war leads him astray. He argues that *Concordia*, which binds together opposing elements, is the stabilising force of the universe – the opposite, in fact, of cosmic dissolution – and that when Petreius disrupts this harmony, there is a return to *nefas* which is like dissolution. 'Thus the first encounter of the civil war follows the pattern of the flood which preceded it: as in the flood the accumulation of weathersystems overcame the river-banks and resulted in a mighty *vorago*, so in the battle *rabies* and *furor* overcome the *foedera pacis* and lead to utter *nefas*.' It would be wrong to deny this

---

[71] The same play on *propinquus* is noted by Rowland (1969) p. 205 on 3.305, where Caesar's spacial proximity is made to suggest a relationship of kin.

interpretation completely, but the fact is that it tells only half of the story; a valid half, but a half none the less. Lapidge has a strategy for dealing with those details which conflict with his approach: when he reads 'rupit amor leges' (175) – a clear case of 'dissolution' caused by the very forces which, according to Lapidge, should hold the universe together – he disables the thrust of the line by remarking 'the paradox is characteristic of Lucan: love here breaks the *leges* of war as a prelude to war breaking the bonds of love.' When love breaks bonds, it is merely a paradoxical prelude; when war breaks bonds, it is the real thing. But this depends on the assumption that the bonds of war are somehow less real, less important, than the bonds of love, that a universe based on war rather than on love is illegitimate, a poet's joke. Lapidge has betrayed himself as a partisan; surely the point about Lucan's universe is that the illegitimate is becoming legitimate, that things have reached such a pitch of perversity that conflict is replacing concord as the true binding force, and that disruption caused by love may be as much a disaster, a *nefas*, as disruption caused by enmity: 'omne futurum / crevit amore nefas' (204–5). Civil war is not the dissolution of a system; it is the exchange of one system for another.

So while it is not impossible to agree with Lapidge that the preceding flood finds its parallel in the ensuing *furor* and *rabies* which destroy this *concordia*, we must give proper emphasis to the parallel it finds in the fraternisation itself. As in the flood, boundaries are being transgressed ('audet transcendere vallum / miles' 175–6), and the soldiers' palms are *effusas* (176) like water, there are tears instead of rain ('fletus quid fundis inanis' 183). Everything is mixed up, and cannot be distinguished any more than blended wines can be separated:[72]

> pax erat, et castris *miles permixtus* utrisque
> errabat; duro concordes caespite mensas
> instituunt et *permixto* libamina *Baccho*   (4.196–8)

Further, the structure of the flood-description and the frater-

---

[72] On the imagery of liquids and mixing here, see the excellent Saylor 1986 pp. 150–1.

nisation scene runs parallel: just as Lucan depicts a great flood and then invokes a greater, universal flood, so now he describes an exhibition of love and then invokes the *concordia mundi*.

In the passage just cited, we see that to be *concors* is to be *permixtus*; and when Lucan invokes *Concordia* a few lines before, it is 'rerum *mixti*que salus concordia mundi' (190). Lapidge is forced to gloss *mixti mundi* as 'a universe constituted of opposing elements'. This must be at the least provocative, since *miscere* is a word usually associated with cosmic dissolution and the abolition of boundaries: thus in the flood 'rerum discrimina miscet' (4.104); so the conjunction of *concordia* with *mixti mundi* is paradoxical. *Concordia* itself is a difficult word: a *con-* compound, and therefore carrying connotations of conflict and confusion, of the process of concussion that brings about dissolution and civil war, but on the other hand the force that maintains the defining *nexus*. Truly a *concordia discors*; truly a word at war with itself.

After the flood, boundaries return ('utque habuit ripas Sicoris ...' 130); now there is a floodlike chaos of undistinguished fraternisation, and into it Petreius will reintroduce definition; he goes through the camp *dividing*:

> iunctosque amplexibus ense
> *separat* et multo *dis*turbat sanguine pacem   (4.209–10)

and, since (as we have seen) civil war is not so much about definition as re-definition, he replaces one kind of *foedus*, the 'foedera pacis' (205), with another, one kind of love ('sacer orbis amor' 191) with another ('scelerum amor' 236).[73] While he divides, he also confounds ('concussit' 236).

---

[73] See Johnson 1987 p. 13 for the irony in the repetition of *amor*. He is, however, wrong to suppose that Lucan's prayer to Concordia represents a sublime 'initial inspiration' (the way Lucan would have liked to write his epic), which later 'dissolves into poignancy, then into bitter tragedy and sardonic refutation of the very spirit that had inspired the prayer' (p. 12). The refutation is already in the prayer. Further, it must be some indication of the tongue-in-cheek nature of the prayer that while here Lucan invokes *concordia*, he later invokes *discordia* to finish the war (5.299; Berthold 1977 p. 223).

Afranius and Petreius

Lucan's portrayal of the fraternisation between the two armies
and of the final surrender of the Pompeians has been the occasion for a good deal of critical dissension.[74] Faced with a
Petreius loyal to the Pompeian cause, but denigrated as a per-
petrator of civil *nefas*, an Afranius who betrays the cause but
is showered with authorial approval, and an apparently benevolent Caesar, the commentators have been split over how
to master this ostensibly pro-Caesarian lapse on the part of a
poet who is elsewhere pro-Pompeian. It is to this scholarly
turmoil that I should like to add my own, discordant, voice.

Let us begin with the parallelism of Afranius and Petreius.
In the first section of this chapter I proposed that Lucan's
insistence on the concord of the two Pompeian generals precisely endangered the possibility of our taking him at his word.
While at the time the indeterminate nature of the text, which
was capable of supporting two contradictory interpretations,
led me to make a pointedly arbitrary choice of one over the
other, it should have become clear by now, through the ensuing sections, that there is indeed room in the episode as a
whole for a reading which problematises a simple view of
Pompeian solidarity, and of untroubled oppositions between
Pompeian and Caesarian, love and war, concord and discord,
order and chaos. What we find in the fraternisation and the
surrender is an urgent (but generally underestimated) insistence on the disparity of Afranius and Petreius even (or especially) in the face of a self-unified Caesar: on the one side is a
dux, on the other, two *duces*:[75]

> ... *dux* causae melioris eris. polluta nefanda
> agmina caede *duces* ...   (4.259–60)

Caesar's commentary in fact already foreshadows the fundamental division of character types within the Pompeian
camp. On hearing of the fraternisation, says Caesar,

---

[74] See Saylor 1986 pp. 149–50, reviewing past scholarship.
[75] For *dux* and *duces* see also 4.3, 25, 44.

Afranius ... paratus, ut videbatur, ut, quicumque accidisset casus, hunc quieto et aequo animo ferret. Petreius vero non deserit sese. (Caes. *BCiv* 1.75.1)

Afranius is unconcerned and uncommitted; Petreius is ever vigilant. For Lucan this becomes exemplary: it is Petreius alone who motivates the dis-fraternisation; and Lucan suppresses the 'true account' (which tells that the surrender was a joint decision, and that Afranius happened to be the one to make the supplicatory speech)[76] in making Afranius solely responsible: 'pacisque petendae / auctor ... Afranius' (4.337–8).

This might be mere co-incidence: it might be that Petreius happened to be in command on the first occasion, Afranius on the second occasion, and that even under Petreius the Pompeians would have had to surrender, but Lucan makes it quite clear through the speeches of each commander that the differences of action are motivated by a profound difference of principle: Afranius' speech to Caesar is either a snivelling betrayal of Petreius' severely righteous rebuke of his troops in the fraternisation scene, or at the very least a radical critique of it. Verbal reminiscences reinforce the obvious parallelism. Where Petreius had cried 'trahimur sub nomine pacis' (222), Afranius literally 'drags' his troops into Caesar's camp to sue for peace:

> pacisque petendae
> auctor damnatis supplex Afranius armis
> semianimes in castra *trahens* hostilia turmas
> victoris stetit ante pedes. (337–40)

Damnatis armis in the same passage recalls and perhaps re-interprets Petreius' scornful 'damnataque signa feretis' (217).[77]

---

[76] Caes. *BCiv* 1.84; cf. Appian *BCiv* 2.43.

[77] Haskins ad 4.217 understands Petreius to be referring to the Pompeians' own standards, of which they will have despaired if they surrender to Caesar; hence *feretis* means little more than that they bring the standards with them as gifts: 'will you go to a master and present him with your condemned standards ...?' – of course this is exactly what Afranius does later. But Duff may have a point in understanding 'signa feretis' in the stronger sense of 'carry standards into battle', i.e. 'wage war', and in

With similar scorn Petreius had asked

> utque habeat famulos nullo discrimine Caesar
> *exorandus* erit?   (218–9)

and Afranius duly 'begs' for his life:[78]

> at nunc causa mihi est *orandae* sola salutis
> dignum donanda, Caesar, te credere vita.   (346–7)

It is, further, by a typically Lucanian twist that Afranius makes a *causa orandae* out of a *causa oranda* – not pleading a cause, but giving a cause for making a plea (those who wish to underread 'causa' here, and give it the unemphatic meaning that survives in the English word 'because', should note that until over the half the line is read ('at nunc causa mihi est orand– '), it does indeed sound as if Afranius is saying 'but now I must plead my case'). While Petreius, that is, stands for the *causa senatus* (213) and the *causa aequa* (230),[79] Afranius makes his 'causa' out of his belief in Caesar's worthiness to grant his life; as for the Pompeian cause, 'causaeque priori, / dum potuit, servata fides' (350–1). This 'dum potuit' is an astounding qualifier if we consider the absolutism of Petreius' earlier exhortations:

> non *potes* hoc causae, miles, praestare, senatus
> adsertor victo redeas ut Caesare? certe,
> ut vincare, *potes. dum* ...   (213–15)

making the standards *Caesar's*; hence 'and carry the standards that you once condemned' i.e. as belonging to a former enemy. If this interpretation is the correct one (though perhaps we should not insist), it has an interesting effect: for the severely Pompeian Petreius, it is *Caesar's* weapons that are 'condemned'; for the disloyal and uncommitted Afranius, it is *Pompeian* weapons that are 'condemned'. Compare also 359–60 (Afranius speaking), 'nec enim felicibus armis / misceri damnata decet'.

[78] Ahl, wrongly (1976 p. 196): 'There is no trace of residual nobility in Caesar's Afranius [sc. in contrast to Lucan's Afranius]. It is, perhaps, in the contrast of the verbs *petimus* (in Lucan) and *orare atque obsecrare* (in Caesar) that the difference of manner comes across most clearly'; he does not notice Lucan's *orandae*.

[79] 'Aequa', revealingly equivocal: is the Pompeian cause 'just', or is it just 'equal' to the Caesarian cause?

Just where and when does it stop being possible to resist? According to Petreius the Pompeians should maintain their allegiance to the cause (to continue where we left off) . . .

> dum ferrum, incertaque fata,
> quique fluat multo non derit volnere sanguis (215–16)

Apparently, this means 'for ever', for as long as blood runs in your veins, as long as you can carry a sword . . . but by the time of the surrender it has become possible for Afranius to take Petreius' rhetorical periphrasis literally: fate is no longer uncertain, and there is no longer any possibility of using the sword or shedding any blood because Caesar is refusing to fight. Afranius' words sound like the fulfilment of conditions that Petreius had never seriously proposed:

> nil *fata* moramur . . .
> nec *cruor effusus* campis tibi bella peregit
> nec *ferrum* lassaeque manus. hoc hostibus unum,
> quod *vincas*, ignosce tuis. (351, 354–6)

Afranius' *dum potuit*, then, abides by the letter of Petreius' law, but none the less seems to contravene its spirit. Meanwhile, in place of *servata fides*, Afranius manages at least to preserve his *maiestas* ('servata precanti / maiestas' 340–1); we are to ask, is the exchange of *fides* for *maiestas* a viable transaction?

In conclusion, then, we have seen that when Afranius does not actually deny Petreius' words, he appropriates Petreius' rhetoric and reinterprets it in the new context of the necessity of surrender. The effect of this is to reaffirm solidarity; Afranius would have us believe that *both* commanders are behind the surrender:

> *nos* denique bellum
> invenit civile *duces*, causaeque priori,
> dum potuit, servata fides. (349–51)

But it is solidarity that is only apparent, and it is at the expense of principle. With the example of the Massilians behind us,

and with Vulteius yet to come, we must read this abandon-
ment of *fides* with some perplexity.[80]

The problem of Caesar's *clementia*

If Afranius and Petreius are as opposed as I suggest, this
immediately hamstrings any reading of the episode as consistently pro-Pompeian – self-consistently, that is, and consistently with the rest of the poem. The weaknesses of such a
reading are perfectly exemplified in Ahl's discussion of Caesar's *clementia*, which is the most eloquent attempt to date to
smooth over the contradictions in Lucan's stance.[81] Ahl's
strategy, in fact, is to transfer the perplexity of the reader to
the author, that is, to assume that the difficulties experienced
by the reader in coming to terms with inconsistencies in
Lucan's political message in fact stem from the difficulties experienced by Lucan in coming to terms with the 'uncomfortable truths' of history:

> If the Caesarian account is an approximation of the truth, Lucan is con-
> fronted with an episode that not only shows the Pompeians in a very bad
> light, unwilling to fight and prepared to sell out to Caesar, but is evidence
> of Caesar's clemency. Lucan's task is to reduce the impact of Caesar's
> clemency and of the overall damage the incident causes to the republican
> image. (p. 193)

In support of this hypothesis, Ahl must show that in spite of
Lucan's necessary failure (he must have failed, otherwise we

---

[80] On the *fides* of the Massilians as a good old Roman virtue and an implicit
rebuke of the actual Romans who appear to have forgotten it, see Rowland 1969 p. 205, and note especially 3.301–3:

> Phocais in dubiis ausa est *servare* iuventus
> non Graia levitate *fidem* signataque iura,
> et *causas, non fata, sequi.*

In Vulteius we are faced with an Afranius in negative who is equally
problematic: a *Caesarian* who is *praised* for *preserving* his loyalty. The
commentators are therefore equally perplexed: see Pfligersdorffer 1959
p. 365, Schönberger 1961 pp. 217–23, Heyke 1970 pp. 147–54 for the
question of whether it matters that Vulteius is on the wrong side, and
(with Rutz 1960 pp. 466–8, Ahl 1976 pp. 119–21 and Berthold 1977
pp. 221ff) on whether Vulteius can be considered a positive *exemplum*.

[81] Ahl 1976 pp. 192–7.

would not notice the problem) there is some evidence of 'Lucan attempting to salvage what he can from the debacle' (p. 195, on the surrender of Afranius); but not too much, for Ahl is in the (comfortable) position of being able to attribute the failure of his reading to the failure of the poet;[82] and so the only immediately compelling refutation of his position would consist in showing that Lucan is more successfully pro-Pompeian than Ahl allows. None the less, since this is impossible, we must do what we can.

Consider Ahl's defence of Petreius. In essence, he argues (pp. 194–5) that although Petreius is condemned by Lucan for his breach of *pietas*, he 'has every right to be enraged' at the fraternisation, since Caesar's account shows that in reality this fraternisation was a betrayal of the Pompeian camp – a fact that Lucan alludes to covertly; if Petreius and his troops come off badly in Lucan's account, at least they can be respected for their continued heroic resistance: Lucan's pro-Pompeian intent is undiminished.

What does Lucan gain by this curious treatment of the incident? First, he sidesteps the uncomfortable truth that the Pompeians did not want to fight Caesar at all. He would rather damn them and Petreius for a breach of *pietas* so he can portray them as heroically resisting Caesar until thirst and hunger compel them to capitulate. At the same time, he saves Petreius from total censure by alluding to the real version of what happened, relying on his reader's knowledge of history. (p. 195)

Now, this position raises some important questions which may show how crucially flawed it is. As regards Lucan's relation to Caesar, Ahl wants to tread a thin tightrope: on the one hand, he maintains that Lucan's text *deforms* and *suppresses* Caesar's commentary in the interests of providing a new, pro-Pompeian, interpretation of the civil wars; and on the other, he assumes that Lucan's readers are able to supplement his

---

[82] 'The important thing is not the degree of historical and rhetorical manipulation Lucan uses to minimise Caesar's clemency, but the simple fact that he *is* trying to play down Caesar's moral qualities. *His portrayal of Caesar in Spain seems favorable not because he intended it to be so but because, despite his efforts, he could not make it unfavorable.*' (Ahl 1976 p. 197; mostly my italics).

text with their detailed knowledge of Caesar's commentary, wherever appropriate. Both: Caesar's text is erased; and: Caesar's text is present. From a purely theoretical point of view, this 'having your cake and eating it' must be something like the reader's true position. Caesar's text is, *and* is not, a relevant context for Lucan's – *both at the same time*. What is disturbing in Ahl's reading of the episode is the way in which he dictates when and where exact knowledge of Caesar's account is to be ignored, and when conjured as a corrective. If, indeed, this 'reader familiar with the Caesarian account'[83] is so attuned to the possibility of allusion that he can comfortably treat the smallest oddity as a signal to overwrite Lucan's account with Caesar's,[84] it would be remarkably docile of him not to see the possibility of overwriting Lucan elsewhere as well; he would bear constantly in mind that Lucan's version of events and Caesar's version of events are different; and would enjoy as one of the pleasures of the poem the implied invitation to compare the historian's 'truth' with the poet's 'lies'. Such a position would at all times threaten to undermine our reception of the new *Bellum Civile* as corrective because a rewriting of the old. That is, Lucan proclaims in effect (through his title, through his choice of subject) that he will give a true account of civil-war history which will remove the subtle bias that contaminates Caesar's commentary, and which will re-

---

[83] Ahl, 1976 p. 194: 'The reader unfamiliar with the Caesarian account must surely find these lines inexplicable ... The reader familiar with the Caesarian account will know that Petreius has every right to be enraged.'

[84] For Ahl, this signal consists in the words '[sc. Petreius] seque et sua tradita venum / castra videt' (206–7). It seems to me that he exaggerates the perplexity that these lines should cause, when he suggests that the reader can only explain them if he has recourse to the Caesarian account. We might provisionally assume that (a) Petreius *thinks*, mistakenly, that his camp has been sold, or, more likely, that (b) Petreius treats the fraternisation as if it were a betrayal: such is the height of his republican fervour that to him a spontaneous exhibition of brotherly love is on a level with treachery through bribery. To be sure, the words have their origin in the Caesarian account; but if we interpret them as I suggest, they need be no more than a derisive gesture towards that origin.

instate the dignity of the losing side.[85] Let us not underestimate the priority of that reading; but at the same time, let us agree that Lucan's extremes of pro-Pompeian partisanship, his often wilful distortion of received fact, and his lacunic, elliptic twists of narrative ensure that we can never ignore the account which he claims to displace. The excitement of reading the *Bellum Civile* consists partly in our experience of the tension involved in the question of which of the two authors we should priorise. Or, who do we believe? And who do we want to believe?

The tension is all: to break the tension and come down definitively now on one side and now on the other is to misrepresent the power of the text to authorise a single true reading. Ahl, who weaves an intricate course through this particular sea of indeterminacy, attempts to provide a single pro-Pompeian reading, such a reading as we know cannot be 'true'; and if we ask what other criterion motivates it, we discover that, profoundly, he wants to show that Lucan is *consistent*, presumably on the grounds that inconsistency is commonly held to be a sort of incompetence. So important is this criterion (which has implications beyond the scope of our discussion) that, to ape Ahl's words out of context, he sidesteps the uncomfortable truth that Lucan favours Caesar and does not approve of Petreius at all; and he would rather damn Lucan for an isolated poetic failure so he can portray him as maintaining a consistent political stance even in opposition to a 'true' Caesarian account.

> Lucan's treatment of Caesar's activities in Spain ... seems, at first glance, thoroughly inconsistent with his attitude to him in the rest of the epic ... It would, I think, be overhasty to assume a temporary change of heart on Lucan's part. The difference is, rather, the by-product of dealing with an irrefutable case of Caesarian *clementia*. (p. 192)

To the 'irrefutability' of Caesar's *clementia* (which is irrefutable because it appears in Caesar's own version) we must return in a moment. But to continue. Even as he accounts for one major inconsistency, Ahl discovers (correctly) that Lu-

---

[85] See Rambaud 1960; and my own discussion in chapter 2 pp. 17–19.

can's approbation of Afranius' 'selling out' to Caesar, which leads to his voicing the opinion *in propria persona* that non-involvement is the only good course in the civil war, is a flat contradiction of Cato's stance in book 2. Ahl's republican (and pro-Catonian) reading of the poem has compelled him to read Cato's words as a statement of 'Lucan's own avowed position', and, perhaps absurdly, he continues to privilege this Catonian position over the position that the author himself actually does avow, here. Be that as it may, Ahl is forced to admit an inconsistency:

> As we shall see [sc. in a later chapter] this is a flat contradiction of Lucan's own avowed position in *Pharsalia* 2, and of his justification for Cato's entry into the civil war. Lucan has sacrificed the overall consistency of his theme in a vain attempt to salvage a patently unsalvageable episode. (p. 197)

So the inconsistencies proliferate; he cannot control them all, and here finally he must appeal to the paradox that one inconsistency (the flat contradiction) is the price that must be paid for a consistency (pro-Pompeianism); or to phrase the absurdity more plainly, Lucan has sacrificed the overall consistency of his theme in a vain attempt to maintain the overall consistency of his theme. Ahl is tying himself up in knots.

It is time to begin to propose an alternative approach. Let us release Lucan from the duty of being anti-Caesarian and pro-Pompeian. The good staunch loyal Petreius is authorially condemned; his speech, a faultless classic of republican rhetoric, which should align him with the great heroes of early republican Rome, does no more than inspire a love of crime:[86]

sic fatur et omnis
concussit mentes scelerumque reduxit amorem. (235–6)

Nefas ensues (243): once again Lucan shows that in civil war the highest Roman values are inevitably misdirected – this *nefas* is the result of the *fides* that Petreius held so dear ('fecit monstra fides' 245). Petreius aligns himself with (for instance) Scaeva, who mistook crime for virtue. Even if Ahl is correct in

---

[86] Cf. the same paradox in 2.323–5 (Cato's advice to Brutus).

arguing that we must bear the Caesarian account in mind, and that in fact the Pompeian troops 'have been doing everything of which Lucan's Petreius accuses them', it is not legitimate to deduce that therefore 'Petreius has every right to be outraged', since the notion of 'right' is precisely what is being attacked, confused, inverted, redefined by civil war – the point of this passage (among others) is to show how the most understandable, the most apparently 'right' actions, when torn from their usual context and set in a civil war, become the opposite of right.

While Petreius is condemned, Afranius is condoned. It is, however, impossible to read Lucan's praise of Afranius as pro-Pompeian in motivation (which is what Ahl tries to do), since the point about Afranius is that in abandoning his *fides* to Pompey, he denies that he (or Petreius) had ever really supported Pompey in the first place:

> non partis studiis agimur nec sumpsimus arma
> consiliis inimica tuis. nos denique bellum
> invenit civile duces, causaeque priori,
> dum potuit, servata fides.   (348–51)

It is a position which anticipates the argument of Curio, who fears for the loyalty of his troops (who had previously been Pompeians):[87]

> eripe consilium pugna: cum dira voluptas
> ense subit presso, galeae texere pudorem,
> quis conferre duces meminit, quis pendere causas?
> qua stetit inde favet.   (4.705-8)

In any case, Afranius' obsequious submission to Caesar is a total negation of the position of the haughty (but authorially favoured) Domitius, who considered the gift of his life the worst possible punishment. Domitius lived to fight and die (for

---

[87] In the following passage, Duff mistranslates *eripe consilium pugna* as 'snatch from them [i.e. the enemy] by battle the power to form a plan'. Surely better in context would be 'snatch consideration [from yourselves] by battle', i.e. 'don't think, fight'.

Pompey) another day; Afranius, who never fights again, is no true Pompeian.[88]

Ahl makes much of the argument that the historical sources compel Lucan to treat the incident in the way he does. So, if Caesar appears to be good, and Petreius bad, and if Afranius' position of selling out contradicts those positions which Lucan elsewhere appears to endorse, if, in other words, Lucan fails, it is not for want of trying; but certain 'irrefutable' facts of history stand in his way. This is clearly absurd, as the briefest examination of Lucan's treatment of his sources would indicate. My discussion of the Massilia episode in particular will have shown just how cavalier is his attitude to history; while he generally does not tell utter fictions, he is quite capable, by means of rearrangement, imputation of unlikely motivations, and particularly omission, of twisting the most obstinate historical fact to suit his needs. Ahl manages to give evidence of some such distortion in the scenes we are discussing (e.g. he is successful in showing that Lucan tones down the importance of Caesar's clemency as a catalyst for the fraternisation, pp. 193–4); what is remarkable is that there is not more. Now, while it is always dangerous to hypothesise about what Lucan *might* have done, none the less would it not make more sense, for a poet with avowed pro-Pompeian aims, to make Afranius into a criminal, a Judas who betrayed the cause behind the

---

[88] Contrast Afranius' demand for pardon,

> supplex Afranius ...
> semianimes in castra *trahens* hostilia turmas
> victoris *stetit ante pedes* ...
> ... et *veniam* securo pectore *poscit*   (4.338–43)

with Domitius' demand for death:

> ecce, nefas belli, reseratis agmina portis
> captivum *traxere* ducem. civisque superbi
> *constitit ante pedes.* voltu tamen alta minaci
> nobilitas recta *ferrum* cervice *poposcit*.
> scit Caesar poenamque peti *veniamque timeri*   (2.507–11)

Note that in Plutarch's *Cato Minor* (66.2), Cato commits suicide as a rejection of Caesar's potential clemency.

back of the noble Petreius? Would it not have been better to disown Petreius too, rather than make him voice such obviously 'virtuous' sentiments, only to surprise us at the end with the information that we must read those sentiments as evil? Or, if Lucan wanted to rescue Petreius, could he not have implied that fighting broke out spontaneously against Petreius' will? In fact, could Lucan have not avoided treating the fraternisation at all? – certainly Plutarch and Cassius Dio make no mention of it.

What is perhaps equally remarkable is the extent to which Lucan has imported a gratuitous pro-*Caesarian* tone into the surrender scene. No 'uncomfortable truths' of history compel Lucan to include the detail that, in response to Afranius' plea,

> [dixerat.] at Caesar *facilis voltuque serenus*
> flectitur atque usus belli poenamque remittit. (363–4)

We *must* compare this with the last time we caught a glimpse of Caesar's face, also in response to a speech of supplication, at Massilia:

> sic Graia iuventus
> finierat, cum *turbato* iam prodita *voltu*
> ira ducis tandem testata est voce dolorem. (3.355–7)

We see then that the serenity of Caesar's face in Spain is uncharacteristic for being a positive feature.[89] But further, this comparison with the Massilian campaign has the virtue of underlining a fact that should otherwise be obvious. For the Massilians' embassy (to which Afranius' speech is parallel) is *not* negotiating a surrender, and their eventual surrender, which should come later in the episode, and in response to which we know Caesar displayed his characteristic *clementia*,

---

[89] Typically, Thompson and Bruère (1970, p. 160) seek to defuse this oddity by appealing to Lucan's incompetence: 'In granting Afranius' plea with uncharacteristic disinterestedness Caesar for an instant is divested of his Lucanian *furor* and made by his conduct to reflect the *pietas* of Virgil's Aeneas. This would appear to be an incidental effect of Lucan's allusion which the poet did not foresee.'

is pointedly absent in Lucan's account.[90] If Lucan could cut Caesar's *clementia* from his Massilian episode, why not here in the Spanish episode? We can conclude that the surrender scene is there not because history imposed it, but because Lucan wanted it there.

There is a possible objection. Perhaps it can be shown that, in contrast to the petition of the Massilians, Afranius' speech manages to find exactly the right kind of rhetoric to overcome the possibility of Caesar's anger. The toadying 'dignum donanda, Caesar, te credere vita' (347) sets the tone for Afranius to play the Latins to Caesar's Aeneas:[91] perhaps Caesar is so flattered by the implications of Afranius' speech that he is prepared not to exercise his usual cruelty; Afranius probably knows this, and has recognised that he must sacrifice his principles to make a ploy of his obsequiousness. In answer to this objection: an ironic reading of Afranius' speech, which shows Afranius accepting the degrading position of flatterer as a necessary evil, will have some trouble showing how this squares with *servata maiestas*, which implies precisely the reverse: dignity in defeat. And secondly, though we may question whether 'facilis voltuque serenus' *on its own* shows a pro-Caesarian bias, none the less, authorial approval is behind Caesar (and Afranius) all the way, from the gratuitous gloss 'iustae' (365) for 'foedera pacis' (which implies that if the 'foedera pacis' of the fraternisation (205) were wrong, *these* 'foedera pacis' are right), to the Virgilian-sounding *laudes* of the non-military life,[92] which come across as a hymn of gratitude to the mercy of Caesar, from the incredible 'dux causae melioris eris' (259), whose irony cannot be (objectively) gauged, to the late recurrence of *liber* in 4.384

> tunc arma relinquens
> victori miles spoliato pectore tutus

---

[90] Caes. *BCiv* 2.22.6; see Rowland 1969 p. 205.
[91] On Lucan's allusions to the embassy of the Latins in *Aen.* 11 see Thompson and Bruère 1970 p. 160.
[92] For allusions to Virgil's *laudes vitae rusticae* in *Georgic* 2, see Thompson and Bruère 1970 pp. 161–2.

innocuusque suas curarum *liber* in urbes
spargitur. (4.382–5)

showing that for all the liberty the Pompeians think they protect, only Caesar seems to be able to make men free.[93]

The fractured voice

At last, it is time to draw some conclusions. What I have
argued is that, at least from the fraternisation scene until the
end of the episode, Lucan has fairly consistently showered dis-
approval on Petreius, who is loyal to the Pompeian cause, and
approval on Afranius, who abandons the Pompeian cause.
Further, although the cruelty of Caesar does come out (more
than it need do) in his policy of refusing to fight,[94] by the end
of the episode he too comes in for unusual praise. In this section of the poem, therefore, our narrator has, it might appear,
changed his stance, and temporarily become a supporter of
Caesar. These things are all obvious: they are only difficult
because everyone has recognised that they do not square with
a pro-Pompeian reading of the poem. Given all of this, we
have a choice of roughly two strategies: first, to claim that, in
some cases, the political alignments of Lucan's *exempla* are
irrelevant; it does not matter, for instance, that Petreius is
Pompeian, since he exemplifies in abstract the *nefas* that comes
from the paradoxes of civil war, and rhetorical effect is more
important than the promulgation of a political message. The
alternative strategy is to suppose that Lucan intended to engi-
neer a pointed contradiction.

With the first approach I have more sympathy than I ought,
for it seems to me that Lucan is a less passionately dedicated
republican than is usually supposed, and the extent to which
we may draw conclusions about his political stance from his
involvement in the Pisonian conspiracy has certainly been ex-

---

[93] Cf. Saylor 1986 p. 156.

[94] Caes. *BCiv* 1.71–2: Caesar avoids battle (even though his men urge him
on) because he wants to prevent unnecessary bloodshed on both sides.
Lucan's Caesar is significantly less humanitarian: he knows that staying
the sword is sometimes crueller than using it.

aggerated.[95] On these grounds it would be *prima facie* reasonable to be less surprised by the capriciousness of Lucan's allegiance to Pompey. But in the present case we must be rigider. It will not do to posit an impartial Lucan because his stance here is so obviously *calculated* to confuse us: in the course of my discussion I have gestured towards parallels in the Vulteius episode, the Scaeva episode, the Corfinium episode, the Massilian embassy and Cato's justification for entry into the war. Were a detailed comparison to be undertaken, it would emerge that not only do the *speeches* show through their parallelism an embarrassing disagreement between Pompeian and Pompeian, and a frightening agreement between Pompeian and Caesarian, but also the *connecting narrative* evinces an inexplicable disparity of authorial 'point of view'. And the effect of these active contradictions is, quite simply, to fracture the solidarity of the narrating voice.

For Lucan has become a character in his own poem: we discover that, more than any other epicist before him, Lucan makes of himself not only a knowing narrator, but a subjective and enthusiastic spectator of his war.[96] Consider a passage like Lucan's invocation of Concordia in the fraternisation scene. When he writes

---

[95] On this question I oppose myself to the almost unanimous agreement of the commentators (for a review of the relevant scholarship see Rutz 1985 pp. 1481–8 and add Sullivan 1985 pp. 143–52, Martindale 1984). The main problem with the use of the Pisonian conspiracy as evidence of Lucan's republicanism is that it assumes too easy a relation between a poet's life and his work; and besides, what we know of the conspiracy suggests that it was not an ideological struggle, so much as an attempted coup motivated by personal ambition (Sullivan 1985 p. 148 and Griffin 1984 p.159). Certainly we know that Tacitus believed Lucan's involvement in the conspiracy stemmed from personal animosity (*Ann.* 15.49); if it has in the past been claimed that Tacitus was wrong, and that Lucan joined the conspiracy in a glow of republican ardour, this is because it has been assumed that Lucan's poem is pro-republican (because, circularly, Lucan joined a republican conspiracy). It is time to put a stop to this circularity; here; now.

[96] See chapter 1 n. 14.

nunc ades [sc. Concordia] ...
        ... magnum nunc saecula nostra
venturi discrimen habent. periere latebrae ...   (189, 191–2)

we may, at a pinch, manage to read past the shifter *nunc* without too much discomfort: more likely than not he means 49 BC, rather than the 60s AD (though surely the abrupt juxtaposition of the present [*nunc*] *habent* with *periere*, perfect, should ruffle us a bit). But with 'saecula *nostra*' he has gone too far: it takes a great deal of determination not to interpret *nostra* initially as 'mine, the poet's, and yours, the reader's', since the sentence seems to set out as if to say, 'this fraternisation could be a crucial moment in the genesis of the Neronian age'. But *venturi* eventually forces us to take the unlikely step of reading *saecula nostra* as 'the time of the civil wars' – the time that is being recreated in front of us, and in which poet and reader participate: Lucan is shown to be a contemporary bystander, but not without our being reminded (through the difficulty of the interpretation) that this is a striking anomaly.

It is useful, though not quite true, to say that Lucan the character is on a level with all the other characters in the poem, partisan, rhetorically proficient, but not thereby authoritative. That is, *as* a character, as a contemporary of civil war, it is right that he should be afflicted by all the paradoxes and divisions that civil war entails; swallowed and caught up in a war where *no-one* is right, and where every position is a paradox, a contradiction, it must be that Lucan's position is wrong, a paradox, a contradiction. That is not mere critical sophistry: that is the way things *must* be, for to have an author with an uncomplicated, single, *true* point of view would be to suggest that the civil war had a single, uncomplicated and true solution – and that, I think we must all agree, is entirely foreign to the paradox-ridden picture of civil war that Lucan paints for us.

But Lucan is somewhat more than a character; it is not quite true to say that he is just one more voice to add to the polylogue, though certainly we may interpret his subjectivity as a gesture towards the abdication of authorial tyranny. It can, however, only be a gesture: the author remains, by a definition that rests, I suppose, on the law of the genre (i.e. it is the way we read), the authority of the poem. So: Lucan is the voice that comes back again and again, each time slightly different. The connecting narrative is split by speeches into speech-like parts, and just as Lucan shows a (typically 'Silver age'?) fondness for arguing two sides of a case in the speeches of his characters,[97] so too the 'speeches' that are Lucan's form an interesting internal dialogue. But he is also the moral, philosophical and political authority of the poem, and for that reason we must be disturbed by his internal contradictions. But – and here is the crucial point – that is exactly why he contradicts himself. The poem, the civil war, is and takes as its subject the internal fracturing of authority. It is a world where what should be one is many, where the unity of the Roman state is painfully divided, and where, until the final victory is won by one side or the other, there will be many potential authorities each vying for supremacy. A Pompey, a Caesar; more frightening than this dichotomy, an Afranius, a Petreius (even men on the same side are on different sides). It is, therefore, mimicry of civil war, of divided unity, *concordia discors*, that has produced this split in the authorial, dominating, legitimising persona, this one poet many poets, this schizophrenia, the fractured voice.

[97] Schönberger 1961 pp. 75ff.

4

APPIUS AND THE DELPHIC ORACLE

The business of civil war is dissection and antithesis – Rome is divided, and each half fights against the other. So, analogously, Lucan's poem of civil war features the antithetical doubling of epic topoi and epic characteristics as its device *par excellence*. We have seen this device at work, with all its paradoxical complications, in our examination of the Ilerda episode, and we have discovered that not even the authorial persona, that most fundamental and stable of literary features, is immune. Now we will see it operating more specifically and on a slightly grander scale. It has long been known that Lucan's Delphic episode (book 5) and his Erictho episode (book 6) play extensively on allusion to Aeneas' consultation of the Sibyl and his descent into the underworld in *Aeneid* 6.[1] But although it has been recognised that Lucan's two episodes in some sense run in parallel,[2] the Delphic episode has been regarded as poor stepsister to the more impressive necromancy,[3] and has consequently not received the attention it deserves. For practical reasons this is not surprising: to spend too much time on the Delphic episode is to risk repeating in anticipation a discussion of Erictho; and the Erictho scene, with its gruesome horror and black pessimism, has always been a favourite *locus* for those who would read the poem as a product of the baroque and macabre age of madness in which it was written,[4] and, more recently, an anti-Aeneid. Virgil's 'nekuia' occurs in the sixth book of the *Aeneid*; Lucan's pseudo-nekuia in the sixth

---

[1] On Lucan's Pythia and Virgil's Sibyl, see section 4. On Erictho's necromancy and Aeneas' descent to the underworld, see chapter 6 n. 1.

[2] Ahl 1976 pp. 130–2; links are noted in passing remarks by Schrempp 1964 p. 28 n. 42, Morford 1967 p. 66, Le Bonniec 1970 p. 186, Luck 1985 p. 280.

[3] See Morford 1967 p. 66 ('gusto').

[4] So e.g. Bourgery 1928B; Baldini Moscadi 1976 (esp. pp. 189–92).

book of the *Bellum Civile*. That is more than a coincidence: if that sort of parallel between book numbers finds no place else-where in the poem (unless, perhaps, we read Marius' and Sulla's sacks of Rome in *BC* 2 as an antithetically doubled version of Virgil's sack of Troy in *Aen.* 2),[5] the parallel be-comes in fact all the more striking for its uniqueness. Viewed from this perspective, it is not to be wondered at that the Delphic episode, which is shorter and has been relegated to an unassuming position at the beginning of book 5, should be regarded as merely prefatory.

The bias in favour of the Erictho episode leans a little on the hypothesis – nowadays almost taken for granted – that the poem is unfinished and that if it had been completed it would have ended with the suicide of Cato in a proposed book 12;[6] which would give the *Bellum Civile* the same number of books as the *Aeneid*. If that is the case, the coincidence of Lucan's and Virgil's episodes occurring in books with the same number is not merely numerical, but structural: a point of contact at the centre.[7] Let us instead assume for a moment that the poem is complete as it stands (a position I will develop more fully in chapter 7). In a poem ten books long the Delphic episode and the Erictho episode, at the beginning of book 5 and the end of book 6 respectively, act as a frame for the central core of the poem; and further, they stand on either side of the divide between books 5 and 6, that is, between the two halves of the poem. Virgil's underworld episode ends exactly on the dividing-line between the two halves of the *Aeneid*; in Lucan the episode is torn in two, the pieces positioned in such a way as to mimic the centrality of Virgil's original whilst importing division and opposition.[8]

---

[5] Albrecht 1970 p. 282 proposes a parallel here on the grounds that both are flashbacks; less convincingly he proposes that both *Aen.* 4 and *BC* 4 feature a 'fraternisation' that sharpens the conflict.

[6] Most convincingly Ahl 1976 pp. 306–26.

[7] So Fauth 1975 p. 335; similarly Narducci 1985 pp. 1549–50 (used as proof of a twelve-book structure); the position is attacked by Marti 1970 p. 30 (who believes in a sixteen-book structure).

[8] Compare, perhaps, the already existing tradition of imitation by 'dé-doublement'; on which, Knauer 1964 p. 137 n. 1 (etc. – see his index).

Arguments from structure are often facile; this one, I think, carries some weight. But whatever the state of Lucan's poem, complete or incomplete, one thing is clear: that Lucan's Delphic and Thessalian episodes, split off from the same source, form a contending pair, and it is ultimately as a pair that we must understand them. It is to the first half of this pair that we now, slowly, turn.

The setting: the senate at Epirus

In the first line of his Delphic ἔκφρασις τόπου Lucan tells us that Delphi stands at the centre of the earth:

Hesperio tantum quantum summotus Eoo   (5.71)

It is a standard known about Delphi, and the ecphrasis is a standard epic phenomenon; but we should not allow this to deaden our sensitivity to the game Lucan is playing here. The centre of the world, at this point in the poem, has become a very pertinent concept. In the long term, the narrative has played on our desire to see the two leaders confront each other 'in the centre' like gladiators, on the Emathian plains; tension has been generated because the action has continually veered away from the centre to the extremes of the earth, avoiding the promised implosion at Pharsalus. Geographically, the sequence of events runs as follows: Caesar comes from the northern extreme against the senators in the centre (at Rome); Pompey escapes eastwards, and his forces are assembled from the eastern extreme[9] while Caesar takes the centre (Rome). Caesar besieges Massilia (in the West), and after a short while moves to the western extreme ('versus ad Hispanas acies *extremaque mundi* / iussit bella geri', 3.454–5). Book 4 opens with a reiteration of Caesar's extreme position: 'At procul *extremis terrarum* Caesar in *oris* . . .' (4.1); and in fact, before the campaign is over the Pompeians will have escaped even further west: 'Petreius Ilerdam / deserit . . . et tendit in *ultima mundi*' (4.144–7) – the edge of the edge. At this stage we are to imagine (albeit contrary to fact) a scenario which puts Caesar on

---

[9] So 2.632 'mundi iubeo temptare recessus'; in Pompey's catalogue of forces, 3.229, 'movit et Eoos bellorum fama recessus'.

the western extreme of the world, and Pompey on the eastern extreme; so Petreius:[10]

> ... nunc toto fatorum ignarus in orbe,
> Magne, paras acies *mundique extrema* tenentis
> sollicitas reges, cum forsan foedere nostro
> iam tibi sit promissa salus.   (4.232–5)

As the book goes on, we see the action sucked centrewards; gesturing towards the notion of *ultima mundi* as if to remind us how far we have come away from the edge, Lucan puts Antony on an edge of sorts, in Illyricum:

> clauditur *extrema* residens Antonius *ora*   (4.408)

(certainly alluding to 4.1), playing out another version of Actium[11] – we are a long way east of Massilia, the other 'Actium' in which the Caesarians were victorious (antithetical doubling again). Turning next to the Curio episode, we see clearly that the edges are coming to the centre (the centre of Africa, at least). Juba is an African Pompey, who like Pompey calls on troops from the extremes of the earth:

> ... *extremaque mundi*
> signa suum comitata Iubam.   (4.669–70)

Concurrently with this movement – the action pushed to the edges and back again, never quite reaching a conflict that is geographically central – Lucan has been telling us with disturbing regularity that civil war has not really started yet: hence, for instance, the suggestion of a beginning at Ilerda, implying that all that came before was not quite civil war. Even as late as the end of book 4 Lucan is willing to make it appear that

---

[10] Pompey was in Greece at this time, not, as it happens, any further east. I am not accusing Lucan of inaccuracy here, since Lucan does not say that Pompey was further east, and even if he did, the words come from the mouth of Petreius. I do however maintain that Petreius' words *imply* a contrast of 'We are on this edge, Pompey is on the other edge'. That, for the moment, is all that is important.

[11] The Vulteius episode pits an Antony (*the* Antony) against an Octavius on the western shore of the Greek mainland. How can we not think of Actium (Antony versus Octavian)? Cf. later, Antony already premeditating an Actium, 5.478–9.

nothing has really happened yet, that Curio's war in Africa, even though it involved an actual battle with a Roman enemy (incredibly, glossed over in Lucan's account), was an inadequate dry run, and that Curio was killed before he had a chance to see civil war:

> ante iaces quam dira duces Pharsalia confert
> spectandumque tibi bellum civile negatum est.   (4.803)

We could, naturally, compel this to mean 'you were denied the chance to watch the *whole* civil war (though you watched part of it)'; but the force of the sentence lies in the equation of *bellum civile* with *Pharsalia*; the civil war begins finally at Pharsalus – until we reach Pharsalus, and concomitantly, until we reach the centre of the world, nothing has really happened.

Our desire to see the promise of 'Bella per Emathios ... campos' fulfilled, our desire to be done with all that is prefatory, to read our way out of that tension-building postponement which is so clearly the hallmark of Lucan's narrative technique, and to get on to the real business of the war, will, I believe, temporarily mislead us when we come to the first lines of book 5:

> Sic alterna duces bellorum volnera passos
> in Macetum terras ...   (5.1–2)

Meaning, in Fishian terms,[12] is an event. One of the first events in this sentence is that we construe *sic* only with *passos*, and take *in* naturally as meaning 'into (a place)'. After *terras* we await only an agent (*fortuna*? *bellum civile*? *causarum series*?) and a main verb, e.g. *contulit* (if we compare 4.803). So the sentence begins as if to say '[Fortune?] brought the leaders into the land of Macedonia after they had suffered alternate wounds of war in this way.' Have we then at last reached the *Emathios campos*? No, for the surprise comes in the next line:

> ... miscens adversa secundis
> servavit fortuna pares   (5.2–3)

which forces us (eventually) to reconstrue the sentence retrospectively, to take *sic* with *passos*, *miscens* and *servavit*, and

---

[12] See, for instance, Fish 1980 pp. 22–67.

read *in* impossibly as a 'final' preposition[13] – 'It was in this way that Fortune ... kept them equal for [the] Macedonia[n conflict].' What starts as a promise of Emathian plains turns out to be a signal for more postponement. As the passage continues, there is more gesturing towards placement: locations are named, suggested, implied, as though they were clues to the setting of the next scene: 'iam sparserat Haemo' (5.3) is another illusory reference to Pharsalus, being a part of Lucan's Philippi / Pharsalus nexus;[14] by association with Haemus, Olympus (5.4) may be the mountain,[15] but is easier (eventually) to understand as 'the sky', even if *gelido* is more usually (in Lucan) a mountain-attribute.[16] With references to the first of January, the calendar, the *fasti* (and note how, yet again, we are presented with an image of new beginning), we could be forgiven for thinking that the action had returned to Rome, picking up *urbem*, the last word of the previous book. The unsettled vagueness of placement is finally resolved with an explicit 'elicit Epirum'.

[13] Barratt 1979 ad 1–3 seems to make light of the difficulty of reading *in* in this way: the final use of *in* may be legitimate (if unusual) Latin; but none of the parallels she cites, nor indeed any of the examples cited in Kühner and Stegmann 2.1 p. 345 Anm. 4 (misleadingly referenced by Barratt?) has *in* governing a place-name; and in our passage the confusion is positively encouraged by the postponement of the main verb. In the end it is difficult to see what our example has in common with phrases like 'in praemium', 'in praesidium', and 'in auxilium'; with *servare*, in fact, it seems closer to the Greek σώιζειν εἰς ... in the sense 'bring safely to (a place)' (LSJ s.v. σώιζω II.2).

[14] Haemus in Thrace, the 'blood' mountain, is closely associated with the Emathian plains in Virg. *Georg.* 1.492. In Lucan, the logic of the Philippi/Pharsalus confusion is pushed to extremes so that Haemus is either explicitly or implicitly located in Thessaly: see 1.680 (the crossover point: the matron says Philippi but she 'means' Pharsalus), 6.576, 7.174, 7.480, 10.449.

[15] As it is in a surprisingly similar passage, 7.173–4 – as here, Haemus and Olympus are on successive line-ends.

[16] Of the Alps, 1.183, 2.535; of Taygetus, 5.51–2. There is no parallel in Lucan for the coldness of the sky; Barratt's citation of *gelido* ... *sidere* (6.393) is subtly irrelevant, since the star itself is not cold (though the adjective should shock: stars are normally fiery); rather, it is associated with a cold time of year (when the sun is in Sagittarius).

Epirus, ἤπειρος, the mainland, the continent. Let us stress the name, since it involves a possible historical distortion. Appian, it is true, implies that the reconvening of the Pompeians and Pompey's speech of encouragement took place immediately on arrival in Epirus.[17] However, the senatorial meeting mentioned by Plutarch in *Pomp.* 65 (although it has nothing in common with the meeting described by Lucan)[18] takes place in Beroea in Macedonia; and the meeting described by Cassius Dio happens in Thessalonica (i.e. Macedonia).[19] Lucan gives us no indication that the Pompeians came anywhere near Macedonia at this point in the war: so far as we can tell, the journey from their camp in Epirus to Dyrrachium (also in Epirus) is just a local shift of position. *Historically*, in fact, Caesar crossed to Epirus precisely because the Pompeians were not there to guard it;[20] but this fact is suppressed by Lucan. It is probable, then, that Lucan is using the same technique that characterises his use of history throughout the poem: the compression of many similar events into one exemplary event. Of the three possible sites for a meeting mentioned in the sources (Beroea, Thessalonica, Epirus),[21] Lucan has chosen one, and combined the features of each into a single speech; just as, at Massilia, two sea battles were melded into one, and, later in the book, two mutinies of Caesarian troops will be compressed into one.[22] Why choose Epirus, then? Because to bring the action to Macedonia at this time, or even to mention so obviously portentous a name as 'Thessalo-nica',

[17] Pompey crosses to Epirus from Brundisium, App. *BCiv* 2.40; when next we hear of him (2.49) there is no indication that he has moved on, so it is presumably in Epirus that he makes his speech. After the speech, the forces are sent out to winter in Macedonia and Thessaly (2.52).

[18] *Pace* Barratt 1979 p. 1 who cites Plutarch rather too uncritically.

[19] Dio 51.43.   [20] Dio 51.44.2.

[21] In my discussion of the relevance of Dio, Appian and Plutarch I will appear to imply that Lucan is using them as his sources. That is of course not the case; but it is admissible as a working method on the assumption that those three historians are late representatives of sources that *were* available to Lucan.

[22] On Massilia see chapter 2 p. 23; on the mutinies see Fantham 1985 pp. 123–6; and compare the compression of two hillock battles at Ilerda (discussed in chapter 3, pp. 55–6).

would be to anticipate things: the movement centrewards, Emathia-wards, must be slow and deliberate. And on the other hand, Epirus carries positively the right connotations: knowing that Emathia is on this same continent, we can feel the pull of the 'mainland' here; we can hear in the name that centripetal urge of the narrative, away from what is way out in the middle of nowhere to a place that is *main*, near the middle of somewhere. Something solid; a perfect setting for the re-grouping of wandering, scattered fragments of senate, for the re-ordering of the senatorial *ordo* (5.13, 29, 34). We are not quite at Emathia yet: but we are nearly there.

Involved in the establishment of Epirus as a proper base for recuperation is the decentralisation of the Roman world. That world has Rome as its centre; so in the proem to book 1, a passage that precedes book 5 in the reading order (establishing it as a preliminary norm) while succeeding it in chronological order (suggesting that that norm has in fact yet to be established), Lucan plays on the geographical centrality of Rome, the Romanocentrism of the Caesarian universe, in which for Nero as Caesar to move away from Rome would be to upset the balance of the world.

> sed neque in Arctoo sedem tibi legeris orbe
> nec polus aversi calidus qua vergitur Austri
> unde tuam videas obliquo sidere Romam.
> aetheris inmensi partem si presseris unam
> sentiet axis onus. librati pondera caeli
> orbe tene medio ...   (1.53–8)

It is an image of balance, structure and order, post-civil-discord stability; one, therefore, which we should expect to see challenged by the discourse of civil war. Here in Epirus, the senate, the ruling body of Rome, has in fact done precisely what Lucan begged Caesar not to do: abandoned Rome itself, and reassembled in a different place. If Lentulus is at pains to explain that the city of Rome is not the important thing, that the senate can convene outside Rome, that Rome is wherever its senate convenes, and if Lucan himself appears to endorse that view ('nam quis castra vocet tot strictas iure securis, / tot fasces?' 5.12–13), the device, which is Themistoclean in origin,[23] does not quite work:

> omnia rursus
> membra *loco* redeunt. (5.36–7)

Here, with the mixing of metaphors,[24] Lentulus audaciously begs the question he is trying to answer. It is not just that the senate is reassembling into a body, but that they are reconvening into a place. *Rursus, redeunt*: a return – to Rome? Where else?

From the comparison with the Nero-elogium we can make two possible deductions. One: the senate is just as weighty as Nero, and its migration to Greece does, metaphorically at least, upset the balance of the world – Nero's position in the centre portends stability, while the senate's displacement from the centre reflects the instability of civil war; Lentulus's speech, which insists on order, law and stability, is just wishful thinking. Or two: Lentulus is wrong: in comparison with Nero (or Caesar) the senate have so little importance (weight) that they can convene wherever they wish, and it will make no difference at all. This second option seems to go so much against the author's undoubtedly pro-republican stance in the passage, that it requires a lengthy defence.

The nothingness of Pompey

The scene in Epirus is, in all of its details, tailored to suit the moral that the senate, the group, is more important than the single leader, Pompey. There is such grand resonance in Lucan's climactic

> docuit populos venerabilis ordo
> non Magni partes sed Magnum in partibus esse. (5.13–14)

that we may recognise here the rhetoric of sincerity in the service of a republican vision. For the reader already convinced that this vision is central to the message of the poem, the lines are very quotable: they read like a contextless *sententia*, and

---

[23] Explicitly so in Appian 2.50.
[24] Barratt 1979 ad loc.: 'this is a mixed metaphor ... one would expect "corpori" instead of "loco"'.

can be cited without further comment to prove a point.[25] But we know better. We know that it is rare for Lucan to be so openly positive about anything or anyone, least of all Pompey and the Pompeians. Here, in effect, Lucan dons his republican mask. Some of the cracks we will not notice immediately: we will only realise later, for instance, that the episode forms a pair with the mutiny of Caesar's troops a little further on in the book,[26] so that we will be invited to view this democratic electoral procedure as a process analogous to mutiny; the leader must realise that he is no more powerful than his supporters; so in the Caesarian mutiny, Caesar

> scit non esse ducis strictos sed militis enses. (5.254)

a sentiment that is deliberately patterned after *non Magni partes sed Magnum in partibus esse*; Caesar's position is a position of weakness, and retrospectively implies that Magnus' position as one of the senate rather than a leader in his own right may be *his* crucial weakness; gives us the reason for his failure to be a real match for Caesar. But already within the episode's immediate context we can see a tendency to demonstrate the nothingness of Pompey. Most strikingly, Pompey himself never speaks, and indeed there is no indication that he is even present at the meeting;[27] Ahl sensitively (and correctly) observes that at the end of the episode the reader will surely

[25] E.g. Ahl 1976 p. 161, 'Cicero is going too far in his zeal to demonstrate what Lucan points out in 5.14: the senators are not on Pompey's side; Pompey is on their side.'

[26] A connection made by Fantham 1985 p. 121 n. 7, who suggests that 'this is a contrast of legitimate and illegitimate command, of authority given and authority almost withdrawn'.

[27] This affords another interesting comparison with the Caesarian mutiny, at which Caesar *seems* to be present although the sources tell us he was not; see Fantham (1985 p.125): '... they [the mutineers] voice their protests against him, apparently to his face. But where are they, and where is he? No hint that they are separated by the distance between Massilia, from which Caesar hurries to join his forces, and Placentia; no hint yet that he is not with them, and no naming of the legion; they are apparently isolated, face to face as the crisis approaches ...'.

expect to hear something of Pompey, and must be thoroughly bemused to find the attention shifting suddenly to Appius.[28]

Pompey's absent presence is all the more emphatic in view of what the historical sources have to say about the episode. In Appian 2.49–52, Pompey is very much at the forefront: he calls an assembly (συναγαγὼν ... ἐς ἐπήκοον, 2.50 – no suggestion that this is a senate meeting: everyone, senate, knights, soldiers, is invited; and Pompey would have had no legal right to convene the senate anyway), delivers a rousing speech and is answered with rapturous applause. He is the total leader, a personality comparable with Caesar, whose speech to his soldiers at Brundisium is obviously juxtaposed with Pompey's as a parallel (App. *BCiv* 2.52–4). Whether or not this meeting is pure invention on Appian's part – for Appian might have invented it precisely in order to parallel Caesar's at Brundisium[29] – it is obvious that, for this historian at least, any meeting of the senatorial forces was unthinkable without the dominating, controlling presence of Pompey. In Plutarch's *Pompey* (65.1), there is a passing mention of what seems to be a senatorial meeting (βουλή, the technical term) at Beroea, from which we can deduce that the senate must have been officially convened at least once (though this particular meeting has nothing in common with the meetings as described by Appian, Cassius Dio or Lucan). In Dio's account of the assembly at Thessalonica, the insistence on the fact that this is a genuine meeting of the senate conducted by the observance of all the proper procedures is as pronounced as it is in Lucan:

... καίτοι τῆς τε ἄλλης βουλῆς ἐς διακοσίους, ὥς φασί τινες, καὶ τοὺς ὑπάτους ἔχοντες, καί τι καὶ χωρίον ἐς τὰ οἰωνίσματα, τοῦ δὴ καὶ ἐν νόμῳ δή τινι αὐτὰ δοκεῖν γίγνεσθαι, δημοσιώσαντες, ὥστε καὶ τὸν δῆμον δι' αὐτῶν τήν τε πόλιν ἅπασαν ἐνταῦθα εἶναι νομίζεσθαι (Dio 41.43.2)

But in contrast with Lucan, we find another insistence on the sham and self-deception involved in these procedures: the senate is just going through the motions of being democratic, while in fact it is Pompey who is in control of things:

οὐ μὴν ἀλλὰ τῶι μὲν ὀνόματι οὗτοί σφισιν ἑκατέροις ἦρχον, ἔργωι δὲ ὁ Πομπήιος καὶ ὁ Καῖσαρ, τῆς μὲν φήμης ἕνεκα τὰς ἐννόμους ἐπικλήσεις, ὁ μὲν τὴν τοῦ ὑπάτου ὁ δὲ τὴν τοῦ ἀνθυπάτου, ἔχοντες, πράττοντες δὲ οὐκ ὅσα ἐκεῖναι ἐπέτρεπον ἀλλ' ὅσα αὐτοὶ ἤθελον. (Dio 41.43.5)

What it all comes down to is this: the senate almost certainly convened *as* a senate at some time during the winter of 49 / 48 BC; this meeting (or meetings) probably took place in Macedonia rather than Epirus, since Appian is the only historian to use Epirus as a setting, and he is also the only one *not* to speak of a *senatorial* meeting. But no matter what the formalities, Pompey was very much the centre of things. With Pompey central to the accounts of the sources, his near absence from Lucan's version is nothing short of stunning.

Lentulus' speech in Lucan combines the motifs of Dio's senate meeting (emphasis on law, order, precedent, the still-pertinent power of the legally elected representatives of the state), of Pompey's hortatory speech in Appian (the parallel with Themistocles, the Camillus exemplum), and, oddly, the much earlier meeting in Rome at which Pompey was elected as military leader for the senators.[30] It is obvious, particularly with respect to the substitution of Lucan's Lentulus for Appian's Pompey, that our good republican author has seen fit to curb the power and ambition of his hero by denying him a controlling position in the episode; but it is equally obvious that he has gone further than he needed. Pompey should not have been denied a voice (he should at least have taken a part in the senatorial debate). And Lucan is quite prepared to signal the denigratory implications of his treatment of Pompey: when Lentulus concludes his speech by recommending Pompey for the leadership, it should be with a dim sense of recognition that we hear the response of the senate:

'... consulite in medium, patres, Magnumque iubete
esse ducem.' laeto *nomen* clamore senatus
excipit et Magno fatum patriaeque suumque
inposuit. (5.46–9)

---

[30] Plut. *Pomp.* 61.1; App. *BCiv* 2.34; Dio 41.3.3–4; how official this 'meeting' was seems open to question.

Once again, even at his moment of triumph, when he receives the applause he has always desired, Magnus is no more than a *nomen*; and even that *nomen* tussles as it always does between the noun and the adjective: command Magnus to be the leader, tell the leader to be great like his name.[31] The tragedy, the irony, continues: what Magnus receives is the booby-prize, *fatum*, Henderson's 'deathstiny', fate or death – but undoubtedly death.[32] Next, the absurdly irrelevant and, so far as we can tell, unhistorical, conclusion to the episode, in which honours are liberally conferred on deserving peoples and kings, reinforces the point. The gifts are like the honour Pompey receives: Rhodes, a great sea power (*pelagi potens*, tying in with Pompey's famous successes at sea), is 'donis exornata' (50–1), a phrase that recalls the oak-tree simile describing Pompey in book 1:

> qualis frugifero quercus sublimis in agro
> exuvias veteris populi sacrataque gestans
> dona ducum ... (1.136–8)

The reward for Athens is praise (*laudantur*). Why *is* Athens singled out for special praise when, according to the catalogue of Pompeian troops in book 3, the Athenians were only able to send three ships (3.181–3)?[33] Presumably, for old time's sake: *fama veteres ... Athenae* (5.52). The wording points to Lucan's characterisation of Pompey as a man relying on his past glory, resting on his laurels long after he has ceased to be an active force.[34] And finally, at the very end of the list is Ptolemaeus, whose name is explicitly linked to the murder that will bring out the 'death' in *fatum*.

The scene as a whole, then, impresses us with the extent to which it tames and undervalues the figure of Pompey. It can be argued that Lucan must show Pompey in a lowly position in order to fit him for his role as defender of republican *libertas*, since as *leader* of the senate without the senate's authorisation he would be just as much a potential tyrant as Caesar. But

---

[31] So Feeney 1986(A) p. 240.
[32] Henderson 1988 p. 124; cf. Dick 1967 p. 236.
[33] Gassner 1972 pp. 141–2.   [34] Feeney (1986A) p. 240.

when the importance of Pompey is denied in the name of hard-line republicanism, the senatorial party must lose more than it bargained for. The point comes across most clearly in Lentulus' appeal to the Camillus exemplum:

> Tarpeia sede perusta
> Gallorum facibus Veiosque habitante Camillo
> illic Roma fuit.   (5.27–9)

It is one of a number of senatorial sneers at the 'invasion' of Caesar: though this is a civil war, the Pompeians continue to represent Caesar as a foreign invader. Here it is obvious enough that Caesar fits into the role of the Gauls (conveniently, Caesar did invade from the North with troops drawn from Gallic outposts; and furthermore the torches which burn the 'Tarpeian seat' connote Caesarian lightning), and that the senators would wish to identify themselves with Camillus.[35] Now, the success of Lentulus' rhetoric depends on his appealing to the 'grand old republican connotations' of the figure of Camillus;[36] but these connotations, especially in the age of the principate, are hardly dependable. As many-time dictator and military tribune with consular power, and as a 'Romulus ac parens patriae conditorque alter urbis',[37] Camillus is a strange figure to choose as an exemplum to *counter* the apparent monarchic ambitions of Caesar, and in fact it is well known that he figured prominently in pro-Sullan and pro-Augustan propaganda; Livy's account of the Camillus story manifestly fits him into the mould of a proto-Augustus.[38] Lucan read Livy; how can he have been so careless as to allow Lentulus to conjure a proto-princeps in support of an anti-Caesarian stance? How can an emphatically single leader appear to exemplify an emphatically multiple and leaderless senate?

[35] Harrison 1979.
[36] Barratt 1979 ad 27–9 cites 1.168, 2.544, 6.786 and 7.358 to demonstrate Camillus' symbolisation of 'the traditional virtuous Roman warrior'. However, if my argument here is correct, it is likely that those instances will be afflicted by the same conscious irony as I detect here.
[37] Livy 5.49.7, reporting a popular sentiment with which the historian agrees ('... haud vanis laudibus appellabatur').
[38] Momigliano 1942 passim.

The answer, of course, lies in Pompey, and it is by considering Pompey a little further that we can perceive Lucan's deviousness in his treatment of historical sources. In the tradition on which the Epirus speech is based, the Camillus exemplum does in fact get an airing, but only in one place: Pompey's harangue in Appian's account:

καὶ ἡμῶν αὐτῶν οἱ πρόγονοι Κελτῶν ἐπιόντων ἐξέλιπον τὸ ἄστυ, καὶ αὐτὸ ἀνεσώσατο ἐξ 'Αρδεατῶν Κάμιλλος ὁρμώμενος. πάντες τε οἱ εὖ φρονοῦντες τὴν ἐλευθερίαν, ὅπηι ποτ' ἂν ὦσιν, ἡγοῦνται πατρίδα. (App. *BCiv* 2.50)

The first thing to notice from a comparison with Appian's rather standard version of the exemplum is that the place of Camillus' exile has become blurred in Lucan. The situation (as we know it from Livy) is that Camillus is in exile at Ardea, while the Romans, displaced from Rome, convene at Veii to elect him dictator. Interestingly, Lucan conflates the two kinds of exile, and places Camillus in Veii. No doubt this need not contradict the Livian story, since Camillus came to Veii when he left Ardea; but none the less, Ardea is a famous element in the Camillus myth, and considering that Appian includes it in Pompey's speech, it is surprising that Lucan suppresses it. The effect is that Camillus is made to supplant the Roman people; their place of exile becomes his place of exile; the single man outweighs the collective state. Furthermore – and here is the important point – in Appian the motivation behind citing the Camillus exemplum is entirely different: for there, it is Pompey who speaks; as the man totally in control, the leader of the senatorial forces, Pompey promises, in effect, to be a new Camillus, to be a new saviour of the Roman state. That is undeniable. When Lucan transfers the exemplum to Lentulus' speech, making it serve the end of proving that the senate is the senate, and Rome is wherever the senate decrees it to be, it becomes a remarkable instance of rhetorical ineptitude; all the more so because the original point of the exemplum (the establishment of Pompey as leader) is displaced, delayed till the end of the speech. In effect, Lentulus as speaker for the senate attempts to usurp Pompey's dictatorial rhetoric for anti-dictatorial ends – but it shows.

In sum, the Camillus exemplum precisely begs the question, Where is Pompey in all of this? Without a strong Pompey, does the senate have any right to see itself as reviving the memory of Camillus? What is the senate, if Pompey is nothing?

The site and origins of the oracle

Lucanian language inhabits a paranoiac world. A pseudo-Stoic cosmos in which everything connects; a poetic, symbolic nexus in which every element – history, myth as aetiology, natural phenomena, and, above all, the word – *conspires*. It is the vision of a total system, in which nothing is unresounding, unportentous. Everything signifies. If we respond to this paranoia we will produce a spectrum of uneases whose range extends from obvious functional connections which constitute the surface argument of the poem, to shadows so vague that even to state them is to overstate them.

And at the centre (one centre) of this interconnected universe stands Delphi. Literally at the centre of the world, it seems to offer us the end of the narrative's centripetal implosion, seems in fact to offer us a premature Pharsalus. That is an important point, and I will want to return to it later. But for the time being the Delphic exegesis forms a dense knot of allusions, symbols, analogies, which need teasing out.

On the lowest level (the level of shadow) the Delphic episode finds a vague prefiguration in the Epirus scene. How much should we read into the fact that the senate 'hear secret things' in their ersatz senate house? –

> peregrina ac sordida sedes
> Romanos cepit proceres, *secretaque rerum*
> hospes in externis *audivit* curia tectis. (5.9–11)

How unaffected can we be to find Appius later consulting the god who knows all secret things, and to hear the poet's punning prophecy that Appius will soon 'hold secret things' himself ('deus omnia cursus / aeterni *secreta tenens*' 88–9, cf. *secreta deum* 222; '*secreta tenebis* / litoris Euboici memorando condite busto' 230–1)?[39] The senatorial obsession with 'clos-

[39] See p. 149.

ing' ('*clausus*que vaporibus axis' 24; '*clausa*que iustitio tristi
fora' 32; 'nostrum exhausto ius *clauditur* anno' 44) is contrived
to prefigure the closing of the oracle (5.69, 111–16, 120–1,
131–40), the god shut into his cavern (*inclusum* 87), the voice
of the priestess which is locked in her throat (197), and the part
played in the episode by Appius *Claudius* Pulcher.[40]

Of course, this latter emphasis on closing (as 'finishing') has
the effect of colouring this part of the poem with a *fin de siècle*
feeling, a feeling that we have reached another end point, and
that another new beginning is being set in motion. As the last
legally elected magistrates of the republic conclude their term
of office, so the Delphic oracle is about to give its last prophecy;[41] Brutus, Rome's *extremum nomen* (7.589), the name
that comes into prominence at the beginning and the end of
the republic, will have found his parallel in Phemonoe, the last
Pythia, who bears the same name as the first.[42] But more generally such echoes work to produce that paranoiac atmosphere
so important to Lucan's vision: scenes echo one another because they *can* echo one another, because nothing is so dissimi-
lar or divided that it cannot be a mirror of something else.

And so back to where we began: Delphi at the centre of the
world. How affronted should we be to find in line 72 that the
centre of the world, the subject of *summotus* (71), is not Delphi, but Parnassus? Not a great deal, perhaps, since Delphi is
situated at the foot of Parnassus, and Ovid had gone some way
towards making the two places synonymous.[43] But on the other
hand, while we may in general grant the poet his licence, the
geographical distortion implied here, minor as it may appear,

---

[40] The pun on Appius' name was suggested to me by Prof. D.C. Feeney.

[41] Historically, of course, the Delphic oracle continued to function, albeit
in a limited way, after the civil war (see p. 137). Lucan, as often, distorts
history for his own ends.

[42] We know the name of the first Pythia from Strabo 9.3.5, Paus. 10.5.7;
see Dick 1965 p. 461; and some good remarks on the irony of the name
'speak-think' from O'Higgins 1988 p. 214 (cf. Morford 1967 p. 66).

[43] In Ovid *Met.* 4.643 Themis is given the epithet *Parnasia*, presumably on
the grounds that she had once possessed the Delphic oracle. Cf. Val.
Flacc. 3.618, 'vox ... Parnasia', the Delphic oracle.

is of a rather different order, and should not pass unremarked. For the centre of the earth was a precisely fixed spot, marked by the world-famous omphalos: the well-defined nature of that spot therefore makes any distortion of whatever degree very surprising; and in this case what is most striking is that implicit in Lucan's description of the twin peaks of Parnassus lies the assertion that it is these peaks, rather than the omphalos (which is never mentioned), that mark the centre-point of the earth:

> Hesperio tantum quantum summotus Eoo
> cardine Parnasos *gemino petit aethera colle*   (5.71–2)

Neatly, the single point is made into two points; at the very centre of Lucan's universe, a universe which, as we know, participates (by a kind of pathetic fallacy) in the divisive conflict that it houses, we find no centre – no one centre, a single omphalos, but two centres, a doubled, split Parnassus.

Parnassus is *the* civil-war mountain; one mountain, two mountains (*gemino colle*, not *gemino cacumine*, as if the peaks were themselves mountains); twinned peaks that recall the two-hill imagery of the Massilia episode: the *tumulus* that forms a contending pair with the city (3.375–80, n.b. *par*, 3.380), and the twin towers that are moved up a rampart to the walls, equalling their height ('geminasque aequantis moenia turris' 456); imagery which we have seen continued and complicated in the Ilerda episode: the twinned hills outside the city which together oppose the city itself on a hill (4.11–18), and the twin crags at Octagesa ('attollunt campo geminae iuga saxea rupes' 4.157). When we reach Parnassus in book 5, then, we have been well prepared to respond to it within this imagistic framework.

We have been prepared in other ways, too. Let us glance briefly at Lucan's one previous reference to Parnassus, in the catalogue of Pompey's eastern forces:

> proxima vicino vires dat Graecia bello.
> Phocaicas Amphissa manus scopulosaque Cirrha
> Parnasosque iugo misit desertus utroque.
> Boeoti coiere duces ...   (3.171–4)

Why does Lucan start the catalogue with Amphissa, Cirrha, and Parnassus (all near Delphi)? In the first place, as Rowland rightly remarks, Phocaean Amphissa begins the list in order to show Phocis at the forefront of Pompeian support: this will assume some importance in the episode immediately following the catalogue, the siege of Massilia, since Lucan consistently (if incorrectly) asserts that the Massilians were colonists from Phocis.[44] In the second place, the area around Delphi is a good place to start a catalogue of world-wide dimensions: the progress of the catalogue will be from the central area of the world to the outskirts (*recessus*, 229).[45] But why Amphissa? Surely because of the resonance of the name: Amphissa is the city which is ἀμφίς, apart, divided, the city of civil war. The pun will immediately be picked up by the twin peaks of Parnassus (bringing out the notion of duality), emphatically so because Parnassus' position in the catalogue is utterly absurd: what soldiers could it send from its twin peaks? *Did* anybody live there? It is hard to see why Lucan would want to include the mountain in the catalogue unless because of its symbolic connotations; connotations that are underlined by the punning in its own name. As PAR-nassus it is one of the more significant in Lucan's nexus of *par* puns that play on the all-important imagery of the gladiatorial pair, which range from PAR-*thi* (a blanket term that covers both Parthians and ancient Persians, mentioned as one of the causes of civil war in that they killed Crassus and so set Pompey and Caesar against each other[46]) to *pars* and *partes*, and, with the addition of an *h*,[47] from P(H)AR-*os* (vaguely the place of Pompey's murder and

---

[44] Rowland 1969 p. 204.

[45] Gassner 1972 p. 167 n. 4.

[46] See 1.103–8; see also 3.264–6:

    inter Caesareas acies diversaque signa
    pugnaces dubium Parthi tenuere favorem
    contenti *fecisse duos*.

where *fecisse duos* reads almost like a gloss on PAR-*thi*.

[47] See Ahl 1985 p. 59 for the interchangeability of *ph* and *p* for the purposes of word play. See also ibid. pp. 107ff for plays on the syllable *par* in Ovid's telling of the story of Pyrrha and Deucalion.

burial,[48] and the setting of the poem's final scene) to *P(H)AR-salia* itself. Parnassus, with its twin peaks and PAR- name (the peaks are set against each other like gladiators?), is easily subsumed into the imagery of civil war. By the time we reach 'Boeoti coiere duces ...', where an apparently innocent *coiere* ('came to join [Pompey's forces]') manages to suggest internal conflict ('came together against each other'; cf. 1.129 'nec coiere pares'), we will have no doubt that the determining design behind this catalogue is the game of using geography and ethnography to mirror the features of civil war – division, duality, chaos: it will be shown that civil war is so pervasive as to be reflected in everything.[49] It will not surprise us, then, to find Parnassus resuming its civil-war connotations when we arrive at the Delphic episode in book 5.

What is not twinned about Parnassus? *Two* gods have made it their sacred place (*mons Phoebo Bromioque sacer*, 5.73). The pairing of the gods is rigorous:

> Delphica fatidici reserat penetralia Phoebi. (70)

and

> Delphica Thebanae referunt trieterica Bacchae. (74)

lines strictly parallel in metre, beginning with exactly the same word, and ending with a word related (at least) to the name of each god; both within five lines of each other, framing three lines on the twinness of the peaks and the two gods themselves. But with Phoebus and Bacchus we are given something more: in a line whose confusion of singular and plural takes us back to the lines on Afranius and Petreius in 4.4–7, we see the disparate gods not only twinned on Parnassus but *mixed* so that they become a single (singular) *cui*:[50]

---

[48] *Pharos* and *Pharius* linked with Pompey's death: 2.733, 4.257, 6.308, book 8 passim, 9.1, 53, 141, 209 ('Pharium scelus') 10.343 ('scelus ... Pharium').

[49] See chapter 5 for a more extensive analysis of symbolism in catalogues.

[50] The crucial word, *cui*, has in fact been a minor object of concern on the part of the textual critics. Do we supply *monti* or *deo*? If the former, then we must tolerate what is possibly a factual inaccuracy (so Barratt claims

mons Phoebo Bromioque sacer, *cui numine mixto*
Delphica Thebanae referunt trieterica Bacchae.   (73–4)

We know by now that the word *miscere* is one of the prime ambiguities of civil-war discourse: on the one hand suggesting mixing as harmonising, unifying, and on the other, mixing as the bringing-together-into-conflict of hostile elements. On the one hand, peace, love and the brotherhood of man; on the other, the battlefield.[51] The information contained in this relative clause (*cui ... Bacchae*) is either a distortion or an irrelevance; either Lucan has gratuitously transported a Bacchic festival to Mt Parnassus,[52] or he has thrown in a line and a half of useless religious lore by the way. Either case must force us to look for an ulterior motive; we will find it, if we want to, in *miscere* (and in the parallelism of lines 70 and 74); and we will conclude that Lucan has selected and ordered his material on the principle that everything must be made to coordinate with his system of civil-war imagery.

Let us go on. The merging of duality into unity that we witnessed in the lines on Phoebus and Bacchus extends its influence to the mountain itself. *How* many peaks does Parnassus have?

(1979 p. 29), citing Ovid *Met.* 6.587ff); if the latter, we must tolerate the singular *cui* for two gods. Hence Schrader's emendation *quis* (i.e. *quibus*); but Housman (ad loc.) sensitively pronounced in favour of the strained singular.

[51] See my discussion of the flood and the fraternisation scene in chapter 3 pp. 52–3; note especially 'pax erat, et castris miles permixtus utrisque / errabat' (4.196) as compared to 'miscendae copia mortis' (4.283), 'miscet proelia' (7.510) and 'tela manusque Romanae miscent acies' (1.681–2).

[52] See note 50. I believe however that Barratt (1979 p. 29) is being hasty when she pronounces that 'the festival was held on Mt Rhodope, see Ov. Met VI 587ff', as if that was the only place such a festival could happen in. To be sure, the Bacchic *trieterica* was often associated with Thrace, as Barratt's other parallels show; but it is counterintuitive to suppose that other parts of Greece did not have their own *trieterica* – Virgil mentions one which took place on Mt Cithaeron (*Aen.* 4.302–3). None the less, there is no evidence of a Delphic *trieterica*, and it is possible that Lucan has invented it.

hoc solum fluctu terras mergente cacumen
eminuit pontoque fuit discrimen et astris.
tu quoque vix summam, seductus ab aequore, rupem
extuleras ... (75–8)

From the look of it, only one: *hoc solum ... cacumen*. For a while, too, we will read *summam ... rupem* as equivalent to this singular *cacumen*, 'the rocky height' (rather than, as later turns out, 'the highest peak [of the two]'). There is, in other words, a delay in our comprehension of *summam rupem* that will temporarily reinforce the impact of the oddity in *cacumen* standing for *cacumina*,[53] and which will not be resolved until we are part of the way through line 78:

... unoque iugo, Parnase, latebas.

Shall we, in order to escape the effect, cite the familiar, desensitising notion of 'poetic singular for plural'? I think not. In the first place, Lucan's work elevates the exchange of plural for singular and vice versa from the level of poetic licence to the level of an article of faith, declared, as it were, even in the opening lines of the poem, where *bella ... civilia* stands for *bellum civile* (immediately opposing the poem's title both by its plurality and by the intensifying *plus quam*), where *Emathios ... campos* stands for *Emathium campum* and *canimus* stands for *cano*. To be sure, the 'poetic plural for singular' is always available as a device by which to ease the constraints of metre, and as such it will tend to allow us to pass by it with little disturbance; but in the case of a poet who piles examples on one another in quick succession (as in the proem), who uses the device almost as often as he does not, and who frequently chooses to bring it in at just those points where it is calculated to be most disconcerting; and finally in the case of a poet whose subject is, in abstract terms, the confusion of unity with duality (the single state fighting itself as if it were two warring states), the plural for singular and singular for plural cannot be entirely neutral. My second point is that in this specific

---

[53] For Parnassus' peaks as plural *cacumina*, see Ov. *Met.* 1.316–7: 'mons ibi verticibus petit arduus astra duobus / nomine Parnasus, superantque cacumina nubes'.

instance Parnassus, whose doubleness is made an explicit and significant feature of Lucan's ecphrasis (as often in Roman literature), *cannot* be referred to as having a single peak without compelling some sense of contradiction.

It is as if to signal the relevance of motifs of merging and separating that Lucan recalls the story of the great flood. We will remember from our reading of the Ilerda episode that flooding – and the great flood in particular – stands as an analogy for (as well as in opposition to) civil war, since it entails the submerging of all individual features and the abolition of boundaries. These characteristics of flooding reappear here: the earth is submerged in water, and there would be no division of sea from sky (or rather stars, provocatively suggesting a confusion of water and fire) were it not for the one peak of Parnassus poking from the waves. In other words, flood has effaced all dividing lines except Parnassus' peak, which is a *discrimen*, and, ironically, this peak is victim to a confusion of division. *Discrimen* is a puzzling word, not least because it is very difficult to visualise: how exactly does a tiny uppermost point of a mountain showing above the waves become a dividing-*line* between sea and stars?[54] But *discrimen* is another civil-war catchword with a meaning that lies somewhere between 'division' (civil war as division of the state) and 'crisis point' (the battle or war that will decide the fate of Rome).[55] Finally, it is not too hard to see (when eventually we realise that Lucan has not forgotten the second peak) that the position of the two peaks reflects in some sense the position of the two civil-war parties (or their leaders). Reading flood as civil war (as we may, hesitantly, do) we will be willing to see the symbol of one peak achieving eminence above the waves while the other is submerged, translating into the 'reality' of one leader achieving pre-eminence over the other.

So there it is. What we are told about Parnassus (the infor-

---

[54] *Discrimen* in a concrete sense is always used of a separating line, space, structure, such as a wall, a strip of land, etc. *OLD* s.v. *discrimen* 1a; *TLL* s.v. *discrimen*, 1356.16ff

[55] See chapter 3 n. 50.

mation that has been selected, the manner in which it is told), and the fact that we are told about Parnassus rather than Delphi, make of this ecphrasis a profoundly resonant symbolic *locus*. And we could go on: as we hear of Apollo's battle with Python, and the founding of the oracle (79–85), we may hear *ultor* (79) as an allusion to Pompey's rhetoric of justification (Pompey is the avenger of Caesar's crimes – 2.531ff – as Sulla is the avenger of Marius', 2.139); we will see the conflict of the heavenly god with the earth-born snake as a proto-gigantomachy[56] (gigantomachy itself being a mythical pre-enactment of the Roman civil war),[57] and noting the portentousness of words like *regna* (= tyranny) and *Themis* (= *ius*) in 81, we will understand that Apollo's violent appropriation of the oracle in some way parallels the motifs of appropriation, conquest, redefinition of law, in civil-war discourse.[58]

At the very least, the symbolic complexity of the Delphi / Parnassus ecphrasis argues a considerable (and hitherto underestimated) degree of poetic subtlety and control on Lucan's part. And it is possible to let it rest at that. I have not, for instance, been particularly concerned to *interpret* these symbols at any great length, as if by translating them into real terms we could gain any profounder understanding of the issues which mould the main body of the poem, as if we could regard the 'meaning' of these symbols as a more or less unique key to the poem (though in fact I believe this could be done); none the less, having demonstrated that the ecphrasis is so replete with 'civil-warness', it will be useful to be able to show how this

---

[56] See Fontenrose 1959, index A (themes and motifs relating to the myth of Python), theme 7G.

[57] Chapter 2 n. 70.

[58] See Paschalis 1986 for a discussion of the pointed absence of the Delphic oracle in the *Aeneid*: it is excluded precisely on the grounds of the Delphic Apollo's association with violence. See also Lucan's incomplete gesture towards Virgil in 106ff: when Lucan says that the oracle 'saepe dedit sedem totas mutantibus urbes', we must of course think of the foundation of Rome, the most famous example. Lucan, however, does not mention Troy or Rome, but only Tyre, which led to the foundation of Carthage, Rome's deadly enemy and dark shadow in the *Aeneid*. This is surely to point obliquely to the fact that Aeneas never consulted Delphi when 'changing' *his* city; it is also a characteristic snub against Virgil.

kind of symbolic power contributes to a more powerful reading of the broader framework. In other words, I will be concerned not with the meaning but with the fact of symbolism at this point in the poem.

I began by proposing that the Delphic episode was contrived by various means to suggest that we had arrived at a premature Pharsalus. I showed that the narrative played on geographical marginality and centrality in such a way as to make centrality a *sine qua non* of the final conflict, and that even though the first lines of book 5 at first imply and then, specifically, deny that we have reached the scene of that conflict, nevertheless the centrality of Delphi and Parnassus makes them at least a candidate for that position. At first glance it may seem absurd, even perverse, to make such a proposition. Not so. I am not suggesting for a moment that any reader could be deceived into believing that a battle will take place on Parnassus, much less the final, climactic battle. Anyone who knows anything about history, anyone who has read the poem so far, will know full well that that distinction is reserved for Pharsalus. What I *am* proposing, however, is that Parnassus *could have been* an ideal site for the final battle; and that is the point I wish to develop now.

What do I mean by an 'ideal site'? Look at Lucan's battle-scenes. What I have argued for especially in the case of the Ilerda campaign (and to a lesser extent in my discussion of the Massilian siege) is true for every battle in the *Bellum Civile*: the site of any battle is shown by the poet to be (let us say) *compatible* with a civil-war conflict; whether the cosmos reflects civil war or civil war reflects the cosmos, battles always take place on sites that are ideal for them; the terms of this 'ideal-ness' are geography, topography, history, mythology and name. Thus, to take an obvious example, the portion of Africa in which Curio fights with Varus and then with Juba is marked out as a site for such conflict right from the beginning of the episode, first by the story of Hercules and Antaeus,[59] then by Scipio's

---

[59] The story's status as an analogy for the coming conflict is well recognised. See Thompson and Bruère 1970 pp. 169–70; their crude position is justly questioned by Ahl 1976 pp. 91–103 and Martindale 1981; for a more sophisticated assessment of the analogy, see Saylor 1982.

historical victory over the Carthaginians, and, further, by the conflict of the names which derive from the two stories themselves: the place is called first *Antaei regna* (4.590), then we are told of *maiora cognomina* (4.656), that is the *castra Corneliana*;[60] the one name has conquered the other; and the stealing of names, or the privileging of one name over another, is one of Lucan's most extensively used civil-war leitmotifs. Topography too plays its part.[61] But I have chosen this particular example because it is here that the question of the relevance of battle-sites (in terms other than the purely tactical) is made explicit. For when Curio has heard the native's account of the place's history, he is delighted:

> Curio laetatus, tamquam fortuna locorum
> bella gerat servetque ducum sibi fata priorum,
> felici non fausta loco tentoria ponens
> indulsit castris et collibus abstulit omen
> sollicitatque feros non aequis viribus hostis. (4.661–5)

The significant thing here is not that Curio was wrong to imagine that the land would help him to win his victory (though in fact he was); the land was ominous, appropriate, an 'ideal site', whose power Curio either misused (see Saylor 1982) or misunderstood (i.e. overestimated).

My point, then, is simple: the Parnassus ecphrasis uses the same topographical (opposed hills) and mythological (Apollo and Python) symbolism as features in Lucanian accounts of battles. Now if, as I repeat, I do not wish to suggest that Parnassus is in any real sense a potential battleground, why is

[60] See Caes. *BCiv* 2.24. Martindale (1981 p. 76) asserts that Lucan's phrase *maiora cognomina* implies contempt for the myth of Antaeus in favour of the historical achievement of Scipio; but there is huge irony in the fact that this greater name is not actually quoted by Lucan; equally, Caesar does not mention *Antaei regna*: the greater name may have won out in Caesar's version, but Lucan will see to it that the earlier, weaker name is the only one to reach our ears. There is a useful discussion in Ahl 1976 pp. 96–7 and n. 32, showing that it is not even clear that *Antaei regna* and *castra Corneliana* are the same place: Lucan has invented the conflict.

[61] Ahl 1976 p. 99, 'The *sangre y arena* of the gladiatorial munus could find no better landscape than the desert of Libya'. A more developed discussion of the topography can be found in Saylor 1982 pp. 171–3.

this point worth dwelling on? Let us say that I am trying to legitimise a full-scale parallel between the Delphic episode and the Erictho episode in book 6. For Sextus' consultation of Erictho takes place in Thessaly, near the site of the coming battle. As we shall see when we come to it (chapter 5), the long prologue to the episode establishes Thessaly, in terms of mythology and geography, as the civil-war land *par excellence*; and then expatiates on the nature of the peculiar form of prophecy it is home to (paralleling 5.86–120 in the Delphic episode). Since the Thessalian episode is deeply coloured by our awareness that Pharsalus is, so to speak, just around the corner, then the Delphic episode must, as a full opposite member of the pair, at least gesture towards its status as a rival battleground. Phemonoe, Erictho; Par-nassus, P(h)ar-salus.

Parnassus is also a poetic mountain. A bland, unremarkable statement of fact: since it is a home of the muses, and sacred to Apollo in his musical capacity, the poetic connotation of Parnassus is a basic given; the three basic givens (it is double-peaked; it is associated with the Delphic oracle; it is associated with poetry) so effectively constitute the set of 'what every schoolboy knows about Parnassus' that it *may* be impossible for the name to appear in a poem without these connotations coming through – if only for a moment. A provocative assertion; but let us be more guarded. Let us say merely that these connotations are always *available*, but that the contract between poet and reader is such that the poet must always give some sort of signal if he wishes them to be incorporated into a reading. Here, now, two of Parnassus' attributes have been brought explicitly to our attention; the third, its poetic attribute, may be important, but we require independent confirmation if it is not to fall by the wayside as an irrelevance. In what follows (to turn things the other way around) it will be shown, in fact, that Parnassus' status as the home of poetry is one of many elements that contribute to a reading of the Delphic episode as an extended piece of metapoetic discussion; each element, in itself shadowy, and by itself proving little; but taken together, forming a mutually supporting nexus of considerable strength.

Lucan's Phemonoe and Virgil's Deiphobe

Lucan's Delphic episode is, as I stated earlier, obviously patterned after Virgil's Sibylline episode in *Aeneid* 6. This fact is well known,[62] but until now no full examination of Lucan's relationship to his predecessor has been attempted for this scene. Here therefore I propose to assemble the scattered comments in Lucanian scholarship and combine them with a few remarks of my own, and see how clear a picture emerges of the extent and purpose of Lucan's Virgilian allusion.

The two episodes start in a very similar way: in each case the protagonist is named, and his quest briefly delineated, in a few preliminary lines:

> at pius Aeneas arces quibus altus Apollo
> praesidet horrendaeque procul secreta Sibyllae,
> antrum immane, petit, magnam cui mentem animumque
> Delius inspirat vates aperitque futura.
> iam subeunt Triviae lucos atque aurea tecta. (*Aen.* 6.9–13)

> ... solus in ancipites metuit descendere Martis
> Appius eventus, finemque expromere rerum
> sollicitat superos multosque obducta per annos
> Delphica fatidici reserat penetralia Phoebi. (*BC* 5.67–70)

And at this point in each case the narrative is delayed by a lengthy ecphrasis containing aetiological material: Daedalus' temple in Virgil (*Aen.* 6.14–33), and Parnassus and the Delphic cave in Lucan (*BC* 5.71–85); Lucan's ensuing discourse on the nature of the oracle has no exact parallel in Virgil,[63] but this does not affect the basic point that in both cases the narrative situation is first sketched out, then delayed by a descriptive passage.

After this delay both narratives follow a broadly similar pattern: the priestess is introduced, the temple entered, a pro-

---

[62] See Pichon 1912 pp. 228–9; Bayet 1946 p. 57, Amandry 1950 p. 21, Schrempp 1964 p. 22, Dick 1965 pp. 464–5, Fauth 1975 p. 341, Ahl 1976 p. 127, Fontenrose 1978 p. 210, Barratt 1979 p. 24 and 27 (citing Henry 1877–92 vol. III p. 221), Parke and McGing 1988 p. 147.

[63] For Pichon 1912 p. 229, Lucan's divergence from Virgil here becomes a point of reproach.

phecy requested; the priestess enters a frenzied state and delivers her prophecy. But of course, while the basic outline of the episode is the same in Lucan as it is in Virgil, we do not have to go very deep into Lucan's version to see that he has consistently distorted and negated his original. In the first place, while in Virgil's episode the Sibyl comes to rebuke Aeneas for his tardiness (*Aen.* 6.33–41), in Lucan the positions are reversed: it is the priestess who is idling away her time, and Appius who comes to find her in order to force her to prophesy (*BC* 5.123–7). Aeneas is given orders by the Sibyl ('nec sacra morantur / iussa viri' *Aen.* 6.40–1), while Appius orders the *antistes* to unbar the temple doors ('*iussus* sedes laxare verendas / antistes' *BC* 5.123–4).[64] And Phemonoe's unwillingness to prophesy is of course one of the basic points of Lucan's negative imitation, in contrast with a Sibyl who repeatedly urges Aeneas on and reproaches him for lingering.[65]

In fact, Lucan's ability to delay the natural progression of the episode defies belief; once again, a quick examination of the topographical layout is instructive. Henry long ago argued that Lucan's picture of the Delphic temple was modelled on Virgil's Sibylline temple:[66]

Compare Lucan 5.71, *et seqq.*, where we have the similar hill, 'iugum Parnassi' ... with its similar 'rupes' or rocky side containing the similar 'antrum'; the similar 'templum' entirely dependent on, more modern than, and affording access to, the 'antrum'; the identical term 'limen' applied ... to the entrance, not of the temple, but of the 'antrum' ...

Now it is fairly clear that Henry is right to suppose that Virgil's *limen* (*Aen.* 6.45) is not the entrance to the temple, but is inside the temple and is the entrance to the cave: the Trojans are called into the temple at 41, and are approaching the cave described in 42–4 when they come to the *limen*; afterwards the

---

[64] Ahl 1976 pp. 125–6 is surely wrong to suppose that this *antistes* (and the presumably identical *sacerdos* in 145) is Appius himself – an allusion to Appius' augurate; for how can Appius *be ordered* to open the shrine?

[65] Ahl 1976 p. 127. Lucan is accentuating a tradition of struggle in the prophetess (see Luck 1985 p. 276) though not in the Delphic priestess (see pp. 144–5).

[66] Henry 1889 p. 221. See also Parke and McGing 1988 p. 147.

frenzied Sibyl is in the cave (77). But whether the 'identical term' *limen* is in the identical place in Lucan's version remains moot. First, we are told that the *antistes* finds Phemonoe wandering carefree by the Castalian spring, seizes her and forces her to break into the temple; then she approaches the *limen*, but fearing to go any further she tries to dissuade Appius from his quest for a prophecy:

> iussus sedes laxare verendas
> antistes pavidamque deis inmittere vatem
> Castalios circum latices nemorumque recessus
> Phemonoen errore vagam curisque vacantem
> corripuit cogitque fores inrumpere templi.
> limine terrifico metuens consistere Phoebas
> absterrere ducem noscendi ardore futura
> cassa fraude parat. (*BC* 5.123–30)

So far so good: the situation appears to be exactly as in Virgil, with the *limen* situated inside the temple and outside the inner sanctum; the priestess has entered the temple and stands on the verge of an inner *limen*. But what are we to make of the following lines, which occur a little later?

> haerentem dubiamque premens *in templa* sacerdos
> *inpulit.* illa pavens adyti penetrale remoti
> fatidicum prima templorum in parte resistit ... (145–7)

Is Phemonoe inside or outside the temple when the priest thrusts her in this second time? It is a tricky point, but it seems natural to interpret the phrase in *templa ... inpulit* as 'forced her to *enter* the temple',[67] rather than 'forced her to *go further into* the temple'; the priestess hesitates outside the temple, is pushed inside, and then fearing to go further (into the *penetrale*) she puts up a struggle 'in the first part of the temple'. If this is the case, we may be compelled to revise our reading of the earlier passage (127–8): does the *antistes* in fact fail to force Phemonoe through the temple doors? Is the limen *terrificum* perhaps the outer threshold of the temple? If so, that would explain how Phemonoe can still be outside the temple when she is thrust in the second time. As a logical solution it

---

[67] So translated by Duff ad loc., and Luck 1985 p. 282.

serves its purpose, but it is unsatisfactory, not least because it is hard to see why the *outer* threshold of the temple should be *terrificum*. And if that is the situation Lucan wants us to envisage, he has certainly given us no help; there is no suggestion that Phemonoe did *not* enter the temple the first time, and we are only driven to this recourse when a later portion of the text implies a contradiction. For the reader who knows Virgil's Sibylline episode there can be no doubt (at first) that when Phemonoe stands on the *limen terrificum* in 128, she has reached the same stage as the Sibyl when she comes to the inner *limen* of the Cumaean cave ('ventum erat ad limen' *Aen.* 6.45). There is no room for uncertainty: as far as the reader is concerned, Phemonoe enters the temple and hesitates before the inner *limen* in 127–8, and then later enters the temple and hesitates before the inner *penetrale* again, at 145f. Lucan has, quite simply, repeated himself.

I do not for one moment believe that this is an oversight on Lucan's part. On the contrary, this repetition of the entry into the temple seems a deliberate ploy to put obstacles in the way of the narrative. Lucan uses a similar ploy a little earlier in the episode: after the four-line introduction in which Appius is named and we are briefly told of his quest, the long, delaying ecphrasis and digression on the nature of the oracle is concluded with the lines

> sic tempore longo
> inmotos tripodas vastaeque silentia rupis
> Appius Hesperii scrutator ad ultima fati
> sollicitat. (120–3)

words which are little more than a paraphrased repetition of 67–70, a fact which must be brought emphatically to our attention by the actual repetition of the word *sollicitat* in the same position at the beginning of a line. The effect is to bring us suddenly back to where we had started, and to re-emphasise that during the intervening digression we have really progressed nowhere at all. So too, then, the repetition of Phemonoe's entry into the temple actually works to further Phemonoe's ends: she wants to avoid having to prophesy, and in the intervening passage she attempts to deceive Appius into believing that the oracle no longer functions; when at the end of her deceitful speech we see that she is in exactly the same position as before the beginning of her speech (even though the narrative implied otherwise), we sense a Sisyphean inertia, and we realise that the narrative too is prepared to deceive so as to avoid the prophecy; just when the story seems to have moved forward, we discover that it has moved nowhere at all.[68]

In Virgil, immediately on arriving at the *limen*, the Sibyl goes into a prophetic frenzy with the approach of the god:

> cui talia fanti
> ante fores subito non vultus, non color unus,
> non comptae mansere comae; sed pectus anhelum
> et rabie fera corda tument, maiorque videri
> nec mortale sonans, adflata est numine quando
> iam propiore dei.   (*Aen.* 6.46–51)

By an exact reversal, Phemonoe in the same position precisely does not enter a prophetic frenzy: in a typically Lucanian 'negative enumeration'[69] we hear that all the normal symptoms of frenzy are *absent*, because Phemonoe is faking it:

> atque deum simulans sub pectore ficta quieto
> verba refert, nullo confusae murmure vocis
> instinctam sacro mentem testata furore
> haud aeque laesura ducem cui falsa canebat
> quam tripodas Phoebique fidem. non rupta trementi
> verba sono nec vox antri conplere capacis
> sufficiens spatium nulloque horrore comarum
> excussae laurus inmotaque limina templi
> securumque nemus veritam se credere Phoebo
> prodiderant.   (*BC* 5.148–157)

We may note that while some of these symptoms derive from the Sibyl's frenzy (raging heart, flowing hair, huge voice),

---

[68] For a similar case, see chapter 1 p. 2.
[69] The phrase is borrowed by Martindale 1980 p. 374 from Kenney 1973 p. 129; see Bramble 1982 pp. 544ff for 'negation antithesis', an overlapping technique; and on this passage see Luck 1985 p. 280: 'by telling us what she did not do, Lucan lists the characteristics of a real trance'.

others come from a later passage in which the ground shakes and the woods sway just before Aeneas and the Sibyl enter the underworld (*Aen.* 6.255–8).

This parallel is one that has received no comment in Lucanian scholarship to date; it is more commonly argued that the Sibyl's frenzy is the model for Phemonoe's *genuine* frenzy as depicted in *BC* 5.161ff.[70] Certainly this is true; but there is something to be gained from insisting on more precision. For we can see that when Phemonoe first pretends to go into a trance, and then, after Appius' threats, goes into a real trance, this responds to *two* depictions of the Sibyl's trance (6.46–51 and 77–82), separated by Aeneas' request. To a certain extent, Phemonoe's un-frenzy is made up of the (absence of the) same elements that will come to the fore in her real frenzy (for instance, the wildness of her hair in 154 and 171; possession by the god in 148 and 165ff; her madness and the confused quality of her voice in 149–50 and 190–2), whereas the two versions of the Sibyl's frenzy represent two stages of development – first an onrush of excitement at the approach of the god, and last, full possession by the god; but none the less this 'second' frenzy of Phemonoe is particularly closely related to the Sibyl's 'second' frenzy, and it is here that Lucan comes closest to verbal echoing of his model:

> bacchatur demens aliena per antrum
> colla ferens . . . (*BC* 5.169–70)

> At Phoebi nondum patiens immanis in antro
> bacchatur vates . . . (*Aen.* 6.77–8)

And even if Phoebus' possession of the priestess was mentioned in the 'first' frenzy, it is in the 'second' that the idea is particularly dwelt on, paralleling the same idea only in the Sibyl's 'second' frenzy (*Aen.* 6.77–80).

Again, it is a delicate point, but one worth making because it exemplifies what is typically Lucanian about Lucanian imitation: faced with a model in which two vaguely similar pas-

---

[70] Austin 1977 ad *Aen.* 6.47, 48, 77–97; Barratt 1979 ad *BC* 5.169–70, 170–2, 176–7, 190–1, 193; Ahl 1976 p. 127.

sages represent a sequential development, Lucan substitutes two *very* similar passages which are exact opposites, a frenzy and a non-frenzy. We can detect two contrary moves in this operation: on the one hand there are vestigial traces of the original model in which the two frenzies were distinguishable in their function, maintaining a connection with that model; and on the other, a mingling of the two original frenzies into a single collective frenzy which is presented twice, once negatively and once positively. That is a move that should be familiar to us by now; while it undercuts any possibility of narrative *progress*, since it replaces the Virgilian sense of slow development with a 'crude' juxtaposition of episodic blocks which simply mirror and oppose one another, it is also an operation conducted according to the logic of civil war: the mingling of what is different, the opposition of what is, virtually, the same.

Furthermore, by insisting on the idea that Lucan's two frenzies parallel the two frenzies described in Virgil, we preserve one of Lucan's best literary jokes. *Between* the two frenzies, in both episodes, the protagonist speaks – Aeneas in Virgil (6.54–76) and Appius in Lucan (5.157–161). Viewing these two speeches as parallel, at least on the grounds that their positions are parallel, we have on the one hand an Aeneas who eloquently, obsequiously, and at some length supplicates Phoebus and the priestess on behalf of his wandering followers, and requests a prophecy; and on the other, an Appius who curtly and menacingly compels the Pythia to utter her prophecy. In spite of the difference in length of the two speeches (which is in fact one of the main points), it is clear that they are specifically contrastable; most clearly of all in the very last words of each:

> '. . . foliis tantum ne carmina manda,
> ne turbata volent rapidis ludibria ventis;
> *ipsa canas oro.*' (*Aen.* 6.74–6)

Aeneas requests, simply enough, that the Sibyl should not (as she will in the historical future) merely write down her prophecies, but that she should sing them out loud, here, now. In Lucan those last words are torn out of context, negated, and given a completely new meaning:

> ... 'et nobis meritas dabis, impia, poenas
> et superis, quos fingis,' ait, 'nisi mergeris antris
> deque orbis trepidi tanto consulta tumultu
> *desinis ipsa loqui.*' (*BC* 5.158–61)

That is, the priestess must see to it that the words issuing from her mouth come from the god implanted in her breast, rather than from her own (deceitful) mind.[71] We can see immediately what the game is: if Lucan's brief is to construct an episode which obviously relies on the Virgilian scene but is its complete antithesis, then it is a major poetic coup to imitate a climactic line openly, keep it in its climactic place (at the end of a speech and the beginning of a line up to the caesura), insert a negative, and yet construct a context in which it makes perfect sense.

We have seen that Aeneas' lengthy supplication is paralleled by Appius' much briefer threats; it is likely that the difference in length between the two speeches is the main reason why the parallel has been overlooked. But it is obvious that throughout the episode lengthiness of treatment is manipulated as one of the principal factors in Lucan's negative imitation: where Virgil is brief, Lucan is expansive; and where Virgil is expansive, Lucan is brief. Past Lucanian scholarship, obsessed as it was with the notion of Silver Latin rhetorical redundance – a model of literary history in which it is possible to diagnose decadence by its symptomatic bombast, grandiosity, overkill – has tended to see only one half of this relation. And it is true that, in all, Lucan's episode takes up more space than Virgil's (170 lines as against Virgil's 100-odd, if the cut-off point is Aeneas' request to visit the underworld); that Lucan's description of Phemonoe's frenzy is far more detailed than Virgil's

---

[71] Possibly Lucan is accentuating one of the principal differences between Sibylline and Pythian prophecy: that the Sibyl always spoke in the first person, while the Pythia spoke in the person of Apollo. See Parke and McGing 1988 pp. 9–10; this distinction is however called into question by Fontenrose 1978 pp. 206–7.

corresponding treatment of the Sibyl's frenzy,[72] and that in particular the extensively described *subsiding* of Phemonoe's frenzy corresponds to a one-line dependent clause in Virgil ('ut primum cessit furor et rabida ora quierunt', 6.102);[73] that Phemonoe's deceitful speech (5.130–40) is longer than any of the Sibyl's curt exhortations (*Aen.* 6.37–9, 45–6, 51–3); that Lucan's huge emphasis on the fact that Phemonoe is forced to suppress most of what she knows (174–89, 197, 198–208, 210) has grown out of a forceful reinterpretation of a single word in Virgil;[74] and that Lucan's digression on the nature of the oracle, his personal remonstration with the oracle for saying so

[72] Ahl 1976 p. 127; Austin 1977 ad *Aen.* 6.47 and 77–97 (on Lucan's 'extravagance' versus Virgil's 'great economy of language'); Barratt 1979 p. 24; Dick 1965 pp. 464–5.

[73] Pichon 1912 p. 229; Austin 1977 ad *Aen.* 6.102; Barratt 1979 ad *BC* 5.208–11. Notice that even here Lucan must assert his individuality by negating the Virgilian line: even as the priestess is released from possession, we are told that her madness does *not* leave her (5.210–18, note especially 'perstat rabies', 210, and 'nec fessa quiescunt corda', 216–7); in fact Phemonoe's 'calming down' reads almost like a third description of frenzy!

[74] Virg. *Aen.* 6.100–1: 'ea *frena* furenti / concutit et *stimulos* sub pectore vertit Apollo'; Apollo shakes the reins and applies the goad, and both actions have the effect of urging the Sibyl on like a horse. In Lucan, reins and goad are divided and given opposite functions (civil war again!):

> nec verbere solo
> uteris et *stimulis* flammasque in viscera mergis:
> accipit et *frenos*, nec tantum prodere vati
> quantum scire licet.   (*BC* 5.174–7)

The goad spurs her on, while the reins hold her back; and these reins are the starting-point for Lucan's theme of suppression. Barratt 1979 ad 176 proposes that 'Lucan strongly accentuates what is discreetly suggested by Virgil in *Aen.* 6.79f' ('tanto magis ille fatigat / os rabidum, fera corda domans, fingitque premendo'); but if Virgil does suggest *control*, it does not seem to me that he is suggesting the same sort of control as Lucan: the Sibyl is trying to 'shake off' the possession (78–9), but Apollo manages to control her and thereby makes it possible for himself to prophesy through her; while Phemonoe has already been possessed and is being prevented from uttering all the things she sees. I prefer to regard the oracle's silence and the suppression of the prophecy as one of the main original – negative – elements Lucan has brought to his imitation.

little and his own interpretation of the prophecy are passages which are unparalleled in the Sibylline episode. All this is true; but we must not forget the other side of the balance: that, as we have seen, Aeneas' extended request for a prophecy is compressed into Appius' three-line threat; and that in place of the fourteen lines of detailed prophecy uttered by the Sibyl, we are given three stunningly anticlimactic and pointedly irrelevant lines of prophecy from the Delphic tripod, three lines which make a mockery of the Sibyl's enigmatic outline of the whole war between Trojans and Latins (and, profoundly, of the plot of the last six books of the *Aeneid*) by focussing exclusively on the fate of a single and utterly insignificant character who has played no part in the civil war yet[75] and will never play a part, as the oracle predicts.[76]

It is only when we take both factors into consideration – Lucan's expansions *and* his contractions – that we do full justice to the manner and tone of the imitation. Put simply, the longer a passage is, the weightier it is, the more important it is: it becomes an 'event'. In Virgil's episode – and again I am speaking crudely – the main 'events' are Aeneas' prayer and the Sibyl's prophecy: they are, in an obvious albeit superficial way, the *point* of the episode. Lucan completely overturns this emphasis: in his episode it is the preparations, the bridge-passages, the 'build-up', that receive all the attention and become the 'point', while the eventual telos – the prophecy itself – is a matter of indifference. Reading this episode with an eye on its model will produce a weird sensation of dislocation, lost balance, top-heaviness.

As indeed it should: the whole episode is predicated on this kind of dislocation, on delay, frustration, anticlimax. We have already seen how the repetition of Appius' introduction onto

---

[75] Neither in the poem, nor historically: according to Valerius Maximus' account of this anecdote, Appius had still not made up his mind which side to fight for – which is why he consulted the oracle (Val. Max. 1.8.10).

[76] On the anticlimax, see Ahl 1976 p. 128; Morford 1967 p. 66. As Ahl shows, the prophecy is irrelevant because it does not answer Appius' question about the ultimate fate of Rome and the world.

the scene, and the repetition of Phemonoe's entry into the temple, are deliberate ploys to delay the progression of the narrative; we have seen how a false frenzy precedes a true frenzy of which it is practically a negative repetition, and have seen how both frenzies outweigh in their superfluity of detail anything in Virgil. Now, as the episode draws to its (anti)climax in the final frenzy, Lucan plays his last card: a series of 'now at last' words, spread out over a paradoxically wide interval:

tandem conterrita virgo	161
confugit ad tripodas vastisque adducta cavernis	162
haesit et insueto concepit pectore numen ...	163
*tandem*que potitus	165
pectore Cirrhaeo [sc. Paean] ...	166
[23-line gap]	
spumea *tum primum* rabies vaesana per ora	190
effluit ...	191
... extremaeque sonant domita *iam* virgine voces	193

To say 'now at last' is one thing; to say it four times over a space of some thirty lines, making those thirty lines bear the weight of the expectation they produce, is another thing entirely: Lucan blatantly points toward a conclusion while mercilessly delaying that conclusion; it is the artistry of suspense in its *reductio ad absurdum*: action prolonged to its limit and then beyond; and, I would argue, self-consciously so.

Sibyls and Pythias

We have seen, now, how Lucan's imitation of Virgil works in detail. On a more general level, the fact that the Pythia is frenzied at all suggests Virgilian influence; as Fontenrose shows at length,[77] the evidence we have suggests that historically, at least, the Delphic priestess remained calm and sane during her prophetic sessions. Hence comes the assertion that Lucan's frenzied Pythia must be essentially Sibylline and Virgilian. That assertion is probably correct, but we should add a cautionary note. In the literary tradition, we do occasionally find frenzied Pythias: Plato (*Phaedr.* 244A *et seq.*) pursues the pun μανική/μαντική indiscriminately through many forms of pro-

---

[77] Fontenrose 1978 pp. 204–12.

phecy, resulting in a Pythia who is frenzied because she is classed with other frenzied prophetesses. It is easy to see this distortion becoming traditional; we do not *have to* resort to Virgilian influence to explain its appearance in Lucan, though other considerations make that likely.[78]

But there is one factor that makes it absolutely certain that the Sibylline episode is behind the Delphic episode: the comparison of the two is authorised by Lucan himself, twice. In the first place Phemonoe suggests that the oracle no longer functions because the gods consider that the Sibylline prophecies should be enough to satisfy the world:

> ... seu sponte deorum
> Cirrha silet farique sat est arcana futuri
> carmina longaevae vobis conmissa Sibyllae ... (5.136–8)

and, in the second place, Lucan draws an explicit parallel between the Pythia and the Sibyl in the final build-up to the uttering of the prophecy:

> qualis in Euboico vates Cumana recessu
> indignata suum multis servire furorem
> gentibus ex tanta fatorum strage superba
> excerpsit Romana manu ... (5.183–6)

As the commentators repeatedly remark,[79] the two passages amount to nothing less than an authorial directive to view the Pythia in terms of her Virgilian predecessor, the Sibyl. The

---

[78] We do find a frenzied Pythia in Phaedrus (Appendix 6), who wrote in the first century AD; the influence of Virgil can be discerned here too, but even more clearly than in Lucan, the poem – particularly the pun on *furens* ('crazy' / 'frenzied') – seems to reach back beyond Virgil to the traditional conceits of prophetic *furor*. See Henderson 1976.

Bayet (1946) cites a story in Plutarch (*Def. Or.* 438A–B) which tells of a single instance of frenzy followed by death during a consultation of the oracle, and suggests that it may have inspired Lucan's Delphic scene. The point of the story is that something went disastrously wrong that day (see Fontenrose 1978 p. 208), so although it is possible to allow that Phemonoe's *death* may have been suggested by Plutarch, the one-off frenzy will not have been enough for Lucan to regard frenzy as the norm.

[79] Henry 1889 p. 221, Amandry 1950 p. 21, Ahl 1976 p. 127, Barratt 1979 p. 27, Parke and McGing 1988 p. 151 n. 24.

gesture, I must emphasise, is metapoetic – an important point for when we come to discuss the literary self-consciousness of the episode as a whole (section 6).

But even as Lucan provides us with a straightforward 'clue' for the interpretation of the episode – a clue so explicit that for some readers it is, I suspect, a little embarrassing – he cannot resist twisting this clue with his characteristic irony. Consider the earlier passage: these 'songs of the aged Sibyl which were given to you' are clearly not the same as, or of the same order as, the prophecies heard by Aeneas (to this extent the parallel is not exact). Although in earlier times the Sibyl may have prophesied *ex tempore* in response to consultation like a Delphic priestess,[80] certainly by late republican times Sibylline divination was confined to written prophecies of supposedly ancient origin.[81] An official collection of these written prophecies, the *Sibyllini libri*, was housed in the Capitol under the charge of special officers whose job it was to consult and interpret them in times of emergency when directed by the senate;[82] later, after the destruction of the original collection, Sibylline prophecies were eventually moved by Augustus to the temple of Apollo on the Palatine.

There are two features of the history of the Sibylline books that I want to emphasise. First, that from the start they were closely guarded; access was restricted to a small number of officials (originally two, then ten, then fifteen); consultation was extremely rare, and it would seem that under the principate the Sibyl was strictly under imperial control – and silent.[83] In other words, the closing of the Delphic oracle and the fear of kings which Lucan discusses in 5.111–14 would seem to apply as much (if not more) to the Sibyl as it does to Delphi. The second feature of Sibylline books is that they had a habit of getting burned. Indeed, from their very origin they were the remnants of a larger collection that had gone up in flames: the story of Tarquinius (Priscus or Superbus) and a mysterious old woman who offered him nine books of prophe-

---

[80] Parke and McGing 1988 pp. 80–1.   [81] *Ibid.* p. 9 and passim.
[82] Dion. Hal. 4.62.5   [83] Parke and McGing 1988 pp. 209–10.

cies at too high a price, and burnt six before Tarquinius was persuaded to buy, is famous.[84] In 83 BC even these remaining three books perished by fire when the Capitol was burned down during the Sullan civil war. The collection was replaced some years later by prophecies scraped up from unofficial sources across the empire.[85] Finally, in 12 BC, Augustus called in all prophetic books that were being circulated unofficially, and had most of them burned, retaining only a small number of 'genuine' Sibylline prophecies.[86] Given this history, a history of restricted access and diminution by burning; and adding to this the fact that in the last years of the republic the prophecies were often manipulated for purely political ends[87] – notably Suetonius records a rumour that Lucius Cotta was intending to 'leak' a prophecy to the senate which would suggest that Caesar should be made a king[88] – there must be some irony in Lucan's allowing Phemonoe to suggest that the Sibylline prophecies should be 'enough' for the Romans.

It may be objected that such a complicated set of connotations cannot have been in Lucan's mind when he wrote the passage, and that he was alluding solely to the Virgilian Sibyl. This, as I have shown, must be wrong: although it is clear that Virgil's Sibyl is in Lucan's mind throughout the episode, and that in such a context merely to mention the word Sibyl is to point in Virgil's direction, it is equally clear that Lucan has sidestepped Virgil by speaking of a pseudo-historical Sibyl, of historical prophecies – as befits a 'historical' epic; in the simile, too, the Sibyl selects prophecies for the Romans, while in the Aeneid the prophecies are for the Trojans; that is a pointed gesture, a double assertion of dependence *and* independence.

---

[84] Dion. Hal. 4.62.1–4.
[85] Dion. Hal. 4.62.6; Tac. *Ann.* 6.12; see Parke and McGing 1988 pp. 138ff.
[86] Tac. *Ann.* 6.12; Suet. *Aug.* 31.
[87] A note of caution: this is part of a *mythology* of Roman republican 'decline and fall'. In reality, with the Sibylline prophecies so much under state control even in earlier republican times, it is difficult to imagine how they could ever *not* be used for 'purely political ends'.
[88] Suet. *Jul.* 79.3; Plut. *Caes.* 60; the same story is alluded to by Cicero (*Div.* 2.110).

Furthermore, there is something to be made of Phemonoe's alluding to the burning of the Delphic temple in 278 BC in the lines immediately preceding our first passage:

> ... seu, barbarica cum lampade Python
> arsit, in inmensas cineres abiere cavernas
> et Phoebi tenuere viam ... (5.134–6)

This is proposed as a reason for the silence of the oracle: the caves have become blocked with ashes. It is reasonable to suppose that this excuse is facetious: while we can parallel two of Phemonoe's four excuses in Plutarch's *De Defectu Oraculorum*[89] (the third is under discussion), this remaining one, the blocking of the god's passage with ash, is both unparalleled and unlikely; not only that, but there is no evidence that either Delphi or the temple was ever burned during the Gallic attack,[90] nor does it appear that the oracle went into a decline after the attack. If the excuse of ashes at Delphi is unhistorical to boot, what led Lucan to include it here? Partly – this is obvious – because a facetious excuse underlines Phemonoe's deceitfulness; but partly, I propose, because Lucan wishes to remind us of the burning of the Sibylline prophecies particularly in the fire which destroyed the Capitol in 83 BC.

In sum, Phemonoe's suggestion that the world should give up on the silent, burnt-out Delphic oracle, and turn instead to the silent, burnt-out Sibylline prophecies must be ironic. Pushing delicately on: if at the same time as making one of his most explicit gestures in the direction of the Aeneid Lucan loads his gesture with an irony that suggests the uselessness of the Sibyl, it is not unlikely that we are to read this as something like an indication of contempt. To put it more strongly: by referring

---

[89] For the first, the disappearance of prophetic vapours (5.132–4), see Plut. *Def. Or.* 434B; for the second, that the wickedness of men has caused the oracle to withdraw its prophecies (5.139–40), see *ibid.* 413. See Dick 1965 p. 460.

[90] *Pace* Cortius, quoted by Barratt 1979 ad 5.134–6; see Parke and Wormell 1956 pp. 254ff for a discussion of the attack. Lucan may be thinking of the earlier sack of Rome – both were led by a man named Brennus – in which a large part of the city *was* burnt (Livy 5.41.10 et seq., and Lucan 5.27–8, 'Tarpeia sede perusta / Gallorum facibus').

to the Sibyl at this point, Lucan says, in effect, 'Go and read the Aeneid' (so far all would agree). The Sibylline *carmina* begin to stand symbolically for the poem in which the Sibyl most famously figures. So: Read the Aeneid, *that should be enough for you* ('farique sat est ... carmina ... Sibyllae'); don't bother with the *Bellum Civile*, with this particular prophecy-scene. But then the irony (the implied uselessness of the Sibyl) ensures that we know the Aeneid *is not* enough; it is not a better alternative, it will not tell the truth any more than Lucan can; and so the prophecy-scene *will*, hesitantly, continue; the Delphic shrine *will*, reluctantly, open.

We are on the fringes of a metapoetic interpretation of the episode. It is now time to turn to the question at greater length.

Lucan in disguise?

Let us take a closer look at the introduction to the episode, where we first hear of Appius' intention to consult the oracle:

> quae [sc. arma] cum populique ducesque
> casibus incertis et caeca sorte pararent
> solus in ancipites metuit descendere Martis
> Appius eventus, *finemque expromere rerum*
> *sollicitat superos* multosque obducta per annos
> Delphica fatidici reserat penetralia Phoebi.
>   Hesperio tantum quantum summotus Eoo
> cardine Parnasos gemino petit aethera colle
> *mons Phoebo Bromioque sacer* ...   (*BC* 5.65–73)

We may start by noting the collocation *solus in ancipites*, which looks forward to the tension between singular and plural that we noted in the discussion of Parnassus' peaks: the twin peaks (*gemino colle*) are here anticipated by the word *ancipites* which in spite of Lucan's extensive gloss (*casibus incertis et caeca sorte*), bringing out its metaphorical sense, still retains its basic sense of 'doubleness', and in particular 'doubleheadedness',[91] appropriate of course in the context of a war between two 'heads'[92] whose end will be the establishment

---

[91] See Barratt 1979.

[92] One thinks in particular of the two 'heads' on the innards of the sacrifice in 1.627–8. Caesar is a *caput* in 5.365; both Caesar and Pompey are

of a *princeps*, but more immediately appropriate for the prelude to an episode set on the double-headed mountain;[93] while *solus* looks forward to the difficult 'hoc solum cacumen' (75). But none of this should surprise us: we have already seen how these key civil-war concepts invade the poem at every level, and how much Lucan is keen to reflect the broader issues of the war in the most casual verbal effects. What I wish to bring to the fore at this point is something of a rather different order.

The critics have not been kind to the Delphic episode. From its dismissal by Heitland as 'the padding' of book 5,[94] through Bayet's casual judgement that it is 'hors-d'oeuvre sans rapport à l'un ou l'autre des protagonistes, sans portée générale, sans liaison avec l' action ...',[95] to Morford's impression of 'triteness',[96] the episode has been made to stand or fall – and hence fall – on its 'relevance'. Ahl's detailed, and in many ways excellent, study of the episode[97] struck a blow in its defence, concluding that 'the story of Appius ... is anything but a digression; it is carefully dovetailed into the thematic structure of the epic' (p. 130). To some extent, I feel we should exercise caution: Ahl's need to establish the relevance of the episode may have swamped his precious insight that the shortness of the prophecy and 'Lucan's own expression of astonishment as to why the gods could reveal nothing more important than this on the eve of Pharsalia and the imminent collapse of the republic' are 'nothing less than an admission that the whole episode leads nowhere'. Nowhere *is* exactly, pointedly, defiantly, where the episode goes, and that at great length. From the initial surprise of introducing a heretofore and hereafter unmentioned character onto the scene (when we expect, perhaps,

heads in a civil war that will 'alterutrum mersura caput' (6.8). The metaphor (which is linked to the imagery of dismemberment; see chapter 5 n. 36) is common in Lucan, and pointed: when Pompey loses his position as 'head' in the battle of Pharsalus, it is not long before he loses his head literally, too.

[93] Ov. *Met.* 2.221, 'Parnasusque biceps', later imitated by Silius 15.311. Cf. the wobbling of the priestess' head on an 'ancipiti cervice' (5.172).

[94] Heitland 1887 p. xxiii.   [95] Bayet 1946 p. 53.

[96] Morford 1967 p. 65.   [97] Ahl 1976 pp. 121–30.

Pompey)[98], a character who pointedly withdraws from the main action of the poem in order to consult the oracle ('while the peoples and leaders were preparing their arms ... Appius alone ...,' 65–8), and who will afterwards be *tanti discriminis expers* (194); from our knowledge that the episode is anecdotal, even apocryphal, in origin;[99] and from our immediate recognition that Lucan has included the episode as an imitation of Virgil's Sibylline episode (hence, I would hazard, a suspicion that that is ultimately the *only* reason it is in the poem); from all of this we see that the episode is quite carefully marked out as something apart, outside the narrative, perhaps a self-contained literary exercise, certainly a literary cul-de-sac. But given these rather striking characteristics, which amount to something like an assertion of the right to be irrelevant, if Lucan so pleases, the episode continues to beg the question of its relevance; and, with Ahl, though in rather different terms from his, I should like to answer it, positively.

We begin to get a glimpse of a possible direction of enquiry when we realise that the episode's introduction, quoted above, alludes clearly but surprisingly to a part of the book 1 proem, that part in which he invokes Nero as his inspiration and sets his poem in motion.

> sed mihi iam numen; nec, si te pectore vates
> accipio, Cirrhaea velim secreta moventem
> sollicitare deum Bacchumque avertere Nysa:
> tu satis ad vires Romana in carmina dandas.
>   fert animus causas tantarum expromere rerum
> inmensumque aperitur opus, quid in arma furentem
> inpulerit populum ...   (*BC* 1.63–9)

The similarities between the two passages are clear enough: *sollicitare deum* (1.65) responds to *sollicitat superos* (5.69), both at the beginning of a line; for Appius' *finemque expro-*

---

[98] Ahl 1976 pp. 121–2.

[99] The story is told by Val. Max. 1.8.10 and Orosius 6.15.11. It is suggested that it *may* ultimately derive from Livy (Bayet 1946 p. 53, Syndikus 1958 p. 36; not so Morford 1967 p. 65), but even if that is the case I find it hard to believe that it figured there in any more detail than we find in Valerius' brief account.

mere rerum (5.68) we have Lucan's own *causas tantarum expromere rerum* (1.67), both phrases concluding a line; in the earlier passage Lucan cites two gods as potential sources of inspiration, Bacchus and Apollo, one precisely identified by his function as the god of the Delphic oracle (*Cirrhaea ... secreta moventem*, 1.64), and both these gods make their appearance in the later passage as the ruling gods of Parnassus (*mons Phoebo Bromioque sacer*, 5.73).[100] We may, finally, note again that as Parnassus is at the centre of the world, so in the proem and just before the quoted passage Nero is beseeched to remain at the centre of his world, Rome.

It is undeniable, then, that Lucan wants to establish a link between Appius' enquiry in the Delphic episode and his own poetic activity in the proem. But whatever the purpose of the parallel, we should note at once that it is not exact: Lucan wants to delve into the 'causes', while Appius wants to know the 'end'; and while Appius does 'disturb the gods', Lucan declares that he does not need to, since Nero is sufficient inspiration. The inexactness – even negativity – of the parallel is sufficient to warn us to be cautious: if Appius is *like* Lucan, if the way he proceeds about his consultation of the oracle suggests that he is enacting symbolically the writing of an epic poem – this, surely, is the point – we should not necessarily suppose that Appius 'stands for' Lucan himself, that he is Lucan in disguise. Rather, all we can suppose as yet is that Appius stands for *a* poet embarking on *some* poetic quest; and so far he seems to have proceeded in a direction which is opposed to the one Lucan avowed in the proem; or, to put it more strongly, Appius is doing what Lucan *might have* done, so he is what Lucan *might have* been. But I think we are being *too* cautious. We have no guarantee that Lucan believes what he says or is telling the truth in the proem; and in fact a large

---

[100] Bacchus and Apollo also feature in Lucan's description of the Roman matron in book 1: she is inspired by Apollo (1.677) and compared to a bacchante (1.674–5). Bohnenkamp 1979 has demonstrated an allusion to Hor. *Odes*. 3.25, in which the poet sees himself as inspired by Bacchus; a metapoetic connotation which colours the Roman matron passage (for she too is a kind of *vates*), and by extension our passage too.

scholarly faction has argued that the Nero eulogy and invocation are heavily ironic;[101] therefore we might take it with a
pinch of salt when Lucan says he has rejected the gods in
favour of Nero. In sum, all we are able to say at this point is
that Appius stands for a poet who either is, is not, or might
have been Lucan. But that is surely all we want, and all we
should expect: the joy of this kind of symbolism comes from
the uncertainty.

There is further evidence that Lucan wants us to think of
the writing of epic when we come to the Delphic episode. In
5.69 we are told that the oracle is *multos obducta per annos*
when Appius comes to open it up (*reserat*, 5.70). It is a point
on which Lucan is insistent, since he later devotes some ten
lines to mourning the loss of such a benefit to the world (111–
120); but it is, as far as we can tell, unhistorical.[102] If the
Delphic oracle was not in fact closed during the last years of
the Roman republic (or, for that matter, during the principate), why does Lucan tell us it was? We must recognise here
the recurrence of what amounts to a Lucanian leitmotif, the
motif of 're-use of old things long untouched' – so far we have
seen it exemplified in the weapons in the temples of Ariminum,
the money in the temple of Saturn, the grove and finally the
ships at Massilia. In each case it is possible to discern a
metapoetic intention behind the motif:[103] Lucan stands self-

---

[101] *Against irony*: Nock 1926 p. 18; Levi 1949; Pfligersdorffer 1959 pp. 368ff;
Grimal 1960; Brisset 1964 pp. 196–201; Thompson 1964; Jenkinson
1974; Lebek 1976 pp. 81–3; Bohnenkamp 1977. *For irony*: Marti 1945
pp. 374–6; Griset 1955; Schönberger 1958 p. 232; Rutz 1965 pp. 296–
302; Conte 1966; Ahl 1976 pp. 25–61 (particularly 47f). See also Ahl
1984 for a brilliant defence of the general position that irony was a
standard mode in ancient literature.

[102] See Ahl's clear-headed discussion (1976 pp. 123–4). My only objection
to his account is that in the crucial lines

> non ullo saecula dono
> nostra carent maiore deum, quam Delphica sedes
> quod siluit... (5.111–3)

he is too quick to interpret *saecula... nostra* as 'Neronian times'; bearing
in mind the shifting quality of that phrase, which we noticed in 4.191, we

consciously past the end of the epic genre; in the *Bellum Civile* epic is resurrected, and lives again a weird, grotesque after-life, before it is allowed to die for good. Epic – and his-tory too: all those famous participants in the civil war who now, briefly, parade the stage after their long rest in the tomb.[104]

Such positions are difficult to 'prove' (which is, of course, why they are valuable). But we should be sufficiently im-pressed by the recurrence of this leitmotif to be able to say that, here in the Delphic episode, the Appius who unbars the long-closed Delphic *penetralia* in some way parallels the action of a poet (possibly Lucan) who is turning to a source of in-spiration – to a kind of poetry – which has long been unused.

For the time being we will leave it at that; now we must turn our attention to the Pythia. Phemonoe is referred to repeat-edly as a *vates*,[105] a word that since Virgil's *Eclogues* – and in Lucan as much as anywhere else – can refer to a poet as well as to a prophet.[106] This vates 'sings' (5.151) as a poet may be said to sing – indeed, she sings in hexameters;[107] and receives the divinity into her breast as her source of inspiration:

> ... et insueto *concepit pectore numen*
> quod non exhaustae per tot iam saecula rupis
> spiritus ingessit vati ...   (5.163–5)

should perhaps allow for the possibility of it meaning 'the time in which our poem is set', i.e. the time of Appius. That said, it is perfectly clear that the oracle was no more defunct in Appius' time than it was in Lucan's; it had only gone into a decline.

[103] See chapter 2 p. 28.

[104] See also O'Higgins 1988 pp. 222–3 on this resurrection motif and its connection with Erictho's corpse.

[105] 5.124, 165, 176, 208; so too Delphic priestesses in general, 98, 115.

[106] The relevant literature on the concept of *vates* is collected by the excel-lent O'Higgins 1988 p. 208 n. 1; who, by a different route, comes to conclusions very similar to mine on the metapoetic symbolism of this episode.

[107] Hexameter verse was supposed to have been invented by the Pythia (Plin. *NH* 7.56.205; Paus. 10.5.7). But see Ahl 1976 p. 123, noting that historically the oracle was, by the time of the civil war, prophesying in prose.

... and so on.[108] We are obviously on the same territory as we were when Lucan spoke of his own poetic inspiration:

> sed mihi iam *numen*; nec, si *te pectore vates*
> *accipio*, Cirrhaea velim secreta moventem
> sollicitare deum   (1.63–5)

Whether Lucan's poetic inspiration is patterned after Delphic inspiration or vice versa, it is clear that we are meant to see them as essentially the same sort of operation. Lucan's poem is like a Delphic prophecy; the Delphic prophecy has something to tell us about Lucan's poem. And Phemonoe becomes our second candidate for the position of 'Lucan in disguise'. Again, we note the differences: Phemonoe is a woman (is this important?); Phemonoe is inspired by Apollo, not Nero (but Lucan may be lying). But in all we can be content that something is happening in this episode that has some bearing on the composition of the *Bellum Civile* – or, more accurately, on the way Lucan would like us to conceive of the composition of the *Bellum Civile* (perphaps, the 'composition myth').

The third figure we must take account of is Apollo himself, who is, as much as Phemonoe, a *vates* (5.85).[109] The position here is more complicated. No sooner has Apollo been established as the presiding deity of the oracle than Lucan launches into a discussion of the nature of the oracle in which we recognise the voice of the Stoic scientific enquirer,[110] a discussion which elides Apollo in favour of the anonymous *hoc numen* (97, 102–3) or *deus* (116) who may or may not be part of the Stoic all-pervading deity ('forsan ... totius pars magna Iovis ... conexa Tonanti' 93–6). That this deity is not Apollo (although he has Apollo's traditional functions and can be seen as a Stoic explanation of what Apollo really means),[111] and

---

[108] Up till 5.169; cf. the false possession in 148, and the general description of the process in 97.

[109] O'Higgins 1988 pp. 213–14

[110] Morford 1967 p. 65; Le Bonniec 1970 p. 176; Barratt 1979 ad 88–90, 93–6.

[111] Note that 'conceptum est pectore numen' (97) – the *numen* in this case being the anonymous deity – looks forward to nearly the same phrase used later ('concepit pectore numen' 163), where the *numen* is Apollo.

that the Stoic voice is not the voice which narrates the main bulk of the episode, is marked by the non sequitur in

> sacris se condidit antris
> incubuitque adyto vates ibi factus Apollo.
> quis latet hic superum? quod numen ab aethere pressum
> dignatur caecas inclusum habitare cavernas? (etc.)   (84–7)

Lucan apparently asks a question he has just answered (Apollo dwells in these caves; what god dwells in these caves?); and this is excusable only if it is registered as a break in the sequence of thought – as one voice takes over from another, as one way of viewing the oracle takes over from another. Since, in the episode proper, we revert to the traditional Apollo (named at 152, 156, 167, 174, 187), the effect is both to cordon off the digression *as* a digression, and on the other hand to undermine the authority and omniscience of the *narrating* voice: the narrating voice sees the mantic session as a case of possession by Apollo; the Stoic reasoner suggests other explanations. The two conflict, but do not affect each other in any way (the Stoic voice does not 'notice' that his question has been answered; the narrating voice continues to speak naïvely in terms of mythical gods), but co-exist in their contradiction. It is not a point I wish to develop at any great length, since we have seen that such contradictions within the authorial voice are to be expected: we might note too that Lucan's eulogy of the oracle in this passage (104–114) is very much at odds with his earlier stance on knowledge of the future in 2.4–15, as well as with the position of his 'favourite' Cato at the oracle of Ammon in 9.564ff.

But to resume. Apollo is, as I said, a *vates*. Now, since the anonymous *numen* of the digression is not exactly Apollo but is a Stoic version of Apolline attributes and functions, we may add that Apollo 'sings' (92, 105). But he is obviously in a special position, since he plants himself in breasts, and is never himself inspired (except, perhaps, by prophetic vapours, 82ff). But the point I would like to make with regard to Apollo – and perhaps in this case we should insist on referring to him only as the anonymous *numen* – is that the *numen* occupies a position

> terris inserta regendis
> aere libratum vacuo quae sustinet orbem   (5.93–4)

which is reminiscent of Nero's position – as a *numen* and a *deus*
himself – in the proem (a passage to which we have already
had occasion to refer):

> librati pondera caeli
> orbe tene medio   (1.57–8)

It is true that the sentences are not the same; but between book
1 and book 5 there are no instances of the past participle of
librare, and it will only re-appear once again in book 9;[112] and
whatever differences there are in sense between our two passages seem to me to be outweighed by the similarities. What I
would like to conclude is that things are so arranged that
Apollo and Nero look like counterparts of each other, the one
inspiring the priestess to prophesy, the other inspiring Lucan
to write his poem.

Delphi and the *Bellum Civile*

We have, then, a hierarchy of metapoetic figures: at the top,
Apollo or the anonymous *numen*, corresponding to the inspiring deity (who may be Nero) of the poem; then Phemonoe,
corresponding to Lucan; and finally Appius, also corresponding to Lucan. It is still not certain that this correspondence is
exact – it will not ever be certain – and we must bear in mind
that the relationship between the Delphic session and the
poem's myth of composition may be *dialectical*, the one answering and correcting, or being answered by and corrected
by, the other. In other words, there are three possibilities:
(a) the Delphic episode mirrors exactly the situation in the
invocation of Nero, and can be used as an extra commentary
on the composition of the poem; (b) the Delphic episode contradicts the situation in the invocation of Nero, and will show
us what Lucan really has in mind; and (c) the Delphic episode,
inasmuch as it is contradicted by the invocation of Nero,

---

[112] 9.529. There is only one other instance of *librare* in any form: the infinitive at 3.433, used of swinging an axe.

shows us a way of composing the poem which Lucan might have gone, but did not. There are individual variants of these three positions, including the three positions combined, but they are the basic ones. But now that we have established that metapoetic commentary *of some sort* is definitely at issue in the Delphic episode, we must turn to the obvious question: what does the episode actually tell us about poetry; what model of the composition myth does it symbolise? For the sake of clarity, I will postpone the question of whether this poem is the *Bellum Civile* and speak of the represented poet figure as if he were Lucan.

Let us address ourselves to the question of *furor*. It is a standard word for denoting prophetic frenzy,[113] and naturally enough it is used by Lucan in this episode, to describe the frenzy which habitually afflicts the priestesses (5.118), the frenzy which does not afflict Phemonoe when she pretends to prophesy (5.150), and, by a bold stretching of the sense of the word so that it becomes almost a metaphor for prophecy, the Sibyl's frenzy (in the simile comparing the Sibyl with the Pythia, 5.184). We also need to remember that, much as *vates* can mean prophet or poet, *furor* can refer to both prophetic and poetic frenzy – that is, poetic inspiration.[114] And in fact there is no need to restrict these observations to the single word *furor*: they apply equally to its near synonyms and cognates, *insania*, *vesanus*, etc.;[115] but for the time being we will narrow our view, for a reason that will now be made clear. *Furor* is something of a key concept in the *Bellum Civile*, denoting the madness of civil war: 'quis furor, o cives ...?' (1.8). In the Delphic episode the various senses of *furor* have their place and interact: Lentulus at Epirus speaks of *bellorum ... furor* (5.36); and Lucan's epilogue to the prophecy mentions *poenas furorum* (in connection with Brutus' assassination of Caesar, 5.206). The *numen* of the shrine is apparently uncontaminated by human *furor* (102–4) – and here the primary

---

[113] Virg. *Aen.* 6.100 ('furenti'), 102 ('furor'); see Cic. *Div.* 1.66–7.
[114] Cic. *Div.* 1.80.
[115] Brink 1971 ad Hor. *Ars* 295–8, 296. The idea goes back to Democritus.

sense is difficult to discern; something like 'wickedness', but the notion is clearly affected by the meaning 'civil-war madness'. And finally – surprisingly – Appius himself is *furens*, angry at being deceived, furiously compelling the priestess to prophesy (157).

The case is similar to one we may have observed in book 1: there the frenzied Roman matron prophesies the events of the war to come, and when Lucan finishes her prophecy, and book 1, with a single concluding line ('haec ait, et lasso iacuit deserta furore', 1.695), the strong emphasis that *furore* receives by virtue of its position as the last word of the book allows that prophetic fury to resonate; picks up the matron's prophetic words 'quis furor hic ...' (1.681), themselves a reminiscence of Lucan's initial 'quis furor, o cives ...' And here in the Delphic episode, surely, the point is the same: we hear the madness of civil war in the ecstasy of the prophetess. That madness is also to be found in the poet's inspiration: the poet writing of the evils of *furor* is himself *furens* – like Phemonoe, like Appius.

Two separate points, then: the traditional *furor* of prophets and prophetesses takes on a new resonance in the context of a 'furious' civil war, the Pythia's madness reflects, foreshadows, the storms of fury on the battlefield, in the cosmos;[116] or, as Morford puts it, 'The fifth book is turbulent, the spiritual turmoil of the Pythia is balanced by the physical turmoil of the great storm, both symbolic of the great events that are to be played out.'[117] And second: this turmoil, these storms of fury, are not only what Lucan's poem is *about*; they are what the poem *is*. Matter and manner are inseparable, as the poet finds himself embroiled in the very madness he is describing.

---

[116] Note the 'imagery of cosmic dissolution' (Lapidge's phrase) in the description of the effects of inspiration on the body of a priestess:

> quippe stimulo fluctuque furoris
> *conpages* humana *labat*, pulsusque deorum
> concutiunt fragiles animas. (118–20)

Note too the civil-war keyword *concutiunt*: cf., for instance, 'certatum totis *concussi* viribus orbis' (1.5).

[117] Morford 1967 p. 60; quoted by Barratt 1979 in her introduction.

How the poet's civil-war frenzy manifests itself has been one of the principal themes of this book; but it is worth showing how it is worked out in the immediate context of the episode. The first thing to emphasise is that although Phemonoe and Appius are separate people, in their symbolic function as metapoetic figures *both* correspond to Lucan. To turn it around the other way: the single poet Lucan, who represents himself as a *vates* inspired to enquire into the truth, is split into two figures who each derive from a part of that representation, one an inspired *vates*, and the other an enquirer into the truth. Both, significantly, are in the thrall of *furor*, as we have seen; and, more significantly, they are *in conflict*, as Appius uses force and threats to extract a prophecy from the priestess, and she in turn uses every possible guile to avoid having to prophesy. Here, then, we see the internal discord of the poetic persona graphically symbolised, and played out for us around the Delphic tripod. As if that was not enough, even the third party, Apollo or the *numen* of the oracle, supposedly free from the taint of *furor*, is involved in a raging struggle with his priestess. To be sure, struggle between prophetess and inspiring god, which amounts to a kind of spiritual rape, is a consistent element of the prophetic tradition; but surely Lucan is unique in the extent to which this violence is accentuated – certainly unique in asserting that it was always followed by death.[118] As Phemonoe is forced, on Appius' orders, to 'break into' the temple (*inrumpere*, 127), so Apollo 'breaks into' Phemonoe (*inrupit*, 167), 'expelling' (*expulit*, 168) the mind from the body of one who had been 'impelled' (*inpulit*, 146) into the temple. Clearly there is a parallel to be drawn between the physical violence done to Phemonoe by Appius, and the spiritual violence done by Apollo. And if these three figures each have their place in the symbolism of the poem's myth of composition, when one might reasonably expect harmony and co-operation to be *de rigueur* for a successful poem, then the mutual violence of the three parts is an important statement. Herein represented is a poem written by a poet divided into

[118] See n. 77.

two conflicting halves, further antagonised by a maleficent and eventually murderous inspiring deity.

Let us put *furor* to one side now, and turn to the prophecy itself. There are two sides to this prophecy: what Phemonoe says, and what she does not say. It is the latter that will receive special attention. Under the inspiration of Apollo, the priestess sees, literally, everything:

> venit aetas omnis in unam
> congeriem, miserumque premunt tot saecula pectus,
> tanta patet rerum series, atque omne futurum
> nititur in lucem, vocemque petentia fata
> luctantur, non prima dies, non ultima mundi,
> non modus Oceani, numerus non derat harenae.
> qualis in Euboico ... [the simile of the Sibyl] (177–83)

Now although in accordance with the model we should expect the actual prophecy uttered by the priestess to correspond to the poem written by the poet, there is much in this mass of material not appearing in the prophecy that is very characteristic of the *Bellum Civile*. Here in one heap, thrust, squashed, compressed into the one breast of the priestess, is the total of history from beginning to end. We should recognise the motifs here – the motif of the heap, and of many things compressed into a small space – as Lucanian leitmotifs. Piles, heaps, masses, of dead bodies, wood and earth; ramparts, funeral pyres, gigantic ships; these proliferate in the *Bellum Civile* as in no other epic, marking the poem, as we have seen, as an epic of bigness, tumidity, anti-Callimachean fatness.[119] And, con-

---

[119] See chapter 2 pp. 32 and 34. I offer here a selective list of examples of the 'heap' motif.

CORPSES: 2.201–20 (mass execution of prisoners by Sulla; blocking of the river because of piles of corpses); 3.575 (piles of corpses in water at Massilia); 4.570–1 (corpses heaped up on Vulteius' raft); 6.180 (pile of corpses equals height of Scaeva's wall); 7.597–8 and 721–2 (heaps of patrician corpses at Pharsalus); note, finally, the excellent joke in 9.796: a man bitten by a *prester* snake so swells up that 'ipse latet penitus *congesto corpore mersus*'.

MISCELLANEOUS HEAPS AND MASSES: the many examples in the Massilian episode are omitted. 2.300 (the imaginary funeral pyre of Rome); 2.449 (fortifications in the towns of Italy); 2.661 etc. (blockade at Brundisium);

comitantly, we see several times the idea that everything – or a great number of things – is converging to one point in time, in space. The astrologer Nigidius Figulus says:

> extremi multorum tempus in unum
> convenere dies. (1.650–1)

(a neat conceit: by using 'extremi dies' for 'mortes' he shows us many *times* converging on one *time*).[120] When in book 2 we hear reminiscences of the bad old days of Sulla, we are told of the killing of the citizens of Praeneste:

> vidit Fortuna colonos
> Praenestina suos cunctos simul ense recepto
> *unius populum pereuntem tempore mortis.* (2.193–5)

and similarly, the execution of prisoners who are crammed into the *ovilia* in the Campus Martius – so crammed that there is no room for the dead men to fall (2.196ff). Later, the whole civil war is contained within Caesar's earthworks at Dyrrachium:

> coit area belli:
> hic alitur sanguis terras fluxurus in omnis,
> hic et Thessalicae clades Libycaeque tenentur;
> aestuat angusta rabies civilis harena. (6.60–3)

Finally, there is Pharsalus. As Lucan had prophesied in the book 3 catalogue of troops

> acciperet felix ne non semel omnia Caesar,
> vincendum pariter Pharsalia praestitit orbem. (3.296–7)

so it will be when we arrive at book 7, where the idea that the whole world has come to fight in this one battle is one of the basic colours of the episode. For instance, take these lines from Pompey's hortatory speech:

4.419 etc. (heavy rafts in the Adriatic); 5.316 (Caesar stands on a mound); 6.31ff (Caesar's earthworks at Dyrrachium); 7.649 (Pompey stands on a mound); 8.695 (Alexander's tomb); 9.340 (piles of sand in Libyan sand-storm).

[120] Lucan may have started from an Ennian line, 'multa dies in bello conficit unus' (*Ann.* 258 Skutsch); if so it has been, as usual, twisted nearly out of recognition.

primo gentes oriente coactae
innumeraeque urbes, quantas in proelia numquam
excivere manus. toto simul utimur orbe.   (7.360–2)

One example should suffice; there are more. What I wish to bring out here is that in the moment of Pharsalus, not only is the population of the earth assembled and decimated, but the whole of history is annulled, the whole of the future changed (7.387ff). Pharsalia is a true crisis point: one place, one time, containing the resources, histories, possibilities, of all places, all times. Everything converges.

And so back to the Delphic priestess. Here, at the mythical centre of the world, and in one person, converges total knowledge of the universe; as if in imitation of the battle ranks at Pharsalus, they struggle for pre-eminence (*luctantur*, 5.181); and like the huge destruction associated with the leitmotif, in the Sibyl simile this mass of possible prophecies is spoken of, provocatively, as a 'tanta fatorum *strage*' (5.185). What Phemonoe sees, then, is what the *Bellum Civile* is all about: civil war, everything. The strands of history and fate are collected into one place, one time, one poem of total significance.

And yet Phemonoe says none of these things. All she can utter is three lines of exquisite irrelevance: her prophecy is precisely not about civil war, it is about how a single character will have nothing to do with the civil war. The Delphic tripod does not speak; the poet falls silent, the vast possibilities of his poem unrealised, unwritten.

Epilogue

Phemonoe's silence in contrast with Lucan's all-too-evident willingness to speak – for after all, in the following lines he takes over where she leaves off, he at least knows the future and tells us of Pharsalus, Pompey's death, the assassination of Caesar (200–7)[121] – begs the question we postponed during the last section: what bearing does the Delphic episode have on the *Bellum Civile*? Is this symbolically represented poet actually Lucan? I cannot say; but yes and no, surely. It is

---

[121] A point made by Schrempp 1964 p. 23.

certainly one of Lucan's poses to be the one who knows but cannot speak – this notably at Pharsalus:[122]

> hanc fuge, mens, partem belli tenebrisque relinque
> nullaque tantorum discat me vate malorum,
> quam multum bellis liceat civilibus, aetas.
> a potius pereant lacrimae pereantque querellae:
> quidquid in hac acie gessisti, Roma, tacebo.   (7.552–6)

Duff (1927 ad loc.) drily comments 'Lucan makes this promise and then proceeds to break it' – too drily, I think, for we must recognise in the gesture of ineffability more than a cheap rhetorical ploy; we must recognise a deeper, more extensive rhetoric, a coherent position from which *this war is too vast and too terrible to describe*. That Lucan does go on to describe it is another issue; if by now I can speak safely of the split in Lucan's poetic persona, then one way in which this split manifests itself is in the opposition of a poet who is too horrified to speak, and a poet who, with apparent grisly relish and Silver Latin exuberance, is quite prepared to taint himself with the *nefas* of describing the ultimate *nefas*. For the time being we see only the first half: it is all too much, the voice chokes in the throat, some things just cannot be spoken of ... The second half of the poet we will see when we meet the dazzling figure of Erictho, who stands as the second half of Virgil's fractured Sibyl, in a position in the second half of the poem's split centre.

But I should like to finish with Lucan's little epilogue.

> secreta tenebis
> litoris Euboici memorando condite busto
> qua maris angustat fauces saxosa Carystos
> et, tumidis infesta colit quae numina, Rhamnus,
> artatus rapido fervet qua gurgite pontus
> Euripusque trahit, cursum mutantibus undis,
> Chalcidicas puppes ad iniquam classibus Aulin.   (5.230–6)

Lucan addresses Appius, and predicts that he will fulfil the Pythia's prophecy by dying and being buried on the shore of

---

[122] This passage is well discussed by Johnson 1987 pp. 98–9; see too O'Higgins 1988 pp. 215–16 on not speaking.

Euboea – certainly in *that* way he will have no part in the war. Ahl sensitively points to the ambiguity of the first one-and-a-half lines: as he says, *Euboicus* can refer to Cumae (as it does at 5.183), and *secreta* can just as much mean 'secrets, arcana' as it does a hidden place where Appius will be buried.[123] So in referring to Appius' tomb, Lucan, oracularly, uses language which suggests that he will somehow be in possession of – or understand (Ahl's interpretation) – the mysteries of the Cumaean Sibyl.[124] This should increase our paranoia: Lucan is playing at being a Delphic oracle; how much more is there to this passage than meets the eye? In the site of Appius' tomb we see – what? Glimpses, shadows, ghosts. Consider: of the vast, struggling mass of prophecy, only a tiny part is uttered; so here in the straits at Euboea we see the infinity of the sea, narrowed. 'Qua maris angustat fauces ... Carystos': can we not hear in this the throat of the Pythia ('faucesque obstruxit Apollo' 197); can we not hear in the churning of the sea the foamy outpour from the Pythia's mouth ('spumea ... rabies vaesana per ora / effluit' 190–1)?[125] Looking further afield, does not Appius' tomb on the shore anticipate the more famous tomb of Pompey on the shore of Egypt? And does not the pendent last word of the episode, *Aulin*, look back to what was the beginning – the very beginning – of it all, the Greek expedition against Troy?[126]

---

[123] Ahl 1976 p. 129.

[124] Cf. 'deus omnia cursus / aeterni *secreta tenens*' (5.88–9).

[125] Cf. the marine simile describing Phemonoe's heart after the prophecy, 217–18.

[126] Ahl 1976 p. 129.

5

THE THESSALIAN EXCURSUS

After serious defeat at Dyrrachium, Caesar manages to escape to Thessaly (6.315); and Pompey, rejecting the advice of his comrades that he should reclaim Italy in Caesar's absence, pursues him (6.316–332). Now, at last, both leaders are in the land which will witness the final conflict, and Lucan marks the occasion with a long digression on the mountains (333–42), cities (349–59), rivers (360–80), peoples (381–94), and 'products' (395–409) of Thessaly that is framed by two expressions of the ruling of fate: '... Emathiam, bello quam fata parabant' (332), and 'hac ubi damnata fatis tellure locarunt / castra duces' (413–4).[1] In a narrow sense, Thessaly has been ordained for war and condemned by fate in that it will be the site of the battle of Pharsalus; but in a wider sense, the catalogue will show us that Thessaly has always been an evil and terrible place, and we will see that fate has been at work since the beginning of time to make it a fit place for the culminating battle of the civil war. This function of the digression has, at least in broad terms, been generally recognised;[2] and it is because it is clear, more so than elsewhere, that here we are faced not with an ostentatious and shallow display of learning, but with a passage of sustained connotative significance, that we start from a basic position of agreement with the scholarship without having to defend the necessity of a close symbolic reading of the text. The Thessalian excursus will be an admirable place to begin our reassessment of the Lucanian 'plague of catalogues';[3] but more than that, it will raise some impor-

---

[1] Wünsch 1930 p. 61.
[2] Longi 1955 p. 184; Syndikus 1958 p. 53 and pp. 71–5 (on the relation of such catalogues to the plot); Schönberger 1961 p. 70; Paoletti 1963 p. 12; Gassner 1972 pp. 183–4; Fauth 1975 pp. 329–30.
[3] Heitland's phrase, p. lxxiv.

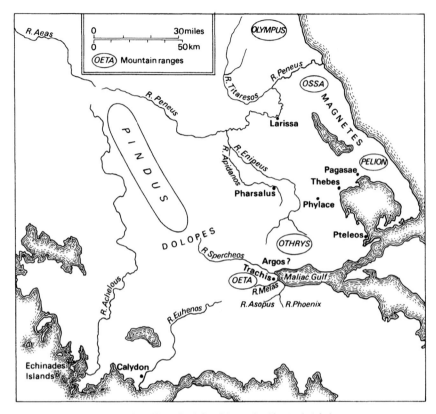

Map 3. Thessaly (after Murray's *Classical Atlas*)

tant questions about Lucan's *doctrina*, which in turn have a crucial bearing on how seriously we take him as a poet.[4]

We begin with the mountains that surround Thessaly on all sides: Ossa, Pelion, Othrys, Pindus and Olympus. Their respective positions are delineated by astronomical and meteorological periphrases, whose complexity has in some cases

[4] General studies, usually brief, of geography in Roman poets (Lucan among them) include Thomson 1951, Mayer 1986, and Syme 1987. On the whole, geographical names are dismissed as ornament; but the studies are valuable in that they show the extent to which geographical lore was transmitted from poet to poet (rather than referring to an external reality). Hence *doctrina*.

151

proved difficult to decipher. Pindus presents no problem: we are told (339–40) that it meets the west wind and the south-west wind and that it cuts short the daylight in the evening; therefore it must be on the western and south-western border of Thessaly, as indeed it is. Similarly, we can readily interpret the position of Olympus (341–2): those who live at the foot of Olympus (presumably on the Thessalian side) have no fear of the north wind, and know nothing of the constellation Arctos – which is always in the south part of the sky; Olympus blocks both, and therefore Lucan is saying, quite correctly, that it is on the northern border of Thessaly. But when we turn back to the first three mountains in Lucan's list, we begin to run into difficulties.

> Thessaliam, qua parte diem brumalibus horis
> attollit Titan, rupes Ossaea coercet;
> cum per summa poli Phoebum trahit altior aestas
> Pelion opponit radiis nascentibus umbras;
> at medios ignes caeli rapidique Leonis
> solstitiale caput nemorosus summovet Othrys.   (333–8)

To understand this passage, we have to know some basic astronomical facts: in winter, the sun rises in the south-east, while in the summer it rises in the north-east; and, winter or summer, the sun verges towards the south as the time approaches midday (these rules of course only apply in the northern hemisphere). So when Lucan says that 'Ossa borders Thessaly in that part where the sun causes day to rise in the winter', he can only mean that Ossa is in the south-east of Thessaly; and if 'Pelion opposes the rising rays with its shade when high summer (or the time towards high summer) draws the sun through its zenith', then Pelion must be in the north-east of Thessaly. Both positions are geographically incorrect, as has often been pointed out: in fact Ossa is in the north-east and Pelion in the south-east.[5] But what of Othrys? Lucan says

---

[5] Pichon 1912 p. 19 (proposing an astronomical, rather than geographical, error); Housman ad loc.; Bourgery 1928A pp. 26–7; Getty 1951 p. 25. Samse, in his indispensable article on the Thessalian excursus (1942), attempts to vindicate Lucan's geographical accuracy by the following

'But wooded Othrys wards off the "middle fires of the sky" and the solsticial head of the parching[6] Lion.' Housman rightly notes (ad loc.) that the sun is not in Leo at the time of the summer solstice; but we should not be so exacting: the solstice stands for summer in general in the same way that *bruma* (= *brevissima dies,* the winter solstice) stands for the season of winter in general.[7] The phrase 'medios ignes caeli' is the subject of some confusion for Bourgery,[8] but Housman (ad loc.) is certainly right to gloss it as 'meridies', the sun at midday. If the sun, even when in Leo, moves south in its journey towards the midday point, then the fact that Othrys 'wards it off'

argument: 'In the winter days the rising sun shines from the south-east into the land of Thessaly and strikes Pelion on the side turned away from Thessaly, and Ossa on the side turned towards Thessaly. Correspondingly, in summertime the rising sun shines from the north-east into the land of Thessaly and then strikes Ossa on the side turned away from Thessaly, and Pelion on the side turned towards it. Consequently the poet is saying that Ossa is the country's boundary-mark in the north-east, and Pelion in the south-east' (p. 250, my translation). An ingenious piece of lateral thinking, but it will not do. If the sun from the south-east strikes the Thessalian side of Ossa in the north-east, it also strikes everything in the same way from north-east to north-west and from north-west to south-west. As a means of fixing a geographical point, it is useless: we must already know where Ossa is. Similarly with Pelion, if the north-east sun strikes Pelion on the Thessalian side, all that tells us is that Pelion is not in the north-east corner of Thessaly; it might be anywhere else. Besides, I can find nothing in Lucan's Latin to support the notion that these mountains are doing anything other than *fending off* the light of the sun from Thessaly ('Pelion opponit . . .' 336; cf. 'summovet Othrys' 338), as Pindus and Olympus fend off winds and block out the light of the setting sun and the northern stars; nothing, in other words, to support the notion that the crucial issue is the light shining on the *Thessalian* side of these mountains. See also note 9.

[6] For *rapidus* as 'parching' rather than 'swift', see Housman ad loc.

[7] Samse 1942 p. 251; *OLD* s.v. 'solstitium' 2b.

[8] 1928A p. 27. If Leo rises in the north-east (which it does, but only visibly so in autumn and winter), this is irrelevant: when the sun is in Leo in summer, its course through the sky invisibly but exactly duplicates that of the sun, so it too is in the south at midday. Hence there is no contradiction, such as Bourgery finds, between north-east and south in the two parts of this astronomical periphrasis. See also Pichon 1912 p. 19.

means that Othrys must be in the south of Thessaly, and this is geographically correct.[9]

In sum, of the five mountains mentioned by Lucan, the first two are in the wrong place, the remaining three correctly sited. Two points: the very beginning of a catalogue is a position of emphasis, and it is remarkable that Lucan should have been so apparently careless as to have made so gross an error in respect of his first two mountains. And second, Lucan certainly knows where Ossa really is. Barely fifteen lines later, referring to the creation of the valley of Tempe by Hercules, he says:

> postquam discessit Olympo
> Herculea gravis Ossa manu   (347–8)

showing that he knows that Ossa is next to Olympus (which he has correctly placed in the North). What on earth has happened? First Lucan perpetrates a major geographical error, then he immediately betrays it. The problem is not solved by further questioning Lucan's capabilities as a *doctus poeta*; rather, I suggest, we are forced to the conclusion that Lucan wishes us to recognise the error for what it is, and by situating it at the beginning of his catalogue, he makes it programmatic of what is to come – a geographical catalogue that will overturn the knowns of geography.

Besides, Ossa and Pelion are in the special position of being somewhat mobile mountains. Their position at the beginning of the catalogue is reflected by their reappearance at the very end of the catalogue (411–12), when their connotations are at last made explicit: they are the mountains of the gigantomachy, which were torn out of their positions in order to make a bridge to the heavens. Their displacement by Lucan can be seen as a symptom of gigantomachic disorder. The gigantomachy is of course supremely relevant to the civil war, and has figured repeatedly in the symbolic fabric of Lucan's

---

[9] Strangely, Samse gets this right (1942 p. 251); one would expect, in the light of his earlier argument (see note 5), that he would interpret the lines as putting Othrys in the north, since at midday the sun would then shine on the side of Othrys turned towards Thessaly.

poem,[10] explicitly so in the proem (1.33–7); and so the Ossa / Pelion frame of the Thessalian excursus marks out the land of Thessaly most emphatically as the site of this archetype of all civil wars. History turns full circle; and for its last, climactic battle, civil war returns to the home of its birth.

Thessaly is a valley of darkness[11] – this is one of the side effects of Lucan's obscure periphrases. Pelion and Ossa oppose the light of the rising sun; Othrys wards off the midday sun; Pindus cuts out the light of the evening sun; and Olympus blocks the shining Arctos (*lucentem ... Arcton* 342) at night. On all sides there are mountains preventing light from getting through. A land, too, of stillness, whose mountains fend off winds from the north, the west and the south-west. More than that, the passage is shot through with language suggesting conflict, oppression: *coercet* (stronger, surely, than the scholiast's gloss *terminat*), *trahit, opponit, summovet, adversos, praecidit*; and, as so often in the poem, a tiny gesture towards Pompey in *umbras*.[12] And finally, this ring of mountains which surrounds and confines the inner part of Thessaly, and which, I suggest, takes some of its colour from Lucan's description of Caesar's earthworks at Dyrrachium earlier in book 6, makes of Thessaly a colossal 'theatre of war' in accordance with the gladiatorial and theatrical imagery so central to Lucan's symbolism;[13] a giant amphitheatre with mountains for stands, Pliny described it in his account of Thessalian geography:

in Thessalia quattuor atque triginta [sc. montes], quorum nobilissimi Cercetii, Olympus Pierius, Ossa, cuius ex adverso Pindus et Othrys Lapitharum

---

[10] See chapter 2 pp. 39–40.

[11] Longi 1955 p. 184.

[12] Note the paradox involved in the line 'Pelion opponit radiis nascentibus umbras', as if light could ever be 'opposed' by shade – that would give shade more substance than it has. The justification is that *umbras* stands for 'shady woods' (see Samse 1942 p. 251 and Commenta Bernensia ad 6. 336); but none the less it remains a paradox (cf. similarly 6. 504). For Pompey and *umbra see* Feeney 1986A.

[13] Conte 1974 ad 6.159–60, 182, 191 (on Scaeva); and Ahl 1976 esp. pp. 84–8 (on Curio).

sedes, hi ad occasum vergentes, ad ortus Pelius, omnes theatrali modo inflexi, caveatis ante eos LXXV urbibus.   (Plin. *NH* 4.30)

Between these mountains, says Lucan, the plains were once covered with an enormous lake (343ff). It was formed by the waters from Thessaly's rivers, which were trapped in the valley with no way of egress; but Hercules separated Ossa from Olympus, so creating the valley of Tempe, and the waters rushed out to reveal dry land. The story of the primeval lake is a well-attested piece of geographical lore,[14] and Lucan chooses the version which ascribes the creation of the valley of Tempe to Hercules;[15] traditionally, the gorge was formed by Poseidon,[16] though Poseidon's agency was easily rationalised as the effect of a catastrophic earthquake.[17] It is remarkable, then, that Lucan, so often the Stoic scientific enquirer, should abandon a long-set precedent for viewing the formation of Tempe in purely scientific terms, and settle for the mythical agency of Hercules;[18] Although Poseidon would seem to be the right figure to perform an operation that involved large quantities of water and required an earthquake, yet Hercules was associated with the cutting of one other major gorge for the passage of water: the Pillars of Hercules, which were supposed to have been the origin of the Mediterranean sea;[19] the *Herculeae fauces* of Thessaly are a natural enough extension of

[14]   See Pauly–Wissowa Vol. 5a pp. 473, 65ff.
[15]   In this he is consistent: cf. 8.1, 'Herculeas fauces'. Cf. Diod. 4.18.6, Sen. *HF* 283–8.
[16]   Philostratus 2.14; Schol. Pind. *Pyth.* 4.246; and Herodotus' report in 7.129.4.
[17]   Hdt. 7.129.4, his own opinion; see also Strab. 9.5.2, Sen. *NQ* 6.25.2, Philostr. 2.17, Baton of Synopus in Fr. Gr. Hist. (Jacoby) 3a p. 78 no. 5.
[18]   Since Seneca as tragedian speaks of Hercules as the cause, where Seneca as scientist in the *N.Q.* speaks of an earthquake, Samse (1942 p. 252) finds in Lucan's version a poetic way of treating the material. This evades the problem. Lucan's scientific and unpoetical approach is notorious elsewhere: see e.g. Lausberg 1985 p. 1608.
[19]   On the parallelism, Diod. 4.18.4–6. For the pillars of Hercules, Plin. *NH* 3.1.4; Mel. 1.27; Sen. *H.F.* 237–8; Lucan mentions the *Herculeae metae* at 3.278.

that feat. Hercules is a central figure in the catalogue: Lucan alludes to his various stories at 353–4, 365, 391–4, and one reason for his presence here is that he figured prominently in the gigantomachy.[20]

The creation of the gorge and the sudden escape of the water from the lake is spoken of as a *ruina*, a favourite civil-war word to describe various grades of catastrophe:

> subitaeque ruinam
> sensit aquae Nereus   (348–9)

and the alert reader will detect a subtle echo from Lucan's account of the Dyrrachium episode, where after a simile describing Pompey's movements in terms of the flooding of the river Po (the flood image connecting with the 'flood' of Thessalian rivers which formed the lake), we read:

> vix proelia Caesar
> *senserat*, elatus specula quae prodidit ignis:
> invenit inpulsos presso iam pulvere muros,
> frigidaque, ut veteris, deprendit signa *ruinae*.   (6.278–81)

We do not have to propose (though we might) that Caesar parallels Nereus as Pompey parallels Hercules. We should be content merely to note that as always Lucan has co-ordinated his digression with the story he is telling so that action and excursus reflect each other. The lake, indeed, is a miniature flood, and as such links with the important motif of universal flood (Deucalion's flood) that I have had occasion to discuss before;[21] the way the lake is described indeed delineates it as a precisely *primeval* lake (*quondam*), and its subsiding, followed by the emergence of towns on dry land, seems to parallel the re-emergence of the earth after the subsiding of the great flood. There is something of a miniature creation-myth in all of this:

---

[20] Hercules is a significant figure elsewhere in the poem too: see Shoaf 1978, Martindale 1981.

[21] See chapter 3 pp. 63–5. Interestingly, Apollodorus (1.7.2) says that the gorge of Tempe was formed at the time of Deucalion's flood, implying a close conceptual connection between the flood and Thessaly's primeval lake.

Lucan's catalogue allows us to witness the creation of a world – an anti-world – from its initial chaotic nothingness, towards the building of its first cities, the development of its first civilisations, and its first discoveries (some of which are common elements in the myth of the passing of the golden age).

The first city Lucan names is, naturally enough, Pharsalus, the precise site of the coming battle: for this reason, presumably, it is *melius mansura sub undis*. A witticism here: it is the native city of Achilles (350),[22] and, as the scholiast noted,[23] Lucan plays on the unusual epithet *aequoreus* for Achilles, which indicates his parentage in the sea-nymph Thetis – better had Pharsalus remained underwater and Achilles remained truly 'watery'. The ships of Phylace were the first to touch the shores of Troy; Phylace, the second town in Lucan's list, is to be taken as a pair with Pharsalos,[24] both alluding to the story of the Trojan war. This war is important in Lucan's poem for two reasons: first because, as in Virgil, Horace and others, the fall of Troy works as a model for the fall of the Roman republic, by the same system of historical parallelism that makes Aeneas an obvious model for Augustus as a re-founder of the old civilisation with some major changes; and second, because it is the subject of Homer's Iliad. Thus the protagonist of the 'last' epic in history, Lucan's Caesar, returns to the home city of the protagonist of the first epic of all. We may note, finally, the suggestion of evil in

> *prima Rhoeteia litora pinu*
> quae tetigit   (351–2)

which looks forward to

> *prima* fretum scindens *Pagasaeo litore pinus*   (400)

referring to the voyage of the Argo, often in ancient literature one of the symptoms of man's audacity and of post-golden-

---

[22] Bruère 1951 p. 111 n. 11.

[23] *Adnotationes* ad loc.; see Gassner 1972 p. 184 n. 2.

[24] The first eight cities in the catalogue are apparently grouped in pairs: see Samse 1942 p. 253.

age wickedness,[25] and cited in the catalogue as one of the *semina Martis*, causes of war among mankind.

We turn to the next two cities in Lucan's list:

Pteleosque et Dorion ira
flebile Pieridum   (352–3)

There is indeed a place by the name of Pteleos, or Pteleon, in Thessaly;[26] but a Dorion in Thessaly does not exist. Dorion is said to be 'ira flebile Pieridum' because it is the place where Thamyris challenged the Muses and was blinded by them when he lost; but in Homer, who tells the story himself in the catalogue of ships, Dorion is located in the western Peloponnese, being one of the cities under the sway of Nestor.[27] But this is clearly more than an ordinary mistake, as we will see if we look at the Homeric passage:

... καὶ Πτελεὸν καὶ Ἕλος καὶ Δώριον, ἔνθα τε Μοῦσαι
ἀντόμεναι Θάμυριν τὸν Θρήικα παῦσαν ἀοιδῆς (Hom. *Il.* 2.594–5)

What has happened is obvious: Homer links together Dorion and Pteleos, both in the western Peloponnese; and Lucan, confusing the Messenian Pteleos with the Thessalian Pteleos, brings Dorion and the story of Thamyris into Thessaly by association. This cannot be accidental, not just the result of carelessness, or foggy geographical knowledge: the story of Thamyris was well known, and its first telling in Homer famous;[28] and the position of Dorion in Homer's catalogue makes it quite clear that Dorion was not in Thessaly. What I propose, then, is this: the appearance of Pteleos, Dorion and the story of Thamyris in Lucan's catalogue alludes directly

---

[25] According to many authorities, the Argo was the first ship. On the 'first ship' topos generally, see Nisbet and Hubbard 1970 ad Hor. *Odes.* 1.3.12, and pp. 43–4.

[26] Hom. *Il.* 2.697; Strab. 9.5.8; Livy 35.43.4; Plin. *NH* 4.8.29; Mel. 2.44.

[27] See Hope Simpson and Lazenby 1970 p. 85.

[28] It should be added that, since Pichon's assertion (1912 p. 217) that Lucan knew Greek authors only indirectly, we have had Lausberg's lengthy study (1985), which puts Lucan's knowledge of Homer beyond reasonable doubt.

and learnedly to the same story and the same towns in Homer's catalogue, and this is an allusion that we should recognise. But when we recognise it, we will simultaneously recognise that it is wrong, and that the story has been illegally transported into new surroundings: we are witnessing a violent, calculated misuse of allusion; an anti-allusion.[29]

Trachis and Meliboea (353–4), the next pair, which is associated with the myths of Hercules' death and of Philoctetes, are correctly placed; so too Larissa and Argos (355–6), a pair exemplifying the well-worn theme of past greatness in contrast with present insignificance. Well worn it may be, but it has obvious parallels with the greatness and decline of Pompey, and the greatness and decline (in Lucan's vision) of Rome after the civil wars. But the Thessalian Argos is a strange choice for such a purpose; it appears once in Homer's catalogue (*Il.* 2.681 τὸ Πελασγικὸν Ἄργος), thereafter to disappear into such obscurity that it became uncertain whether Homer was speaking of a town, a plain, or the whole of Thessaly: if a town, it no longer existed.[30] So while Lucan is undoubtedly right to say 'nunc super Argos arant', it is difficult to see how it ever earned his 'nobile quondam', and it is remarkable that he has brought in a totally insignificant little village to rub shoulders with the likes of Larissa, which *was* a famous and important city, and which remained an important commercial centre even when its political importance had declined. But again it is obvious what Lucan has done: the Thessalian Argos has been given the characteristics of the famous Argos of the Argolid, whose fortunes do parallel those of Larissa. Why? Because Lucan wants to establish Thessaly as the place where *everything* of significance happened. He has been lucky with Pharsalos, Phylace, Trachis, Meliboea and

---

[29] Gassner (1972 p. 184 n. 3), at least, thinks the transference of Dorion to Thessaly is deliberate 'um Unheilvolles auf Thessalien zu häufen'.

[30] See Strabo 9.5.5, commenting on Homer and undecided; Pliny speaks of *Pelasgicon Argos* as one of the alternative names of Thessaly (*NH* 4.7.28). Modern scholarship has decided in favour of the plain in the region of the river Spercheos (Hope Simpson and Lazenby 1970 p. 126; Kirk 1985 p. 228); Lucan, however, clearly thinks of it as a town.

Larissa, which are associated with some central myths; he has stolen Dorion from the Peloponnese by an astonishing gesture of violence to geography; and now by a similar method – a bogus use of Homer's catalogue and a coincidence of names – he has stolen Argos from the Argolid, home city of a web of myth that is absolutely central to ancient literature (and which includes the civil-war precedents of murder within the family and fraternal strife), and has placed it in Thessaly. In a few lines' time he will steal Argos' principal river, too (see below).

One of the many civil-war paradigms that Lucan is in the habit of alluding to is the strife between Polynices and Eteocles, the Seven Against Thebes,[31] which is often seen as a war between Argives and Thebans. Lucan has provided us with an Argos; now, to compound a felony, he goes on to provide a Thebes:

> ubi nobile quondam
> nunc super Argos arant, veteres ubi fabula Thebas
> monstrat Echionias, ubi quondam Pentheos exul
> colla caputque ferens supremo tradidit igni
> questa quod hoc solum nato rapuisset Agave.   (355–9)

By omitting the crucial *Pelasgicon* from his mention of Argos, Lucan ensured that only the reader familiar with Homer's catalogue would understand the manner of his distortion, and would not be led to believe that he had simply made a mistake. Here he goes one step further in dishonesty, for he provides two epithets, *veteres* and *Echionias*, that should actively discourage us from identifying this Thebes with any city other than the Thebes of Boeotia. None the less, it is a Thessalian Thebes he is referring to, a town perhaps not so obscure as Pelasgian Argos, for the geographers know of it,[32] but again, not so famous as the Boeotian Thebes. But here Lucan has changed his game, for he is prepared eventually to make it explicit that the Thebes in his catalogue is not the famous one: it is a different Thebes to which Agave came as an exile (*exul*, the first word, in fact, to suggest that Lucan is not referring

---

[31] Conte 1966 p. 49; Narducci 1974 pp. 102–5.
[32] Strab. 9.5.6, Θήβας τὰς Φθιώτιδας; Plin *NH* 4.8.29, *Thebae Thessalae*.

to Boeotian Thebes) *after* she had torn Pentheus limb from limb, and in which she gave him his funeral. The story of Agave's exile in Thessalian Thebes is, so far as I can tell, Lucan's fabrication: there is a tradition of Agave going into exile after the death of Pentheus,[33] but our only source for the place of that exile puts her in Illyria, where she married the king Lycotherses, later 'piously' murdering him in order that her father Cadmus could possess the kingdom.[34] So while Lucan is, strictly speaking, being honest about which Thebes he is referring to, he is doing everything in his power to keep the more famous Thebes at the forefront of our minds, even if it means altering a myth so as to make Agave murder her son in one Thebes and bury him in another.[35]

With Thebes, Lucan ends his list of Thessalian towns. We began, significantly, with Pharsalus, and we end climactically with three and a half lines on Thebes. Why devote so much space to Thebes, Agave and Pentheus when none of the other towns merits more than a line or two?[36] By starting with Pharsalus we look towards the battle that is to come, the victory of Caesar and the defeat of Pompey; and as we end, focussing on the dismemberment of Pentheus, and Agave bearing his severed head, we look forward to the 'dismemberment' of Pompey, and his severed head in Caesar's hands;[37] to the 'dismemberment' of the senate, of the Roman state, which is to be the result of Pharsalus and the civil war.[38]

---

[33] See Eur. *Bacch.* 1366 etc.

[34] Hygin. *Fab.* 184; see also *ibid.* 240, 254; and the second Vatican mythographer in *Scriptores rerum mythicarum Latini* . . . (ed. G.H Bode) vol. 1 p. 103.

[35] See, however, Shackleton Bailey 1987 pp. 83–4.

[36] Thebes is also the odd one out in upsetting the pairing of towns (see note 24).

[37] The link is noticed by Frank 1970 p. 60. Pompey's decapitation can be seen as a dismemberment: see 10.380–1 'tumulumque . . . / aspice Pompei non omnia membra tegentem'; conversely, the dismemberment of Medea's brother is treated as a decapitation (10.464–7).

[38] For Lucan's obsessive use of the dismemberment image, see Narducci 1973 p. 323; for its precise application as a grotesque extension of the 'body politic' metaphor, see e.g. 'omnia rursus / membra loco redeunt'

When we move on to Lucan's enumeration of Thessaly's rivers – Aeas, Inachus, Achelous, Euhenos, Spercheos, Amphrysos, Anauros, Peneos, Apidanos, Enipeus, Asopos, Phoenix, Melas and Titaresos – various discrepancies have led some scholars to suspect textual corruption; as always we must be grateful for the light that their discussions have shed on the intricacies of the text, but only in one case are the suspicions justified. Not, I think, in the case of the first line of the river-section:

> ergo abrupta palus multos discessit in amnes.
> purus in occasus, parvi sed gurgitis, Aeas
> Ionio fluit inde mari ... (360–2)

The *palus* in question is the primeval lake described in 343–7. When the mountain ring was broken by the making of the valley of Tempe, the waters were drained through what became the river Peneus. Samse, therefore, finds two objections to the lines we read here:[39] first, if line 360 does, as it seems to, form a heading for the list of rivers that follow ('the lake split up into many rivers: first the Aeas ...'), then we are faced with the anomaly that the first rivers he names are those that flow *away* from Thessaly into the Ionian sea (Lucan is explicit on this point) and therefore have nothing to do with Thessaly's primeval lake, which flowed eastwards into the Aegean. And second: *abrupta palus* is surprising when we would expect *mountains* to 'break apart' to allow the water to escape; and it is odd – albeit forgivable – to speak of the lake splitting into many rivers when in fact the rivers all come together into the Peneus before escaping into the sea. Therefore Samse proposes that line 360 is spurious, and that another line must have dropped out; which, he suggests *exempli gratia*,

(5.36–7); 'sparsumque senatus / corpus' (7.293–4) where the context works to ensure that we do not know if Lucan means this literally – 'the dismembered bodies of senators' (so Duff ad loc.) – or metaphorically – 'the scattered body of the senate'. Cf. also the grotesque joke in 5.252, describing the Caesarian mutiny: 'tot raptis truncus manibus [sc. Caesar]', playing on two senses of *manus* (troops or hands) – so Newmyer 1983 p. 235.

[39] Samse 1942 pp. 254–7.

must have been something like 'multi Thessalicis decurrunt montibus amnes' – as heading a list of rivers which flow either westwards away from Thessaly or eastwards through Thessaly.

The first argument has some force: there *is* a logical lapse between 360 and 361, the former reintroducing the topic of the primeval lake, the latter veering away to another part of northern Greece. But since distortions and contradictions are what we have come to expect from Lucan – whether they are deliberate, as I propose, or not – this logical lapse on its own should not be sufficient reason for deleting a line. The second argument has no force at all: the conceptual distortion in 360 is typical of Lucan. It is a credit to Samse's sensitivity as a critic that he was able to see that in *abrupta palus* the lake is spoken of as if it were the mountain-barrier; what should make us certain that the effect was deliberate is the appearance of the word *discessit*, which is repeated from the lines describing the breaking-apart of the mountains ('postquam *discessit* Olympo / Herculea gravis Ossa manu', 347–8), in the same metrical position. The water becomes like the rock that confines it; the distortion is a reverse of one we will have seen in catalogue of Italian geography, where Lucan describes a river-like course for the Appennine mountains.[40] But there is more to it than that. The line describes the splitting apart of a single lake into many individual rivers; coming as it does immediately after the lines on Agave and Pentheus' dismembered body, it cannot fail to associate itself with this dismemberment (Pentheus' single body is split into many limbs and a head),[41]

---

[40] 2.428–38: after a long list of the rivers which flow down either side of the mountains, we are told that the Appennine range 'rises' (*surgit* 2.428) – terminology for the source of rivers; cf. the Nile, 'medio consurgis ab axe', 10.287 – in Gaul, and from there moves down past the Alps, through Italy, and eventually to the sea. Its course may be compared to that of the Nile in book 10; its attribute *ferax* may suggest the irrigation of a river (cf. *fertilis Euphrates* 3.260); and *piniferis ... rupibus* looks back jokingly to the Eridanus, which 'fractas devolvit in aequora silvas' (2.409).

[41] Note too that *caput* is standard terminology for the source or mouth of a river: *OLD* s.v. 'caput' 10b and 11a; in Lucan, 2.52, 3.256, 6.379, 10.191,

and hence with what it symbolises, the dismemberment of Pompey and the division of the Roman state.

On those grounds the line should be kept; and, enjoying the sense of dislocation that comes from a heading which bears little relation to the list it heads, we turn our attention to the rivers themselves. The river Aeas is sufficiently attested for us to know that it is where Lucan says it is;[42] so too the Achelous ('tuus, Oeneu, paene gener' 363–4),[43] and the Euhenos.[44] But the Inachus, second in the list ('pater Isidis' 363), should not be in mainland Greece at all, but in the Argolid.[45] Mendell offers an explanation:[46] in *Met.* 1.569ff (Peneus' council of rivers), Ovid names seven rivers, all of which appear in Lucan's list: Peneus, Spercheus, Enipeus, Apidanus, Amphrysus, Aeas, Inachus. The first six of Ovid's rivers, all on the Greek mainland, are named only by way of example; many other rivers convened at Peneus' council ('moxque amnes alii . . .', *Met.* 1.581), and presumably they came from all parts of Greece; hence it is possible for Ovid to name Inachus in the Peloponnese as conspicuous by his absence ('Inachus unus abest', 583). This collocation of rivers in Ovid, says Mendell, 'leads Lucan into the error of including the Argolid Inachus among the rivers of Thessaly' (p. 20). What, exactly, is being proposed here? It hangs on the delicate distinction between source and model: Mendell's purpose in his article is to show where Lucan got his rivers from; his discussion of the Thessalian excursus forms a subsection to the general heading 'Of the literary sources of Lucan's rivers, Ovid seems to have been the favourite.' No suggestion, therefore, that Lucan is

223, 295 (sources); and 3.202 (mouth). The two senses of *caput* will play an important role in book 10, where Pompey's head is cut off in the land of the Nile, whose 'head' cannot be found.

[42] Plin. *NH* 3.23.145; Mel. 2.57; Vibius Sequester has two rivers, the Aeas and the Aous, but according to Pliny they are the same.

[43] Mel. 2.53; Strab. 8.2.3, 8.3.11, 8.3.26 (mentioning the Echinades); for the silting of the bay, Plin. *NH* 4.1.5 'amnis Achelous e Pindo fluens atque Acarnaniam ab Aetolia dirimens et Artemitam insulam adsiduo terrae invectu continenti adnectens'.

[44] Thuc. 2.83.3; Strab. 8.2.3; Mel. 2.53.

[45] Bourgery 1928A p. 31.   [46] Mendell 1942 pp. 19–20.

ever *alluding* to Ovid as his model, and this, I think, is a mistake. If we view the catalogue (as Mendell does) as a place where information is simply deposited, and if we work on the assumption that this information is ransacked from the work of earlier poets, and, where they are deficient, supplemented with material from geographical manuals, then it is possible that somewhere along the line a river may have slipped in accidentally by a process such as Mendell suggests. If, on the contrary, we view Lucan's rivers as containing an allusion to Ovid's Thessalian rivers, then that kind of error becomes implausible. And there are good reasons for supposing an allusion to the Ovidian passage: we know that Ovid is an important model for Lucan anyway;[47] Ovid's and Lucan's are the only Thessalian river catalogues in Latin literature, and all of Ovid's rivers appear in Lucan's list; and, of course, the very fact that Lucan has decided to include the un-Thessalian Inachus points inescapably in Ovid's direction. If we recognise the allusion, we will recognise the technique of geography by association, by which Inachus is in Thessaly precisely because it is associated with Thessalian rivers in Lucan's model. The technique is similar, though not identical, to the one we observed in the case of Pteleos and Dorion. If we read this 'mistake' as anything other than intentional, then the implications are too unlikely to countenance. The river Inachus is famous in the system of allusive obscurity that is a feature of ancient 'learned' poetry; though often used to identify Io, either by the adjective *Inachius* or the patronymic *Inachis*, Inachus as the mythical first king of Argos and the founder of the Argive royal line is *the* river of Argos (much as the Tiber is the river of Rome, or the Nile the river of Egypt); hence his adjective *Inachius* can be used as an epithet for Argos,[48] or may stand simply for 'Argive'.[49] Since Lucan has given ample evidence

[47] See e.g. Albrecht 1970 pp. 293–7; Linn 1971; Esposito 1987.
[48] Virg. *Aen.* 7.286, 'Inachiis ... ab Argis'; cf. Val. Flacc. 1.107, 3.666; Stat. *Theb.* 1.660.
[49] Virg. *Aen.* 11.286, 'Inachias ... urbes'; Sen. *Phoen.* 444–5, 'Inachio ... muro'; *Agam.* 314, 'stirps Inachia' – a woman of Argos; Val. Flacc. 8.125; Stat. *Theb.* passim, e.g. 2.145.

elsewhere of his intimate familiarity with the basic allusive system of which Inachus is a part – indeed, he displays it here in *pater Isidis* and *tuus, Oeneu, paene gener* – then it is impossible for Lucan not to know that Inachus is Argive. Virgil, his single most important model, knew it; Seneca, his uncle, knew it; and two books ago Lucan himself knew it:

> constitit Alcides stupefactus robore tanto
> nec sic Inachiis, quamvis rudis esset, in undis
> desectam timuit reparatis anguibus hydram.   (4.633–5)

The Lernean hydra: Lerna is in the Argolid; Lucan learnedly conjures Inachus, the river of the Argolid.[50]

In sum, if the inclusion of Inachus in the list of Thessalian rivers is an accident, we have to conclude that, misled by a mildly ambiguous passage in Ovid, Lucan forgot something which everyone knew, which was one of the basic givens of the poetic language he had been using for a lifetime, and which elsewhere he alludes to correctly. The only alternative, then, since this position is untenable, is that Lucan deliberately distorted geography and intended the mistake to be recognised. The special feature of this mistake is that it demands the same degree of reader-alertness as would be demanded by the work of any *doctus poeta*; at a superficial glance it looks like a simple geographical error, a sign of unlearnedness; and it is only when we recognise the Ovidian model that we understand it as more than an error, but rather as a special kind of learnedness: perversion of learnedness served by an anti-allusion.

Having reunited the Inachus with the vagrant Argos in Thessaly, Lucan concludes with ten rivers whose right to be in the catalogue is beyond suspicion. The Spercheos is well at-

---

[50] Lucan would be unusual in placing the fight with the hydra actually on the river Inachus. What little tradition there is locates it either in the swamps of Lerna, or by the springs of the river Amymone, or both (Paus. 2.37.4; Apollod. 2.5.2; Stat *Theb.* 1360, 385, 2.376). Pausanias elsewhere calls the monster τὴν ὕδραν δέ, τὸ ἐν τῶι ποταμῶι τῆι Ἀμυμώνηι θηρίον (Paus. 5.17.11). This leads one to suppose that Lucan's *Inachiis ... in undis* is not Inachus itself, but 'a watery place in the Argolid'; though it is equally possible that he has simply transferred the fight to Argos' most famous river.

tested, and flows into the Maliac gulf as Lucan says (366–7).[51]
Of the river Amphrysus, Strabo tells us that it was in Thessaly,
flowing through the Crocian plain (between Thessalian
Thebes and Mt Othrys) and past the town of Halus;[52] but it is
best known from poetry.[53] Keeping to the line-order of the
manuscripts, the next river is the Anauros, so far as we can tell
unknown to the geographers, and in Latin known only
through Lucan, but none the less with a good poetic pedigree:
probably best known as the river in which Jason lost his san-
dal,[54] it makes its début in Hesiod.[55] The Peneus is Thessaly's
longest and probably best known river,[56] and requires no further explanation. The Apidanus is, as Lucan says, a tributary
of the Peneus, and the Enipeus, which flows past Pharsalus,
meets the Apidanus a little way before the latter's confluence
with the Peneus.[57] Next in the order handed down to us by the
manuscripts are the Asopos, Phoenix and Melas, small rivers
flowing into the Maliac gulf in the vicinity of Thermopylae;[58]
although they are genuinely Thessalian rivers, the line they

---

[51] Hdt. 7.198; Strab. 9.5.9; Plin. *NH* 4.7.28; Mel. 2.44, wrongly having it
flow into the Pagasaean gulf. Of Latin poets, Virgil mentions it once
(*Georg.* 2.486–7), Ovid three times (*Met.* 1.579, 2.250, 7.230).

[52] Strab. 9.5.8, 9.5.14.

[53] Call. *Hymn.* 2.47–9, alluded to in Virg. *Georg.* 3.2, on the connection
with the shepherd Apollo. See also Ap. Rhod 1.54; Orph. *Arg.* 189; Schol.
Lycophr. 900; Virg. *Aen.* 6.398; Ov. *Met.* 1.580, 7.229.

[54] Ap. Rhod. 1.9; Apollod. 1.9.16.

[55] Hes. *Sc.* 477; see also Eur. *HF* 390, Call. *Hymn.* 4.103, and the entry in
the *Etymologicum Magnum*.

[56] See e.g. Plin. *NH* 4.8.30, 'ante cunctos claritate Penius ... [etc.]'.

[57] Most fully, Strab. 9.5.6; see also Hdt. 7. 129; Ap. Rhod 1.38–9 (the
confluence of Enipeus and Apidanus); Plin. *NH* 4.8.30 (not mentioning
any confluence); Ov. *Met.* 1.579–80, 7.228–9 (no confluence); Val. Flacc.
1357 ('segnior Apidani vires ubi sentit Enipeus' – as in Lucan, a contrast
of the fast Apidanus with the slow Enipeus); for Enipeus alone, see Virg.
Georg. 4.368.

[58] The three rivers appear in close proximity in Herodotus' topography of
Thermopylae (7.198–200); so too Strab. 9.4.14; see also Livy 36.22 for
the Asopos and the Melas. They are unknown in poetry (*pace* Mendell
1942 p. 16, presumably mistaking the Melas and the Asopus for their
namesakes in Thrace and the Argolid).

appear in is almost certainly the centre of some textual corruption, and perhaps should be deleted.[59] Finally, the mythical
Titaresos, known only to Homer (in the catalogue of ships),
but identified by Strabo with the Europus, and referred to by
Pliny as the Orcus.[60]

Rivers, then, of every kind; Lucan runs the gamut of cataloguing techniques, from commendably obscure allusions to
myth, a dazzling display of little-known geographical details,
and a dash of etymology,[61] to allusions (climactic, for the
Titaresos) to other catalogues, and plain lies. And on top of
this, Lucan still manages to indulge in those aspects of river-
lore that are his recurrent obsession: their speed and their confluences. Although the topic of the fast river versus the slow
river (which we have seen most recently in Epirus in the form

---

[59] In the line-order of the manuscripts, Asopos, Melas and Phoenix interrupt the list of tributaries of the Peneus. For this reason Housman trans-
posed them to a place before 369. This incidentally removed another
oddity: without the change Lucan seems to be saying, at 369ff, that the
Anauros and the tributaries of the Peneus all 'irrigate the fields which
were Phoebus'' during his servitude'. Samse 1942 pp. 262–6, answering
Housman, and finding the phrase *accipit cursus* too obscure, deletes 374,
but his attempt to find a main verb for 369ff other than the impossible
inrigat is unconvincing (he suggests that we must look back to a main
verb in a line that had dropped out at 360).

There is little to choose: Samse's text leaves the Anauros and the tributaries of the Peneus apparently in the same region as the Amphrysus; the
MSS text (which was early enough to mislead Vibius Sequester) puts the
Asopos, Phoenix and Melas in the wrong place; and Housman's text
preserves a line that is suspicious not, I think, because of *accipit cursus*,
but because the three rivers are unique in the whole catalogue for not
having any attributes (other than the natural resonance of their names,
'Unquiet', 'Red', 'Black') and because the line is simple enough to have
been a scholarly interpolation. The purposeful chaos of Lucan's catalogue makes a final decision impossible; but I incline towards deletion.

[60] Hom. *Il.* 2.751–5; Strab. 9.5.19–20; Plin. *NH* 4.8.31. Both Strabo and
Pliny cite and paraphrase the Homeric passage. Pliny's 'Orcon' seems to
derive from Homer's ὅρκου γὰρ δεινοῦ Στυγὸς ὕδατός ἐστιν ἀπορρώξ
(755): see the note in Rackham's Loeb edition.

[61] The Spercheos is 'amne citato' because of σπέρχω; the Anauros is wind-
less, mistless and dewless because it is derived from ἀν + αὔρα (see the
entry in *Etym. Mag.*). See Samse 1942 p. 258.

of the Hapsus and Genusus, 5.462–7)[62] can be traced in, say, the contrast between the rushing Spercheus and the 'pure flow' of the Amphrysus, the bewildering variety of river-types seems to evade any easy translation of symbol into theme: we have a pure small stream (albeit with a big name, Aeas),[63] another weak stream, a muddy river, a bloody river, a violent river, a pure river, and a river with no breezes, mists or dew. Little suggestion yet of a two- or three-river system, just a wide display of types: as Thessaly is crammed with every important myth, so it is run through by every kind of river, big epic rivers as well as pure Alexandrian streams. The symbolism is focussed more sharply (though it is equally indeterminate) in the final section dealing with Peneus' tributaries.

> ... et quisquis pelago per se non cognitus amnis
> Peneo donavit aquas; it gurgite rapto
> Apidanos numquamque celer nisi mixtus Enipeus.
> [accipit Asopos cursus Phoenixque Melasque]
> solus, in alterius nomen cum venerit undae,
> defendit Titaresos aquas ...   (371–6)

The Enipeus flows into the Apidanos, which flows into the Peneus; the Titaresos meets the Peneus unmediated. Of Enipeus, Lucan uses the word *mixtus*, and knowing the importance of that keyword in the epic, we should ask what kind of confluences are going on here. The answer is, many kinds. Each of the tributaries loses its name ('per se non cognitus amnis'; 'in alterius nomen ... undae'). In 372 they 'give' their waters (*donavit*) generously enough; then we are told that the Apidanos 'it gurgite rapto'. The basic sense of this is surely 'goes with rushing waters', that is, the Apidanos snatches up its own waters, speeding them on; in the same way as an army can move 'agmine rapto'.[64] But although Housman has his

---

[62] See chapter 3 n. 19.

[63] For the suggestion of the hero Ajax in the name of the river, see Samse 1942 p. 258.

[64] 4.35 (assuming that the subject of *cepit* is *hostis*, rather than *terrorque pudorque*); 3.299 (where, strictly speaking, the army is 'raptus' by Caesar as its commander); 3.504 (rushing fire from a torch); 5.483 (speedily prosecuted war); 9.220 (escaping fleet). In our passage, *celer* is to be taken

priorities wrong, his gloss 'gurgite rapto a *Peneo*' represents a strong overtone. Samse objects to Housman's gloss partly on the grounds that it contradicts *donavit*;[65] but *donavit* precisely brings out that overtone in *rapto*, and this is exactly the point: we are given two views of a confluence side by side, one implying a voluntary gift of water, the other implying a violent appropriation of water.[66] Coming to the Enipeus, whose *mixtus* may imply either view, we find a river which actually gains by giving / losing its waters: at first slow, it only achieves speed when it mingles with the Apidanos. Finally, with the Titaresus, a supernatural 'unmixing', a river that may lose its name (Lucan's main innovation in his imitation of Homer's Titaresos is the addition of the name-topos) by flowing into the Peneus, but which keeps itself to itself and does not allow its waters to mingle. Lucan thus separates out the various strands of the imagery of mixing. Two sets of people may mix as an army in battle or as brothers in concord; when one side has achieved pre-eminence, the other may simply lose its identity, or maintain its individuality; the result may be a strengthening of the whole or simply the subsuming of one part into the other. There is no final judgement here: the various alternatives are listed and left to hang. The effect is, as before, to fill the land of Thessaly with every variety of thing, so as to show that land as the central place where anything of importance must happen; but more precisely, by setting up these alternatives at this time and in this place, we see what is at stake in the battle to come; what kind of state will result. We know the result of the war between Trojans and Latins in the *Aeneid*: a mixture of the Enipeus type, where the mingling of tribes produced the greater Roman people. For the Romans of the civil war? Mixing is what must happen when the split between parts is ended by the victory of one part over another. But the fate of the Pompeians is diverse. A new, stronger, Roman state (in all

---

ἀπὸ κοινοῦ with *Apidanos* (Samse 1942 p. 260), and *gurgite rapto* clarifies this.

[65] Samse 1942 p. 261. His other objection is subtler: it is nonsense to speak of river A flowing with its waters seized by river B, for when river A has its waters seized, it ceases to be river A.

[66] Hübner's discussion (1975 pp. 201ff) is helpful.

but name?); Pompeians subsumed into the new regime, or wiped out along with the Pompeian cause; continued resistance, angry refusal to participate in the new state: a pocket of resistance which this poem claims to celebrate.

Having concluded his list of Thessalian rivers with the obstinate resistance of the Titaresos and the funereal overtones of its Stygian source, Lucan initiates a brief ethnography. He tells us first that the newly revealed land was tilled by Bebrycians (381–2). The Bebrycians are a semi-mythical race remembered for only one thing: the boxing contest between Pollux and their monstrous king Amycus which formed part of the story of the Argonauts; and their home is not Thessaly but Bithynia.[67] The Amycus myth made them a byword for ferocity.[68] What of the Leleges (383)? A strong tradition locates them in Caria (eastern Asia Minor), and Homer, followed by Virgil and Ovid, mentions the Leleges alongside the Carians;[69] and the identity, or near-identity, of Carians and Leleges, both of whom were expelled by the early Greek settlers of Ionia, is supported by the prose writers.[70] But peoples, unlike mountains, rivers and cities, can move, and other reports make the Leleges primeval inhabitants of Greece.[71] So although Lucan is unique in making the Leleges specifically Thessalian, there is some precedent for locating them originally in that general area. Next, the Aeolians (384): their home is on the eastern coast of Asia Minor,[72] but their race derived originally from Thessalians and Boeotians.[73] The Dolopes

---

[67] See Ap. Rhod. 2.1ff, Val. Flacc. 4.99ff, and Theoc. 22.27ff for the full story. Cf. *Aen.* 5.373, Ammian. 22.8.14; Plin. *NH* 5.33.127 includes them in a list (derived from Eratosthenes) of Asiatic peoples now extinct; Strab. (7.3.2, 12.3.3, 13.1.8) has some words to say on their origins.

[68] Stat. *Theb.* 3.353; Avien. *Or.* 485 (Berybraces); cf. Val. Flacc. 2.648.

[69] Hom. *Il.* 10.428–9; Virg. *Aen.* 8.725; Ov. *Met.* 9.645.

[70] Hdt. 1.171; Strab. 7.7.2; Vitr. 2.8.12, 4.1.5. Plin. *NH* 5.33.127 lists them (with the Bebrycians) among extinct Asiatic tribes.

[71] Paus. 3.1.1 (in Laconia); 1.39.6 (in the Megarid; cf. Ov. *Met.* 7.443, 8.6); Solin. 7.25 (Boeotia); Plin. *NH* 4.7.27 (Locris).

[72] Plin. *NH* 5.32.123; Vell. 1.4.4; Liv. 33.38; Curt. 4.5.7; Mel. 1.90; etc.

[73] Thessaly: Hdt. 7.176, Strab. 5.2.4, Apollod. 1.7.3; Boeotia: Strab. 9.2.5, Thuc. 7.57.

(384) are a well known Thessalian tribe which inhabited the Pindus range;[74] the Magnesians (385) are similarly well known as the inhabitants of the coastal area between Ossa and Pelion.[75] The name of the Minyae is most famous as denoting the Argonauts (hence 'gens cognita remis' 385); as a primeval tribe their origins are obscure and later movements diverse, but Thessaly is clearly their most famous home.[76] Finally, Lucan gives us nine lines on the *semiferi Centauri* (386–94). The adjective *Pelethronius*, referring to the Thessalian Mt Pelethronion, is known to Ovid and Virgil.[77] Pholoe is a mountain and a district in Arcadia, known to the geographers,[78] which here identifies the story Lucan is alluding to as the fight between the centaurs and Hercules at the time of his hunt for the Erymanthean boar.[79] Since Lucan alludes to the story again at 391 ('hospes et Alcidae magni Phole'), it is reasonable to assume that the intervening lines, portraying Rhoecus at the foot of Mt Oeta, are part of the same story. Another distortion, then: Lucan will have us believe that Mt Pholoe is near Mt Oeta in Thessaly. Again, it is not so much a mistake (it is hard to see how such a mistake could have come about) as a decision not to allow the realities of geography to interfere

---

[74] E.g. Plin. *NH* 4.2.6; Hdt. 7.132; Liv. 33.34; Ov. *Met.* 12.364. In Homer, Phoenix was made their king (*Il.* 9.484), though they do not appear in the catalogue. Virgil uses *Dolopes* (often in conjunction with *Myrmidones*) of the contingent led by Achilles and taken over by Neoptolemus. Pausanias (10.8.3) says that they were extinct by the time of Augustus' foundation of Nicopolis.

[75] E.g. Mel. 2.40; Plin. 4.9.32; Strab. 9.5.1; Hdt. 7.132; Liv. 33.34; Ov. *Met.* 11.408; cf. Val. Flacc. 2.9–10 for the connection with horses.

[76] On the connection with Orchomenos in Boeotia, Hom. *Il.* 2.511, Hdt. 1.146; Strab. 9.2.40, commenting on the Homeric reference, makes the Minyae emigrants from Orchomenos to Iolcos in Thessaly. Indeed, so strong is their connection with Thessaly that Pliny (wrongly) puts Orchomenos in Thessaly because of the Homeric epithet *Minyius*, *NH* 4.8.29. See also Strab. 8.3.3 on the Minyans later settling in Elis, and Hdt. 4.145 on the descendants of the Argonauts (calling themselves Minyans) settling in Sparta.

[77] Virg. *Georg.* 3.115 of the Lapiths; Ov. *Met.* 12.452 of the Lapith Macareus.

[78] Mel. 2.43; Strab. 8.3.1, 8.3.32; Plin. *NH* 4.6.21; cf. Ov. *Fast.* 2.273.

[79] Pholoe is named as the home of Pholus in Apollod. 2.5.4.

with the plan of contracting all possible myths into the bounds of a single land.

Lucan has told us elsewhere that he does not believe in centaurs ('populum Pholoe mentita biformem' 3.198), and his apparent credulity in our passage underlines again one of the unusual characteristics of the whole catalogue. The geographical excursus is the province of historiography[80] – indeed, the closest parallel to Lucan's excursus is in Herodotus' description of Thessaly (7.129), which may well have been one of Lucan's models.[81] Lucan's attitude to myth is notorious; and since the decision to include a geographical excursus may be read as a gesture towards the techniques of historiography, in line with his choice of historical subject-matter, the way he has treated his excursus is remarkable. There is no history in it – nor science. Hercules replaces the earthquake. Lucan ignores any fumbling attempt to explain the non-mixing of the Titaresos in terms of some oily substance in the water, such as we find in Strabo,[82] and (admittedly like Pliny) opts for the mythological account. Now, in the list of peoples, mythological races (Bebrycians, Centaurs, and to some extent Minyans) rub shoulders with prehistoric aborigines (Leleges, Aeolians) and two peoples (Dolopians and Magnesians) whose continued existence is, I suggest, a matter of coincidence. The Herodotean parallel – if it is, as I suspect, an allusion – points in the direction of Xerxes and Thermopylae, but none the less, that allusion is never made explicit, and the excursus remains pointedly mythical, primeval: it is not about Thessaly as it is now, but about the Thessaly lost in the mists of time.

---

[80] Mendell 1942 pp. 4–6.

[81] Haskins ad 6.333; Housman ad 6.374; Wünsch 1930 pp. 59–61; against Wünsch, Gassner 1972 p. 183 n. 4, saying that Herodotus has no list of cities, and that the Herodotean excursus is firmly set in the action (Xerxes is reconnoitering). But whatever the differences, the similarities are striking: the mountains and their positions, the story of the primeval lake, some of the rivers.

[82] Strab. 95.20: τὸ μὲν οὖν τοῦ Πηνειοῦ καθαρόν ἐστιν ὕδωρ, τὸ δὲ τοῦ Τιταρησίου λιπαρὸν ἔκ τινος ὕλης, ὥστ' οὐ συμμίσγεται; an attempt to explain Homer's ἠΰτ' ἔλαιον.

The list of peoples began with the Bebrycians, whose bar-
barity was legendary, and ended with the ragings of the half-
human centaurs, marking Thessaly as a land of primeval violence. Now Lucan turns to a list of things that have their origin
in Thessaly. Appropriately for the site of the worst battle in
history, Thessaly is found to be the land where the seeds of war
were first sown.[83] Here was created the first warhorse, leaping
out from a rock struck by Poseidon.

> primus ab aequorea percussis cuspide saxis
> Thessalicus sonipes, bellis feralibus omen,
> exiluit   (396–8)

Lucan is alluding provocatively to Virgil:

> tuque o, cui prima frementem
> fudit equum magno tellus percussa tridenti,
> Neptune   (*Georg.* 1.12–14)

Provocatively, because he has imported a new violence and a
new emphasis on battle: Neptune did not just create the horse,
he created the warhorse. Virgil does not make clear in what
land Neptune struck the earth; but Servius does place the incident in Thessaly, and there is independent support from the
Etymologicum Magnum.[84] Also in Virgil is the invention of
reins by the Lapiths (*Georg.* 3.115). The voyage of the Argo
from Pagasae as being the first sea voyage (400–1) is, of
course, standard. The invention of coinage by Ionos in
Thessaly (402–5) is unknown elsewhere – though our sources
on the topic are admittedly scanty.[85] These three inventions –
the horse (and reins), the ship and coinage – constitute the
semina Martis. Lucan then breaks off and concludes with two
earthborn monsters. First, Python (407–9), for whose origin
in Thessaly Lucan is our only authority. Other parts of the

---

[83] Johnson 1987 p. 21.

[84] Serv. ad *Georg.* 1.12; *Etym. Magn.* s.v. Ἵππιος ὁ Ποσειδῶν.

[85] Hdt. 1.94.1 says that the Lydians invented the first coinage; in this he is
presumably echoing the opinion of Xenophanes as reported in Pollux 9.83.
Pollux lists other possible inventors: Pheidon of Argos, Demodice wife
of Midas, Ericthonius and Lycus of Athens, and the Naxians. Modern
scholarship settles for the Lydians (Pauly–Wissowa, s.v. 'Münzwesen').

Python myth do suggest a connection with Thessaly: in Plutarch's version the wounded Python fled to the valley of Tempe; alternatively, Apollo went to the valley of Tempe for purification after killing Python.[86] It is quite possible, therefore, that Lucan's version represents a traditional variant of the myth; more likely, though, that he has simply transferred the Thessalian connection to Python's origins,[87] making Thessaly the kind of place where that kind of monster can be born. And finally, the excursus concludes with the sons of Aloeus (Ephialtes and Otus) piling Ossa on Pelion (410–12). Both the Python myth and the Titanomachy are, as we have seen, images of primeval discord which are conjured as precedents for the historical civil war,[88] and it is thus on a climactically symbolic note that the excursus ends – as it had begun – with Ossa.

It is time to draw some conclusions. Critical opinion of Lucan's abilities as a learned geographer has not changed substantially since Heitland's indictment: 'Learning then overpowered imagination in Lucan; and unfortunately this learning was of a loose and inaccurate kind. I propose to give a few instances of blunders inconsistencies and laxity, chiefly in geography, which will suffice to prove how shallow was the erudition so ostentatiously displayed.'[89] My detailed analysis of the geography in the Thessalian excursus paints a rather different picture. This is no hasty, inaccurate collection of raw data from handbooks, clumsily thrust into hexameters, but a highly selective and carefully allusive set piece which displays a knowledge and control of geographical detail that is remarkable and which in many ways outshines the work of extant Roman geographers. But side by side with this geographical

---

[86] Plut. *Quaest. Graec.* 293C, *Def. Or.* 417F–18B, cf. 421C: both versions explain the origin of the Septerion festival. See Fontenrose 1959 p. 20 and 53–4.

[87] So Wünsch 1930 p. 61.

[88] On Python, see chapter 4, p. 114.

[89] Heitland p. lii; see also *ibid.* n. 2, which singles out the long catalogue passages as teeming with inconsistencies. Cf. e.g. Pichon 1912 pp. 7ff. For a defence of Lucan's geography, see Aumont 1968 (on Cato in Libya).

accuracy – and if we discount the kind of minor blurring which can be defended on the grounds of poetic licence (e.g. strictly speaking, Trachis should not be included in the list of cities uncovered, so to speak, by the draining of the primeval lake, since it was outside the ring of Thessalian mountains)[90] – we can detect a contrary movement, a series of gestures towards geographical *inaccuracy* which range from misleadingly phrased elements which turn out on closer inspection to be true (Argos, Thebes) to errors so provocative that they compel us to recognise them as *lies*, as a result of a deliberate policy of doing violence to the order of the world, and profoundly, to the mechanics of learned allusion (Dorion, Inachus). The pointed inaccuracies of the catalogue, in many ways an end in themselves, are none the less at the service of a larger design. Thessaly, as the land of the ultimate battle, must be shown to have been a place of such significance as to make it worthy of such an event, and so must be filled to the brim with grim and portentous myths. A small distortion, bringing Pholoe out of Arcadia, will bring with it the story of Hercules, Pholus and the raging of centaurs who were already Thessalian in origin. Distortions of a greater or lesser kind – whose extent is unfortunately hard to gauge – bring to Thessaly the invention of coinage, and the origin of Python to accompany the already traditional creation of the horse, invention of reins, and the first ship.

In a similar manner, Thessaly is also a fulfilment of the kind of topographical symbolism we have seen throughout the poem. What appeared before as fragmentary instances on a small scale – a pair of opposed hills here, a pair of rivers there, a flooded plain, an amphitheatrical valley – all appear in the Thessalian excursus as a coherent system that is the land of Thessaly. The two-hill motif (with the split between) is found in the valley of Tempe; every possible variation on rivers fast, slow, mingling and losing their names, in the river section; the flood motif in the primeval lake out of which the rivers were born – it is all here, on a colossal scale, as if a consummation of

---

[90] Samse 1942 p. 253.

all the possibilities of civil-war topography. Thessaly, as the place where nearly everything has happened, and where portentous geography is awesomely massed, is an ideal site for the coming battle; fate has chosen well.

6

ERICTHO

The Erictho episode is tasteless, rhetorically overblown, revolting, sensational, macabre, decadent ... but never, ultimately, unreadable. An unrelenting series of adverse critical judgements has done nothing to stem the tide of Ericthonian scholarship; for by a paradox that is eminently instructive, the episode remains – if not the most popular – the most thoroughly explored in the poem. To denounce Erictho is to denounce Lucan; to come to terms with Erictho is to come to terms with Lucan; she has been the very emblem of the poem, a compact consummation of all that we hate or love about the poet. The litmus test.

Consequently, we have learned a great deal about Erictho from a century's worth of criticism, some of it the finest and most subtle in Lucanian scholarship. Sources, literary and non-literary, for Lucan's magic have been investigated, catalogued, analysed; as the fullest account of necromancy in Latin literature, the episode has been scrutinised and commended for its technical accuracy; the black and macabre tone has been (questionably) related to the preoccupations of the Neronian age, and (less questionably) to the ominous atmosphere of the eve of Pharsalus which is the episode's context, or, more widely, to the pessimism and perversity of the poem as a whole; the necromancy has been shown to stand in the tradition of the epic *nekuia*, and in more or less precise opposition to Virgil's underworld scene in Aeneid 6.[1] And yet

---

[1] On Lucan's magic, see Fahz 1904 pp. 42ff; Rose 1913; Bourgery 1928в; Morford 1967 pp. 66–70; Fauth 1975; Baldini Moscadi 1976; Volphilac 1978; Gordon 1987. On the *nekuia* and Virgil's underworld scene, see Guillemin 1951 p. 223; Longi 1955 pp. 186f; Paoletti 1963; Tartari Chersoni 1979; Martindale 1980; Feeney 1986c. Studies of a more general nature include Dick 1963; Schrempp 1964 pp. 25–9; Le Bonniec 1970 pp. 185ff; Ahl 1976 pp. 130–49; Narducci 1985 pp. 1548–51; Johnson 1987 pp. 1–33; O'Higgins 1988 pp. 217ff.

Erictho remains a problem: in Gordon's words (1987 p. 231) 'despite good progress in recent years towards locating the episode within the economy of the *Bellum Civile*, and comparable success in evaluating Lucan's sources for his descriptions of magical rites, the figure of Erictho refuses to be exorcised.' Johnson's remarkable and eloquent eulogy of the episode will have done something to make Erictho more acceptable; in his reading the macabre excesses of the scene are there to be enjoyed: '[Lucan's] Erictho is now absurd, now horrifying, now both horrifying and absurd simultaneously; but she is always as plausible as she is richly comical. It is our incredulous, unwilling laughter, engendered by her grotesque, extravagant wickedness, that wins for her a baffling plausibility' (1987 p. 22).

Johnson's – in many ways admirable – work marks a long-needed shift in the critical perspective: the insight that Lucan can be *funny* is crucial, and so far as I can tell unique in Lucanian scholarship. But, as always, Johnson eloquently sidesteps the close examination of the details of the text which his new perspective should be urging, and which might in turn eliminate some of the glibness of his stance and his rhetoric. The aim of this chapter will be to undertake a reassessment of the Erictho episode with a view to affirming, with Johnson, her importance in the poem, but in such a way as to bring the text back to the forefront where it belongs.

Erictho, Phemonoe, and Virgil's Sibyl

Much valuable work has centred on the opposition between Lucan's episode and Virgil's Sibylline episode (see note 1), but it seems to me that attention to this opposition alone has threatened to obfuscate other major issues of the poem. In this section I propose to examine Erictho's relation to *both* Virgil's Sibyl *and* Phemonoe from Lucan's Delphic episode. What will emerge is that there is, broadly, an alternation of negative imitations of both episodes, the one coming into prominence where the other falls away, so that it is sensible to speak of the Erictho scene as having been constructed from an interweaving of the two; and we will see how carefully overdetermined is nearly every element in the whole.

In the Thessalian episode, as in the Delphic episode, a brief preface introduces us to the enquirer (Appius, 5.64–70; Sextus, 6.417–34), who is in each case male, and a minor figure of whom we have heard nothing before.[2] There is, however, a case for saying that Sextus is less 'minor' than Appius: he is the son of one of the poem's protagonists, and will take part in events recorded later in the poem and beyond, whereas we saw that a main irony of Appius' position in the Delphic episode and in the poem was his total isolation from the plot as one of the few characters who had nothing to do with the civil war. From Appius to Sextus, then, there is a discernible step upwards in 'relevance', in 'importance', which adumbrates what we will discover to be one of the key ostensible contrasts between the two episodes; and which is given added weight by the imminence of the final catastrophe which is Sextus' immediate context ('summique gravem discriminis horam / adventare palam est, propius iam fata moveri', 6.415–16). It is the eve of Pharsalus; the armies are massed and in position; the dreadful day is but a night away; and we expect this prophecy scene to match the importance of the imminent battle.[3] The other noticeable difference is that while Appius is merely pathetic, Sextus is positively evil; blackened into a pirate (along the lines of conventional anti-republican propaganda)[4] who disgraced his father's name (420–2), Sextus emerges as the evil anti-exemplum of the Pompeian cause, in a move which is surprising if we believe Lucan's sympathies to be republican,[5] but which follows the negativising trend of the whole episode. This negativising of course makes Sextus into an anti-Aeneas in the scheme which confronts the Thessalian episode with Virgil's catabasis,[6] but for the time being I wish only to draw

---

[2] Ahl 1976 p. 130.

[3] So Schrempp 1964 p. 25: '[Ericthos] besonderes Gewicht erhält sie durch die Stellung unmittelbar vor dem Buch der Schlachtschilderung'.

[4] See e.g. Augustus *Res Gestae* 25.1; Vell. 2.73; Plut. *Ant.* 32.1. The mud has stuck, even today; but see Gabba 1971 pp. 153ff.

[5] See Ahl 1976 p. 134. He concludes, 'Perhaps [Lucan's] viciousness toward Sextus can be accounted for on the grounds that he felt Sextus had done much to discredit the cause'.

[6] See most fully Tartari Chersoni 1979 p. 31.

attention to the contrast between the innocuous but inert Appius and the more significant but evil Sextus.

Both Appius and Sextus are motivated by *fear* (Appius in 5.67; Sextus in 6.423);[7] but while Appius is alone in his fear (*solus* 5.67), Sextus is one of many (*turbae sed mixtus inerti* 6.419). There is an ironic contrast here between what Lucan says about Sextus and what he has Sextus say about himself later (*non ultima turbae / pars ego Romanae*, 6.593–4),[8] imply-ing that Sextus' position as one of the crowd lowers his status; but it does at least show that Sextus is, in contrast to Appius, a participant, someone connected with events, a representative case of a majority movement. However, what is most striking about Sextus' fear is the way it is further characterised:

> qui stimulante metu fati praenoscere cursus,
> inpatiensque morae venturisque omnibus aeger   (6.423–4)

A typically Pompeian way of expressing fear of the future would surely be to *encourage* delay. Although it is possible to explain Sextus' fear making him *inpatiens morae* as fear of uncertainty, along the lines of his later words to Erictho

> mens dubiis perculsa pavet rursusque parata est
> certos ferre metus: hoc casibus eripe iuris,
> ne subiti caecique ruant.   (6.596–8)

it remains clear that Sextus' response to fear is substantially un-Pompeian, and gives us a further glimpse of how different he is from his father. More than that, by making Sextus view the intervening period between now and the future as just so much unwanted delay, Lucan gives him a perspective that is positively Caesarian. At Massilia, Caesar is 'inpatiens haesuri ad moenia Martis' (3.453) and rushes off to Spain; at Pharsalus, Caesar will be 'aeger ... morae' (7.240);[9] the verbal reminiscences merely reinforce the alignment of the impatient Sextus with a Caesar who is always eager to avoid delay, in contrast with a Pompey who is always slow, hesitating.[10]

---

[7] Ahl 1976 p. 130.

[8] Ahl 1976 p. 132; Tartari Chersoni 1979 p. 31; Narducci 1985 pp. 1550–1.

[9] Tartari Chersoni 1979 p. 32.

[10] On Pompeian *mora* versus Caesarian speed, see chapter 1 p. 9.

So even though Sextus' fear is not itself a Caesarian kind of thing,[11] it manifests itself in an utterly Caesarian way. What effect is Lucan trying to achieve? Put simply, he underlines Sextus' wickedness by aligning him with the archetypically evil character of the poem. But to put it in terms which are more suggestive: if Lucan's poem is founded on a basic duality (often questioned or complicated by further splits or a remerging into unity), whose two elements can be broadly represented as Pompeian and Caesarian, then the Caesarian colouring of Sextus' fear can be seen as a counterpart to the Pompeian colouring (because it is 'weak') of Appius' fear, and what begins to emerge is that the opposition of the one episode to the other is an opposition along the lines of this duality: Delphi as 'Pompeian', Thessaly as 'Caesarian'.

But let me complicate this opposition immediately. In *inpatiens morae* Lucan plays a trick that should by now be familiar. If knowledge of the future can be spoken of as a way of avoiding the delay involved in simply sitting and waiting for the future to happen, it is also clear that, on the eve of Pharsalus, when we are poised on the verge of the ultimate catastrophe in all its imminence, the prophecy scene is itself a huge narrative 'delay'. If Sextus had not decided to consult Erictho, or rather if Lucan had not decided to portray Sextus' consultation, there would be nothing for it but to plunge into the battle itself. So the (Caesarian) impatience of delay becomes a means by which to introduce a (Pompeian) delay into the sequence of the narrative, and, as so often in this paradoxical poem, the narrative's declared sense of urgency is undercut by the reality of its failure to progress anywhere.

It is not long before the already obvious opposition between the two Lucanian episodes is made explicit. The impatient Sextus

> non tripodas Deli, non Pythia consulit antra,
> nec quaesisse libet primis quid frugibus altrix
> aere Iovis Dodona sonet, quis noscere fibra
> fata queat, quis prodat aves, quis fulgura caeli
> servet et Assyria scrutetur sidera cura,
> aut siquid tacitum sed fas erat.   (6.425–30)

[11] See Marti 1945 p. 365.

183

Instead he makes use of evil magic arts, which are by implication not silent but not lawful. Top of the list of the various
methods of prophecy Sextus does not use are three oracles, of
which the second is Delphi: an obvious signal to the reader to
recall the Appius episode for comparison[12] in much the same
way as the Appius episode had directed the reader to Virgil's
Sibylline episode by referring to the Sibyl.[13] But the other elements in the list are instructive. The oracle at Delos is hardly
one of the most famous centres of divination in the ancient
world: attested once in the Homeric hymn to Apollo,[14] in classical times it had disappeared;[15] Virgil alone brought the oracle out of obscurity when he had Aeneas consult it on his
journey across the seas (*Aen.* 3.73–120). As an oracle purely of
the 'Homeric' period, it cannot be thought of as a genuine
option for Sextus in the first century BC.[16] Rather, it is a
distinctly *epic* (or, narrowly, Virgilian) oracle, and for Lucan
to refer to it at this point as one of the prophetic sources Sextus
did not consult is, subtly, a metapoetic gesture which points
again to an opposition between Virgilian and Lucanian
prophecy scenes, and which contributes to Lucan's 'anti-epic'
tone.

Tacitum sed fas: of the Delian oracle it is true to the point of
inadequacy to say that it is 'silent'. It was, simply, non-existent
at the time. As for the Delphic oracle, we have already seen
how Lucan is determined to represent it as defunct.[17] The

---

[12] Ahl 1976 p. 132, 'Not without a touch of irony, perhaps, Lucan criticises
Sextus for not turning to a respectable source of divination such as the
oracles of Delos, Delphi or Dodona ... It is hard to imagine that Lucan
does not have tongue in cheek at this point, knowing full well that Appius'
visit to Delphi is quite fresh in the reader's mind from the previous book.'

[13] See chapter 4 p. 129.

[14] Hom. *Hymn* 3.81: the island of Delos extracts from Leto a promise that
Apollo will have his first oracle there.

[15] Parke 1967 p. 94.

[16] Indeed, so unlikely is the Delian oracle's position in the list that the
reader of the phrase 'non tripodas Deli' will surely interpret it at first as
'the tripod of the Delian god'. Not until the second half of the line will we
be forced to reconsider. I believe Lucan is trying to trip us up, so as to
emphasise how surprising the Delian oracle is in this place.

[17] 5.69 etc. See chapter 4 p. 137.

oracle of Dodona had, like Delphi, gone into a decline in the Roman period,[18] and in the catalogue of Pompey's forces Lucan refers to Dodona as 'quercusque *silentis* / Chaonio ... vertice' (3.179–80), presumably referring to this decline. The three oracles, then, are 'silent' because they are defunct. Not so the remaining methods of divination in Lucan's list, extispicy, augury, the observation of lightning and astrology. Far from defunct, they thrived in the Roman world, and their popularity may in fact be adduced to explain the decline of interest in oracular divination. Indeed, Lucan himself gives us examples of their use, and it is clear that he wishes to refer us back to these as much as to the Delphic episode:[19] Nigidius Figulus uses astrology for his predictions in 1.639–72, and Arruns is called in to perform an extispicy (1.584–638); Arruns is also, we are told, an expert in divination from lightning and the flight of birds (1.587–8). How, then, are these methods 'silent'? They are silent not in the sense that as means of telling the future they no longer had currency, but in the sense that they tell us nothing; everything is wrapped in obscurity, too little is said for it to be of any real use. This is certainly true of Arruns, whose main contribution to the scene is to tell us nothing except that what is to be told is untellable, and who covers the truth with *multa ambage* (1.638); but not so much the case for Nigidius, the astrologer. In the narrow context of the three book 1 prophecies, where Arruns is obscure, Nigidius is clear: he tells what he knows, and what he knows is that the world is to be plunged into a long civil war, at whose end lies tyranny. And yet, if Nigidius is more forthcoming than Arruns, he is less informative than the frenzied Roman matron who follows, and who is able to report names of lands which will witness the events of the coming war. We can conclude that if extispicy is 'silent' because we have seen one of its prominent exponents too terrified to speak, astrology is silent in the sense that its representative did not say as much as there was to know.

---

[18] Parke 1967 p. 132 speaks of 'virtual extinction' after the sacking of Epirus by the Romans in 189BC.

[19] Dick 1963 p. 44.

In short, 'silence' means more than failure to utter a sound, utter a prophecy; it can cover the obscurity of an Arruns who does, at least, speak (and similarly, the thinness and ambiguity of the Delphic oracle's prediction on the one occasion when Appius forced it to open), and in an even more equivocal sense it can cover divination which foretells quite a lot but not everything. If the witchery to which Sextus turns instead of these silent methods of prophecy is *not* to be silent, it has quite a job on its hands: it must outdo every prophecy in the poem; it must be *totally* informative. In other words, *tacitum sed fas* is a narrative promise: dismissing every other prophecy as silent, it guarantees that in the witchcraft scene we will have the ultimate prophecy in which, finally, everything is made clear; and this is a promise which will be reiterated at every stage of the episode's massive preparation, right up to the moment at which the corpse finally speaks (see section 2).

Both Delphic and Thessalian episodes follow the same pattern of introduction – digression – return. Parallel to the digression on Parnassus, the oracle's origin and nature, is the section on witchcraft in general (which includes speculation on how it works, as in the Delphic digression) and Erictho's macabre rites in particular.[20] When we resume the story in 570, we find what is practically a mirror image of the corresponding part of the Delphic episode in which Appius locates the priestess.

> iussus sedes laxare verendas
> antistes pavidamque deis inmittere vatem
> Castalios *circum latices* nemorumque recessus
> Phemonoen *errore vagam* curisque vacantem
> corripuit cogitque fores inrumpere templi.   (5.123–7)

Erictho is found in a similar way, though her name is not mentioned (she has been introduced to us already, whereas this had been Phemonoe's début):

> fidi scelerum suetique ministri
> effractos *circum tumulos* ac busta *vagati*
> conspexere procul praerupta in caute sedentem,

[20]   Ahl 1976 p. 130.

quae iuga devexus Pharsalica porrigit Haemus.
illa magis magicisque deis incognita verba
temptabat carmenque novos fingebat in usus.   (6.573–8)

The details are all there, but they have been put through the Lucanian distorting-mirror. The Castalian *locus amoenus* of the first passage has been nightmarishly transformed into a broken-down graveyard, incidentally at midnight (6.570–2), so that all that remains of the former in the latter is the *circum* in the same metrical position, and the fact that somebody is 'wandering' through it. That somebody is in the first case Phemonoe, but if we expect to find Erictho wandering amongst the tombs we will be wrong: it is the *ministri* who wander, while Erictho is not among the tombs at all, but some way off (*procul*) sitting on a spectacular *praerupta ... caute*. She is just that little bit more elusive than her counterpart. She is also less vague: while Phemonoe was *curis vacantem*, Erictho is intent upon her work; anything but carefree, she is expending her energies on ensuring that the imminent battle does not move to another part of the world, and is planning in advance what to do with the corpses of the leaders (6.579–88). What of the *ministri*? It is clear from the parallel that they are counterparts of Phemonoe's *antistes* (since both are sent out to find the prophetess), and so they ought to be servants of Erictho: *minister*, as a priest's attendant, stands in lowly opposition to the high-priest *antistes*. Besides, for the past seventy lines we have heard of nothing but Erictho's wicked practices, and so it is natural to assume that these *fidi scelerum suetique ministri* are her helpers. It will turn out that that assumption was incorrect: we will find out later that the only extras on the scene are the *pavidos iuvenis comites* (657) – Sextus' servants.[21]

Once Erictho has been found, Sextus puts to her his request, and Erictho replies with an offer of necromancy. This

---

[21] Shackleton Bailey's comment (1987 p. 85), 'These persons are Sextus' *comites* ... employed in any nefarious enterprise he might happen to have on hand, not, as many fancy nowadays, servants of Erictho', is to my mind a little too definite: if they are Sextus' companions, that *should* be a surprise. See also Tartari Chersoni 1979 p. 38, more timidly.

exchange has no precise parallel in the Delphic episode; none
the less Sextus' politeness and Erictho's willingness to provide
a prophecy contrast starkly with Appius' violent compulsion
and Phemonoe's recalcitrance.[22] But, like Appius, Sextus
wants to know the *finis* ('te precor ut certum liceat mihi
noscere *finem* / quem belli fortuna paret' 6.592–3; cf. Appius,
'*finemque* expromere rerum / sollicitat superos' 5.68–9); and,
where Appius 'unbarred' the Delphic 'seat' ('Delphica fatidici
reserat penetralia Phoebi' 5.70; cf. 'iussus *sedes* laxare
verendas / antistes' 5.123–4), Sextus asks Erictho to unbar the
Elysian 'seat' ('Elysias *resera sedes*' 6.600) so as to compel
Death itself to foretell who is going to die. But in structural
terms, if Erictho's speech (6.605–623), in which she admits
that witchcraft is not all-powerful but at least offers what she
can, parallels Phemonoe's deceptive speech (5.130–40), in
which she pretends that the oracle no longer functions and
thereby hopes to escape having to prophesy at all, we lack
a speech of Appius beforehand (i.e. a direct request for a
prophecy) to correspond with that of Sextus.

Turn, therefore, to *Aeneid* 6. Just as the Delphic episode
followed the pattern of the *first* part (the prophecy) of Virgil's
story, so the Thessalian episode follows the pattern of the *second* part (the underworld). In that context a preliminary
speech of Appius was not required, because in Lucan's model,
it is the Sibyl who speaks first (she already knows what Aeneas
wants); similarly here, Sextus speaks first because Aeneas
speaks first in the underworld part of Virgil's episode, immediately after the Sibyl's prophetic frenzy has left her ('incipit
Aeneas heros...' *Aen.* 6.103; cf. 'quam prior adfatur Pompei
ignava propago' *BC* 6.589). To take the parallel further, Sextus asks Erictho to 'unbar the Elysian seat', as Aeneas asks the
Sibyl to show him the way to the underworld ('doceas iter et
sacra ostia pandas' *Aen.* 6.109). Each cites his lineage as evidence of his worthiness for the enterprise (Sextus: 'non ultima
turbae / pars ego Romanae, Magni clarissima proles' *BC*
6.593–4; Aeneas: 'et mi genus ab Iove summo' *Aen.* 6.123).[23]

---

[22] Ahl 1976 p. 130.   [23] Narducci 1985 p. 1549.

The Virgilian allusions continue: here is the Sibyl's reply:

> 'sate sanguine divum,
> Tros Anchisiade, facilis descensus Averno;
> noctes atque dies patet atri ianua Ditis;
> sed revocare gradum superasque evadere ad auras,
> hoc opus, hic labor est.'   (*Aen.* 6.125–9)

The Sibyl's half-hearted witticism – 'If you were prepared to die, it would be easy to descend to the underworld' – becomes Erictho's equally irrelevant advice that if Sextus wished to change lesser fates, it would be easy to do:[24]

> 'si fata minora moveres,
> pronum erat, o iuvenis, quos velles' inquit 'in actus
> invitos praebere deos.'   (*BC* 6.605–7)

In a *variatio* of considerable (humorous) subtlety, Lucan exchanges the Virgilian *facilis* for its near synonym *pronum*, a word which in its literal sense ('downward sloping') picks up Virgil's *descensus*. The parallelism of the Sibyl's speech with the witch's, both following the pattern 'X would be easy, but Y is more difficult', turns out to lead nowhere, for in Lucan it is a case of 'X (which you do not want) would be easy, but Y (which you do not want either) would be impossible'; it is a third alternative, neither changing lesser fates nor greater ones, but merely knowing the future, that Sextus is interested in, and this, says Erictho, is easy. Yet even with this difference Lucan still establishes a parallel with Virgil:

> sed, si praenoscere casus
> contentus, facilesque aditus multique patebunt
> ad verum.   (*BC* 6.615–17)

Lucan's *sed, si*, which introduces the third alternative, picks up Virgil's *quod si*, which reiterates the second alternative:

---

[24] The advice is strictly unnecessary because Sextus has not asked Erictho to change any fates. He has, it is true, referred to her power to alter the future ('quaeque suo ventura potes devertere cursu' 6.591), but has asked for no more than to know the outcome of the war. The irrelevance is motivated in two ways: the first, the Virgilian allusion under discussion; the second will be discussed later.

189

quod si tantus amor menti, si tanta cupido est
bis Stygios innare lacus...
... accipe quae peragenda prius.   (*Aen.* 6.133–4, 136)

Furthermore, Erictho's assertion that there is easy access to the truth (i.e. many methods of prophecy) ironically parallels the Sibyl's conceit that there is an easy way down to the underworld: note the allusion to *facilis descensus* (*Aen.* 6. 126) and to *patet* (*Aen.* 6.127) in *facilesque aditus* and *patebunt* (*BC* 6.616).

In the Virgilian model the episode is interrupted at this point by the burial of Misenus and the search for the golden bough (*Aen.* 6.136–235). Lucan does not interrupt his own episode, but neatly compresses two of the Virgilian elements, an unburied corpse and a search, into Erictho's search for a corpse to use in her necromancy (*BC* 6.619–41).[25] The corpse selected, Erictho and Sextus enter a cave (*BC* 6.642ff). This cave recalls the topography of Delphi, and it is indeed at this point in the parallel that the Pythia is thrust into the temple (for the second time);[26] more urgent, however, and more obviously signalled, is the allusion to Aeneas and the Sibyl in the cave that is the entrance to the underworld (*Aen.* 6.236ff). Erictho's cave is *haud procul a Ditis caecis depressa cavernis* (*BC* 6.642); like Virgil's, it is overshadowed by a dark forest (*Aen.* 6.238; *BC* 6.643–5); the foul air (648) recalls the foul air which kills off birds in Virgil's scene (*Aen.* 6.239–41), and according to Lucan it is worse than the air of the underworld. Erictho's cave is so close to the underworld that she might as well be there:

... maestum mundi confine latentis
ac nostri, quo non metuant admittere manes
Tartarei reges. nam, quamvis Thessala vates
vim faciat fatis, dubium est, quod traxerit illuc
aspiciat Stygias an quod descenderit umbras.   (*BC* 6.649–53)

And if Erictho and Sextus do not in fact descend as far as the Sibyl and Aeneas, Erictho makes it clear that she could pro-

---

[25] Misenus resurfaces at the very end of Lucan's episode: see infra.
[26] See chapter 4 p. 120.

vide something like an actual catabasis – she could show Sextus the rivers of the underworld, the Eumenides, Cerberus, the giants – if she wanted to (662–6). Sextus is terrified: 'exanimi defixum lumina voltu' (658), a phrase which alludes to Aeneas' reaction to the Sibyl's orders, 'maesto defixus lumina vultu' (*Aen.* 6.156);[27] but Erictho rebukes him for being afraid of mere ghosts (659, 666), in a speech which takes its cue from the Sibyl's parallel 'nunc animis opus, Aenea, nunc pectore firmo' (*Aen.* 6.261).

Once inside the cave, Erictho busies herself with her magic (667ff). In Lucan's description are the vestiges of the Virgilian passage in which the Sibyl sacrifices to the infernal deities. Out of Virgil's 'voce vocans Hecaten caeloque Ereboque potentem' (*Aen.* 6.247) has grown a Lucanian invocation, in direct speech, of a whole range of inhabitants of the underworld (695ff). From the description of supernatural noises and quakes that follow on the Sibyl's sacrifice

> ... sub pedibus mugire solum et iuga coepta moveri
> silvarum, visaeque canes ululare per umbram
> adventante dea.   (*Aen.* 6.256–8)

comes a great list of eerie sounds not simply emanating from the environment, as in Virgil, but issuing from Erictho's mouth:

> latratus habet illa [sc. vox] canum gemitusque luporum,
> quod trepidus bubo, quod strix nocturna queruntur,
> quod strident ululantque ferae, quod sibilat anguis;
> exprimit et planctus inlisae cautibus undae
> silvarumque sonum fractaeque tonitrua nubis;
> tot rerum vox una fuit.   (*BC* 6.688–93)

Apart from the typical exaggeration in Lucan's version, supplying nine noises for Virgil's three, we should note the 'civil-warness' of the witch's voice, which is made up of a 'confusion' of dissonance and discord (*confundit murmura ... dissona et humanae multum discordia linguae*, 686–7), picking up two or three civil-war catchwords. Finally, it is possible to read the

---

[27] For Narducci (1985 p. 1550) this allusion contrasts the ignoble terror of Sextus with the pious, dignified despondency of Aeneas.

preparation of the corpse, which involves pouring hot blood –
mixed with various poisons – back into the (newly made)
wounds (*BC* 6.667–9), as a kind of reverse human sacrifice, to
be opposed to the Sibyl's sacrifice of bullocks and cows and
the collection of the hot blood in bowls (*Aen.* 6.243–54).

It is the stage at which Aeneas and the Sibyl plunge into the
cave and into the underworld (*Aen.* 6.262–3) that marks
the end of any precise following of the Virgilian pattern in
the Thessalian episode. It resumes again when we reach the
corpse's prophecy; but meanwhile, as Erictho recalls the spirit
of the dead man back into his body, the Virgilian model drops
away (there is nothing in Lucan's episode to compare with the
journey through the underworld until Aeneas finds his father),
and the Delphic model takes over. The dead man's ghost
is reluctant to re-enter his body (719–25); Erictho angrily
invokes a second time those infernal deities she had invoked
before (730–49); and the corpse comes to life (750–60). This
sequence of events mirrors the stages of Phemonoe's frenzy:
first, a false frenzy (5.148–57), then Appius' threats (5.157–
61), and finally a genuine frenzy (5.161ff).[28] But it is important to note that, precise as this mirroring is, the agents
have been confused. Sextus is the Appius-figure (enquirer);
Erictho is the Phemonoe-figure (prophetess); what of the
corpse? Since Phemonoe's prophetic frenzy is a result of her
body being taken over by Apollo, the corpse stands in an exact
relation to Phemonoe (possessed), and the ghost which rein-
habits it stands in relation to Apollo (possessor). So where in
the Delphic episode we saw the prophetess (as the possessed)
unwilling to be entered by the possessor, and rebuked by the
enquirer, here in the Thessalian episode the possessor is unwilling to enter the possessed, and is rebuked by the prophetess. So the ghost, like Phemonoe, is afraid and hesitates
(Phemonoe: *pavens* 5.146; the ghost: *timentem* and *pavet* 6.721,
722); the ghost fears to enter the *claustra* of his body, and this
picks up the body-as-temple imagery of the Delphic episode,
where Phemonoe's reluctance to enter the Delphic temple pre-

[28] Ahl 1976 p. 131.

figures her reluctance to have Apollo enter her;[29] entrance of
the body is in both cases through the *pectus* (the ghost: *pavet
ire in pectus apertum* 6.722; Phemonoe: *conterrita virgo . . . concepit pectore numen* 5.161, 163), then spreading through the
limbs (the ghost: the blood runs to the *extrema membra* 6.751;
Phemonoe: Apollo gains control over the heart and then *artus
. . . inrupit* 5.166–7); the life creeps into the *desuetis . . . medullis*
of the corpse (6.753), while Phemonoe receives Apollo into her
insueto . . . pectore (5.163).[30] The portrait of the revivified
corpse recalls, in no exact way, the description of Phemonoe's
frenzy (before and after her prophecy); the corpse's jerky
spasms (6.754–7) quickly give way to a stupefied *rigor*
(6.759–60), and so cannot be as violent or dramatic as
Phemonoe's raging career around the cave; but the deathly
pallor is the same (6.759; 5.215–16); and Phemonoe's foaming
mouth (*spumea . . . rabies vaesana per ora / effluit* 5.190–1)
finds a parallel (out of place) in the foaming mouth of the
corpse before the ghost has entered it (*spumantiaque ora*
6.719). The reversal of roles between the two episodes, which
makes victim of aggressor and vice versa, not only typifies
Lucan's opposition technique,[31] but seems well motivated in
this particular case by a context in which the order of things is
overturned by witchcraft (*cessavere vices rerum* 461, etc.),
since Erictho is only able to take over the role of aggressor
because she has, as it were, usurped the place of the gods.

The relation between what the ghost of the dead soldier says
in Lucan and what Anchises says to his son in Virgil's underworld has been the object of much excellent critical discussion,
to which I have little to add. Lucan replaces Virgil's grand
panorama of Roman heroes whose significance is, on the surface at least, optimistic, with a black vision of famous Roman

[29] See chapter 4 p. 144.
[30] Not that there is no difference between the two compounds of *suetus*:
Phemonoe's heart has never before been possessed (because if she had
been possessed, she would be dead); the corpse once did have life, but has
got out of the habit of living.
[31] For instance, the Delphic episode itself pits an aggressive Aeneas figure
against a weak Sibyl figure.

dead conducting their own civil war in the underworld.[32] Virgil's single list of names, all portending the future glory of Rome, becomes in Lucan two lists which represent the two sides; and while Lucan includes names that do not appear in Virgil's list (Sulla, Catiline,[33] Marius, Cethegus), it is none the less clear that one of the points of his reworking is that it divides the unity of heroes listed by Virgil into two opposing camps (on one side, Decii, Camillus, Scipio, Cato, Brutus; on the other, Drusi, Gracchi). Anchises' message of hope and joy ('hanc prolem cupio enumerare meorum, / quo magis Italia mecum laetere reperta' *Aen.* 6.717–18) is replaced by a message of total despair from Lucan's ghost: for the family of Pompey, the only consolation will be death. Virgil concludes his vision of the underworld on a melancholy note with the doomed Marcellus; Lucan, alluding carefully to Virgil's Marcellus, ends with the doom of the house of Pompey, and makes the exception into the rule.[34] Simply, Lucan's pessimism opposes Virgil's optimism; Lucan is an anti-Virgil. Too simply: we have learnt that the darker vision so remorselessly pursued by Lucan was already implicit, already lurking in the shadows of Virgil's text. Lucan is either laying bare the ambiguities inherent in Virgil, or he is setting up a straw Virgil to smash down. No matter, in either case there is a gesture of defiance, of violence – either, simply, a negation of an imagined Virgilian stance, or otherwise an assertion that what is worrying in Virgil's vision should not be left in the shadow.[35]

---

[32] See note 1 for the main scholarly discussions, and add Bramble 1982 p. 543.

[33] Catiline can, none the less, be traced to Virgil's portrayal of Aeneas' shield in *Aen.* 8: see Paoletti 1963 pp. 22–5, who proves a conscious allusion.

[34] Virgil's 'heu, miserande puer' (*Aen.* 6.882) becomes Lucan's 'o miseranda domus' (*BC* 6.819); Virgil's 'ingentem luctum ne quaere tuorum' (*Aen* 6.868) becomes Lucan's 'tu fatum ne quaere tuum' (*BC* 6.812). See Tartari Chersoni 1979 pp. 38–9.

[35] See, notably, Feeney 1986c for the ambiguities in Virgil as well as a useful discussion of the manner of Lucan's imitation; according to him '[Lucan's] presentation again and again magnifies the reservations of Virgil to show that the hoped-for achievement has not come off, to show that Virgil was

And finally, Lucan's brief coda, in which the corpse demands his death in return for services rendered, and Erictho accompanies Sextus back to the real world (*BC* 6.820–30). Clearly we are meant to think of the coda to the Sibylline episode,[36] where Aeneas and the Sibyl leave the underworld and Aeneas returns to his ships. But Lucan's concentration on the *corpse* provides, typically, an extra twist: while Aeneas and the Sibyl escape back to the world of the living, the corpse escapes back to the world of the dead. Simultaneously, the corpse fulfils two other functions: his funeral rites pick up the funeral rites of Misenus from earlier in Virgil's underworld scene (*Aen.* 6.212–35). Note especially the allusion in Lucan's

> tunc robore multo
> extruit illa rogum   (*BC* 6.824–5)

to Virgil's

> et robore secto
> ingentem struxere pyram   (*Aen.* 6.214–15)

confirming the connection between Misenus and Lucan's corpse that we noticed earlier. This gives a new force to the horror of the resurrection; if the corpse is Lucan's version of Misenus, then it is doubly an affront to decency and an affront to the Virgilian model that this neo-Misenus should be denied his proper burial but should on the contrary be co-opted into performing a main role in the rest of the episode. And secondly, the death of the corpse grotesquely parallels the death of Phemonoe at the end of the Delphic episode (*vixque refecta cadit* 5.224; *cadaver / ut cadat* 6.822–3); both dying – one 'tragically', the other eagerly, after their prophecies.[37]

So ends Lucan's most famous episode, a *tour de force* of overdetermination, a masterly synthesis of multiple poetic

mistaken in believing that in the balance of flawed and sound the scale could possibly incline to the good. All that is positive in Virgil is stifled and suppressed by Lucan, while the discordant notes in his predecessor's piece become the leitmotif of his arrangement' (p. 17).

[36] Ahl 1976 p. 147.

[37] Some are not convinced that Phemonoe dies. There is an ambiguity: see O'Higgins 1988 p. 213 n. 18.

threads. We see that the choice of necromancy, far from being motivated exclusively by a Neronian taste for the bizarre, the macabre – as so many would have it – is in fact a necessary response to oracle and catabasis, brilliantly combining possession by a spirit with a Virgilian vision of the underworld, and at the same time managing to oppose itself, morally, philosophically, verbally, to both. That is not to mention the story of Gabienus, which may well have been an important inspiration.[38] And this is only the groundwork; even within the tightness of this schema, the Erictho episode still manages to be its own story, to present its own tensions, perplex us with its own anomalies, impress us with its own pointedness. While we shall not be able to escape entirely the shadows of Deiphobe and Phemonoe, it is to Erictho herself that I would now like to turn our attention. For there is still much to say.

The corpse's prophecy

I remarked earlier that the introduction to the Erictho episode contained an implied narrative promise that the forthcoming prophecy would be the climactic prophecy of the poem; a prophecy that would be *totally* informative, which would say everything that there was to say, because not to do so would amount to what Lucan ironically calls 'silence'. Most critics have agreed that Erictho's is the major prophecy of the poem, and that she is 'infinitely more informative to Sextus than the oracle is to Appius'.[39] Blandly, there is no doubt that that is true: the episode is a long one, and what the corpse says is more expansive than what any other prophet says. But a large reason for our believing in the necromancy as the climactic, all-telling divination scene is that Lucan tells us so; as we continue through the episode we find assurance after assurance that at last everything is going to be made clear. There will be no shirking this time. This time, there will be certainty. Sextus:

> te precor ut *certum* liceat mihi noscere finem
> quem belli fortuna paret.   (592–3)

---

[38] See note 52.
[39] Ahl 1976 p. 131. See also Schrempp 1964 p. 25, 'Die Ericthoszene im sechsten Buch gibt uns die wirkungsvollste Prophezeihung'.

Sextus, unlike Appius, meets with no resistance: Erictho is glad to help. Given the incredible powers of witchcraft outlined in Lucan's introduction, mere prophecy should be child's play for someone like Erictho;[40] and this Erictho confirms as she accepts Sextus' commission:

> sed, si praenoscere casus
> contentus, facilesque aditus multique patebunt
> ad verum... (615–7)

Furthermore, as if to remove all possibility of obscurity, Erictho promises to choose a newly dead corpse for her rites, one that will speak clearly:

> ut modo defuncti tepidique cadaveris ora
> *plena voce* sonent, *nec* membris sole perustis
> auribus *incertum* feralis strideat umbra. (621–3)

Note the recurrence of that word *certus*: a newly dead corpse speaks *plena voce*, but with a corpse that has been too long exposed in the sun there is danger of its message being *incertum*. That danger will be avoided. The corpse is chosen; Erictho finds one with good strong lungs so that it can speak properly (630–1),[41] and preparations begin. Erictho concocts her poisons, and makes her invocation; at the end of which she duly asks for a soul which is recently dead (712–16) and

---

[40] Gordon 1987 p. 232: Erictho is 'far too potent for the insignificant duties she is called upon to perform in the epic itself'.

[41] Housman (ad 6.637) is perplexed that so much care should be taken to find uninjured lungs if the corpse's throat has been pierced. I agree. But I would not therefore, as he does, wish to reinterpret *traiecto gutture* (637) as 'having a noose put around its neck by Erictho'. Such a sense of *traicere* is only barely possible, and Housman's parallels are unconvincing because their own contexts make it impossible to understand *traicere* as 'pierce'. Here however, with a body dead on a battlefield, how that body met its end is an entirely relevant piece of information, and it is hard not to take *traiecto gutture* (with Cortius) as 'cuius guttur traiectum erat in proelio'. Housman's difficulty depends on the supposition that a damaged throat is a hindrance to prophecy. This is not necessarily so; indeed, as Ahl points out (1976 p. 137), the corpse of Gabienus, whose story may be behind Lucan's necromancy (see note 52), had been executed by having its throat cut, and yet was still able to speak after death: presumably Lucan is alluding to that here. Let us therefore preserve the anomaly.

climactically prays that

> ducis *omnia* nato
> Pompeiana *canat* nostri modo militis umbra,
> si bene de vobis civilia bella merentur.   (716–18)

once again promising a total prophecy.

So far so good. There is a minor hitch in the preparations, when the dead man's ghost hesitates before entering his body, but the full force of Erictho's power is too great for anything to resist, and the corpse comes to life. As the witch addresses the ghost, promising him the great reward of undisturbed death if he tells her what she asks him to, the insistence on clarity and certainty reaches fever pitch. Erictho:

> tripodas vatesque deorum
> sors obscura decet ...   (770–1)

A sneer at oracular prophecy that of course reiterates the implied contrast with the unhelpfulness of the Delphic episode. Continuing:

> *certus* discedat, ab umbris
> quisquis vera petit duraeque oracula mortis
> fortis adit. ne parce, precor: da nomina rebus,
> da loca; da vocem qua mecum fata loquantur.   (771–4)

These, the final words of Erictho's address to the corpse, drive home the point to the extent of overkill. But even now, on the verge of our actually hearing what the corpse has to say, Lucan adds a little detail that promises once again that nothing will be left unsaid:

> addidit et carmen, quo, quidquid consulit, umbram
> scire dedit.   (775–6)

With such an emphatic build-up to a clear, omniscient, truth-telling prophecy, the corpse's first words must come as a major shock. Erictho had asked that the corpse 'give a voice by which the fates may talk with me'; the corpse replies:

> 'tristia non equidem Parcarum stamina' dixit
> 'aspexi tacitae revocatus ab aggere ripae ...'   (777–8)

And it turns out not only that the ghost is unable to be the mediator between Erictho and the fates as Erictho had commanded, but that he has hardly even descended far enough into hell to have learnt anything at all. All he can report is what he saw from a distance of the assemblage of ghosts in the underworld (*quod tamen e cunctis mihi noscere contigit umbris ... 779*). Presumably it is precisely because his body is unburied that he has not progressed beyond the near bank of the Styx.[42] None the less, the ghost maintains that the little knowledge he has is sufficient to make it clear what the fates intend:

> quid fata pararent
> hi [sc. dead Romans] fecere palam.   (783–4)

How satisfactory is this? With the word *palam* there should be a sense of having returned to the position we were in at the very beginning of the episode:

> cunctos belli praesaga futuri
> mens agitat, summique gravem discriminis horam
> adventare *palam* est, propius iam fata moveri.   (414–16)

But the difference is that while until now we have only known that the fatal hour was drawing on apace, the ghost will at least tell us which side will win. That, however, is all. Astoundingly, the ghost continues to disclaim the kind of knowledge that we have been promised in the build-up to the necromancy, the kind of knowledge that Erictho demands:

> tu fatum ne quaere tuum: cognoscere Parcae
> me reticente dabunt; tibi certior omnia vates
> ipse canet Siculis genitor Pompeius in arvis...   (812–14)

When Aeneas notices the sad spirit of Marcellus and enquires who he is, Anchises tells him 'o gnate, ingentem luctum ne quaere tuorum'; it is obvious (see note 34) that Lucan has this passage in mind here when he writes *tu fatum ne quaere tuum*. But the difference between the two sentences is significant and instructive. Anchises' *ne quaere* is emotional, rhetorical: do not ask, it is too terrible, it will grieve me to speak it and grieve you to hear it. The *ne quaere* of Lucan's corpse must of course

---

[42] A fact which is, curiously, misrepresented by Paoletti (1963 p. 21), who pictures the ghost as having crossed the Styx, and being crowded round by the other ghosts on the opposite side.

take on some of the colouring of the passage Lucan alludes to (a colouring we cannot easily discard); but, typically, the sense of the phrase has been altered in the transposition from a Virgilian to a Lucanian context. As what follows makes clear, what the corpse is saying is 'Do not ask about your fate *because* I will not tell you.' Incredible: not only is the necromancy shown to be ineffectual because the corpse (in spite of Erictho's spells to make him know the answer to all her questions) has not learned enough in the underworld to say anything precise, but further the corpse falls into the same 'silence' which characterised other, legal forms of prophecy (*tacitum sed fas* 430; *me reticente* 813). Indeed, it is hard to distinguish the obfuscations of the corpse's prophecy from the ambiguities of Phemonoe's oracle. We readers, with hindsight, imagine that we can understand precisely what the corpse is predicting: the defeat and death of Pompey, Caesar's victory and eventual assassination, the deification of emperors, the annihilation of Pompey's sons, Sextus in Asia and Gnaeus in Spain. But how much of this is explicit? None: the corpse provides his consultee with nothing but signs, hardly more than the equivalent of portents we have seen throughout the poem and will continue to see after this episode. These signs may be 'clear', as the portents at the beginning of the episode were 'clear'; but they must be interpreted, and because of that they are liable to be misinterpreted (as Appius misinterpreted his oracle). Sextus cannot know why Brutus is rejoicing; he cannot know which of the *duces* will be buried in Rome and which in Egypt, or when, nor can he be certain of the place or time of his own death (Europe? Libya? Asia? That seems to cover most of the options).[43] The corpse's prophecy turns out to be a concatenation of oracular riddles which, as in the best tradition of oracles, Sextus will be unable to solve until he sees them fulfilled. Worst of all, the equivocal nature of the prophecy seems deliberately to lure Sextus to the scenes of his defeat, just as

---

[43] A similar situation is Aeneas' examination of his shield in *Aen.* 8. *We* understand what it all means; Aeneas does not (*Aen.* 8.730). See Lyne 1987 p. 209.

Phemonoe's oracle lures Appius to his death in Euboea as if it were the place to which he would escape from the dangers of civil war. What exactly does the corpse mean by 'toto nil orbe videbis / tutius Emathia' (819–20)? With hindsight, we understand that although Pharsalus is the final nail in the coffin for Pompey's cause, none the less none of Pompey's house will actually be *killed* there, and in that sense Thessaly will have been safer than any other place in the world. Sextus, however, might be misled into believing that the coming battle will be a final moment of triumph for the Pompeians, or at least a non-event, a minor skirmish of no importance in the great scheme of things; and thus not avoid a battle that will in fact spell the beginning of his doom.[44] In brief, the necromancy, ineffectual, silent and oracular, falls far short of the expectations which the poet has worked so blatantly to heighten.[45]

Instead, then, there is the prediction of another prophecy: Sextus' father Pompey will give him a total prophecy (*omnia ... canet* – notice that this is in the same metrical position as the earlier *omnia ... canat* of Erictho's invocation)[46] in Sicily. The necromancy promised certainty (*certum* 592, *nec incertum* 622–3, *certus* 771); the corpse does not live up to this promise, but adds insult to injury by offering in Pompey a *certior vates* to come. This fuller, clearer, more certain prophecy yet to be uttered is interesting from a number of angles. Helenus, in book 3 of the *Aeneid*, similarly included in his prophecy an injunction that Aeneas should consult the Sibyl when he reached Cumae (*Aen*. 3.441–60), and there can be little doubt that Lucan is alluding to that injunction here,[47] not least because of the reminiscence of Virgil's *ipsa canat* (*Aen*. 3.457) in Lucan's *ipse canet* (814. The other, stronger reminiscence I will deal with in a moment). What does this allusion tell us about

---

[44] In this connection, see further note 51.

[45] This is noticed, but to my mind underplayed, by Schrempp 1964 pp. 25–6 and Ahl 1976 p. 138. It is given more emphasis by Paoletti 1963 p. 19.

[46] See Housman ad 6.716, noticing the contradiction, but wisely not resorting to the weaker *omina*. The crux is also discussed by Ahl 1976 p. 136.

[47] So Morford 1967 p. 72.

Lucan's prophecy scene? It is clear, surely: Lucan's climactic prophecy to end all prophecies is revealed at the last minute to be nothing of the sort; emerging instead as obscure, second-hand, and finally, astonishingly, silent, it now proclaims itself as yet another prelude to yet another, greater prophecy, a prophecy that will *really* fulfil the role of a neo-catabasis (and in which Pompey, Sextus' father, will play the role of Anchises, Aeneas' father),[48] to which the Erictho scene will stand in the same relation as the Helenus prophecy to the Sibylline episode. In short, we were given every reason to expect the necromancy to be parallel in 'importance' to the journey to the underworld; now we discover that it is only as preliminary as Helenus' prophecy.

So be it; the culmination is signalled, then surprisingly postponed, and we have seen enough of that kind of narrative deception in the poem so far to know that it is a standard Lucanian technique. But this time I think we are dealing with a special case. What makes it special is that Pompey's prophecy to Sextus in Sicily, the new climax offered as a postponement of this one, does not exist in the poem as we have it. Again we bump up against the question of where Lucan intended his poem to end, for some critics have argued that the promise of a prophecy in Sicily is evidence that the poem would have continued until it had covered at least the Bellum Siculum in 36 BC, had Lucan lived.[49] Not so; the poem is complete – or, if not, the difficulties involved in extending it far enough to include a Sicilian episode make this one of the least probable of the proposed end-points.[50] There can be little doubt that Lucan never intended to fulfil this promise of a Sicilian prophecy; not only because it is firmly placed beyond the scope of the poem, but for the subtler, though equally profound, reason that it would be redundant. Sicily, the scene of the proposed prophecy, is Sextus' Pharsalus; the place of his final

---

[48] On Pompey and Anchises, see Schrempp. 1964 p. 105 n. 42; Tartari Chersoni 1979 p. 39; Narducci 1985 p. 1551.

[49] E.g. Thompson 1964. But see Schrempp 1964 p. 28 n. 42.

[50] See chapter 7 for a full discussion of the issues.

defeat,[51] from which he will flee towards his execution, mimicking his father's fate. By the time Pompey prophesies to Sextus, most of the events of the civil war in which Sextus is interested will already have taken place. To be sure, Sicily is chosen for the later prophecy in order to recall to the reader the apocryphal story of Sextus and the undead Gabienus who is the archetype for Lucan's reanimated corpse;[52] but it does not require too cold and steady an eye to see that one reason for putting the prophecy in Sicily is that Sicily is the end of the line for the Pompeian house; the fullest, clearest prophecy is therefore reserved for the time when there is no future left. It will, simply, be too late. But there is worse to come. For no sooner are we told that Pompey will be a *certior vates* who will reveal everything, than this promise is immediately – not merely qualified, but contradicted:

> ille quoque *incertus* quo te vocet, unde repellat,
> quas iubeat vitare plagas, quae sidera mundi.   (815–16)

[51] A point brought out by Tartari Chersoni 1979 p. 39. There is an interesting scholion (Marti 1958 ad 6.813): 'Tangit illud quod ipse sompniaturus erat patrem sibi monere ut fugeret, vel sibi dicere: "veni ad me", et in crastina die ab Agrippa fuit in Sicilia interfectus ubi piraticam exercebat'. No prizes for historical accuracy (Sextus was killed in Asia by M. Titius), but the immediacy of Sextus' doom is well understood. The dream (not explicitly a dream in Lucan's text) was probably suggested by the parallel with Anchises in Sicily in *Aen.* 5 (hence *veni ad me*); see below.

The promise of a prophecy in Sicily sounds innocent enough; but is it not a sinister and indirect way of saying that Pompey will have died before Sextus reaches Sicily (who, other than professional prophets and dead heroes, has the power of prophecy?)? And surely it is a crucial, almost criminal omission for the ghost not to have warned Sextus that with the prophecy from his father will come his own final defeat. Is the ghost trying to lure him to his death with promises of omniscience, as Phemonoe lured Appius to his death in Euboea? See Schrempp 1964 p. 28 n. 42.

[52] The story of Gabienus, who was executed by Sextus in Sicily but would not die until he had delivered to Sextus a message from the underworld, is recounted by Pliny *NH* 7.52.178–9. First noticed in this connection by Grenade 1950 pp. 37ff, it is fully discussed by Ahl 1976 pp. 133–7; see also Martindale 1980 pp. 367–8, Gordon 1987 p. 232.

203

'Paradoxical' indeed.[53] The allusion is again to Helenus' prophecy:

> illa [sc. Sibylla] tibi Italiae populos venturaque bella
> et quo quemque modo fugiasque ferasque laborem
> expediet, cursusque dabit venerata secundos.   (*Aen.* 3.458–60)

The Sibyl will foretell and advise on the war with the Latins (in other words, the action of the second half of the *Aeneid*); line 459 (*et quo quemque modo* etc.) is almost exactly repeated in *Aen.* 6.892, but there it is Anchises who is doing the advising. Pompey, as neo-Anchises, will be utterly unable to fulfil the basic requirement of his role. And worse again; the fact that Pompey will appear to Sextus in *Sicily* alludes to the dream in which Anchises appears to Aeneas, also in Sicily (*Aen.* 5.719–45).[54] Worryingly, Anchises' main purpose in the dream is to advise Aeneas to come to him in the underworld for a big prophecy (737). If we take this allusion at all seriously, perhaps we will begin to suspect that Pompey's prophecy in Sicily would similarly turn out to be another preliminary to another prophecy. In any case, as the *vates* who is said to be *incertus* in the same breath that tells us he is *certior*, Pompey is the tool by which Lucan will force us to recognise that his continual postponement of the ultimate, of the climactic, of the full and clear, is a process that will have no end. *There will be no climaxes*, only pseudo-climaxes that look forward to something greater that never comes.

---

[53] Ahl 1976 p. 146.

[54] See Bruère 1950 p. 229, and my note 48. Aeneas' dream seems to be alluded to in the dualistic nature of Lucan's underworld (good guys versus bad guys): from Virgil's original

> non me impia namque
> Tartara habent, tristes umbrae, sed amoena piorum
> concilia Elysiumque colo.   (*Aen.* 5.733–5)

is twisted Lucan's 'Elysias Latii sedes ac Tartara maesta / diversi liquere duces' (*BC* 782–3); 'tristis felicibus umbris / voltus erat' (*BC* 6.784–5); and 'camposque piorum' (*BC* 6.798).

Erictho and Lucan: the poetry of *nefas*

If Appius' visit to the Delphic oracle could be regarded as re-enacting in the plot the poem's 'composition myth', if Appius himself and the Pythian priestess could be seen, cautiously, as two halves of a 'Lucan in disguise', then it is inevitable that the Erictho episode, whose narrative retraces and opposes the Delphic episode so precisely, should be viewed in a similar light. What we do not find is any exact allusion to the proem, which would make it clear that Erictho is (like Phemonoe) a counterpart of the 'inspired poet', or that Sextus is (like Appius) a counterpart of the 'enquirer'; instead the allusions (such as Sextus asking for information about the *finem*) are only to the Delphic episode itself, and we must deduce an indirect correspondence with the proem through that. Let it be said, though, that it would be hard to imagine a Thessalian episode that did allude to the proem as exactly as we might like; in the first place, there would be a danger of bald repetition; and in the second place, Erictho is different from Phemonoe, Sextus is different from Appius, and the basic elements of the basic metapoetic formula (enquirer as a kind of invoker of the muse; spiritual possession as a kind of poetic inspiration) are, in the Thessalian episode, being rather violently turned on their heads, as we have seen. The connection between prophecy and poetry (the poem) has been initially set up in Lucan's treatment of the Delphic oracle; now that it is understood, he is free to take it to the limits of his perversity without having to establish it again.

Not that it is ever unclear that the composition myth is one of the major issues of the episode. Erictho (like the corpse, 628) is a *vates* (651),[55] astonishingly so if we bear in mind the

---

[55] More precisely, a *Thessala vates*, presumably alluding to the Sibyl, who is an *Amphrysia vates* (Virg. *Aen.* 6.398); the Sibyl is so called because she is a prophetess of Apollo, who famously served for a time as shepherd for Admetus around the river Amphrysus; but, significantly for the Lucanian allusion, Amphrysus is a river in Thessaly, a fact that we will have been reminded of by the Thessalian geographical excursus (*BC* 6.368).

sanctimonious connotations of that word. Of course the word had developed much – even, had been much abused – since a time when it might have borne more or less unquestionably the kind of heavily religious and moral meaning that Newman discovers in Virgil,[56] but still, it is stretching a point a bit for Lucan to make a *vates* out of an archetypically evil enemy of gods and civilisation. Such a po-faced appellation naturally urges us to question it; how is Erictho a *vates*? How does she square with the other *vates* in the poem, who include Lucan himself? And if Erictho is admissible as a *vates*, does this affect our understanding of those others? Answers must be various and provisional, and we will return to that issue in a moment; for now I only say, one reason why Erictho is a *vates* is that she is one of many representations of the 'poet-figure'.[57] What else? She sings *carmina*, invents new *carmina*, is well versed in the uses of *carmina*; witches' spells, of course, but in a context which is already marked as potentially metapoetical in significance, we will have no hesitation in hearing in *carmen* the poem of the poet-figure. The correspondence between magic and poetry, and specifically between *carmen* as 'song' and *carmen* as 'spell', has a long history, whose ramifications have been only partially explored.[58] By early Roman imperial times it had become sufficiently commonplace for it to be instantly recognisable as a trope, but sufficiently dynamic to be worth continuing to play on. When Manilius, writing we believe under Augustus and Tiberius,[59] begins his didactic poem on astronomy with the words

---

[56] Newman 1967 traces this development, perhaps unkindly, as a decline.

[57] On the metapoetic aspect of the Erictho episode, see further O'Higgins 1988 pp. 217ff.

[58] For the Greek tradition of the association of magic with poetry and rhetoric, see de Romilly 1975 esp. pp. 3–21. In Latin the *locus classicus* is Ov. *Am.* 2.1.23ff, on which see Reitzenstein 1935 p. 79 and Wimmel 1960 pp. 304–5. Luck (1985 p. 77) casually offers self-referentiality in his discussion of Virg. *Ecl.* 8.

[59] Goold 1977 p. xii (the introduction to his Loeb edition); see also Wilson 1985 pp. 28–34.

Carmine divinas artes et conscia fati
sidera diversos hominum variantia casus
caelestis rationis opus, *deducere mundo*
aggredior primusque novis Helicona movere
cantibus et viridi nutantis vertice silvas
hospita sacra ferens nulli memorata priorum.   (Manil. 1.1–6)

he is, while participating in a number of other topoi (sacerdo-
tal imagery, originality, Orpheus), also punningly alluding to
one of the most well known feats of the magic arts: the 'drawing down' of the moon,[60] which Manilius will achieve in the
sense that he will write a poem about the stars. Dragging them
down onto the page? More than that: *deducere* without doubt
alludes to the Augustan conceit of the *carmen deductum*, as it
does in Virgil and in Ovid.[61] If, in this explicitly programmatic
passage, we can discern an overt allusion to magical *carmina*,
it is no great leap to read Lucan's implicitly programmatic
episode with an awareness of a possible correspondence between Erictho's spells and the poem in which they appear.

Proof, there can be none, nor should there be. But confirmation, albeit dependent on an initial willingness to believe, can
be provided. Let us take a second look at Erictho's reply to
Sextus' request for a prophecy:

... et contra 'si fata minora moveres,
pronum erat, o iuvenis, quos velles' inquit 'in actus
invitos praebere deos. conceditur arti,
unam cum radiis presserunt sidera mortem,
inseruisse moras; et quamvis fecerit omnis
stella senem, medios herbis abrumpimus annos.
at, simul a prima descendit origine mundi
causarum series, atque omnia fata laborant
si quicquam mutare velis, unoque sub ictu
stat genus humanum, tum, Thessala turba fatemur,
plus Fortuna potest...'   (605–15)

---

[60] Cf Virg. *Ecl.* 8.69, 'carmine vel caelo possunt deducere lunam'; Ov. *Am.*
2.1.23, 'carmina sanguineae deducunt cornua lunae'; cf also Lucan himself (6.499ff), 'illis [sc. carminibus] et sidera primum / praecipiti deducta
polo...'.

[61] See the excellent discussion of this passage by Wilson 1985 esp. pp. 289–
90. For the *carmen deductum* see also Hofmann 1986.

It will be recalled from my previous discussion that, strictly speaking, these lines are irrelevant. Erictho is saying that it is possible for her to alter minor events, but not major ones – that is, those that have been planned for since the beginning of time and are inextricably caught up in the *causarum series*. Sextus, however, did not ask to *change* fate, only to know what fate had in store; and the strange redundance of Erictho's reply should force us to ask what Lucan felt he was gaining by having her unnecessarily insist on this limitation to her powers. Seen from the perspective of the kind of meta-poetic symbolism I have been arguing for, the lines take on an interesting new significance, for the impotence of the witch seems to run along lines very similar to the impotence of the poet. Historical fact imposes severe limitations on the *fecunda licentia* of the historical epicist; at every turn the poet must reconcile his fictions with the canonical version of *what really happened* – more so, I think, than in the case of the mythological epicist, though to a certain extent the same restrictions apply even there. None the less, it remains true that the poet who chooses a historical subject (this poet certainly, though it would be counterintuitive to suppose that he was unique in this respect) does *change* history. We have seen that many times. What rules determine the degree of the poet's (Lucan's) historical distortion, what can be changed and what not? Like Erictho, Lucan can change 'minor' events, but he cannot change 'major' ones. The result of Pharsalus cannot be altered, Pompey cannot be saved from assassination, Caesar must cross the Rubicon, everything must happen in accordance with what we might find in a bald summary of the 'main' events of the civil war (a summary no more detailed than, say, the Livian periocha), for these are the events that are decreed as having made the future, as having participated in the *causarum series* to give us the dictator, the end of the republic, the depopulation of the world; these are the events where everything comes together into the balance, where *uno sub ictu stat genus humanum*, the critical, nodal moments. But within the limits of this incorrigible outline, there is fluidity. 'Minor' events, those that in large numbers make the major events, can be omitted, distorted, invented; things that 'history' does not record may be freely improvised (Caesar and Amyclas, Scaeva's exploits at Dyrrachium, Pompey's last night with his wife – only the seeds of these episodes exist in the sources), and other things that history does record may be altered provided they do not affect the main outcome (the course of events at Massilia, Cicero's appearance and Domitius' 'heroic' death at Pharsalus). Indeed, the necromancy itself is a strong example of free improvisation, and Sextus' presence in Thessaly an example of the altering of a 'minor' event, for we know that at this time Sextus was, historically, with his mother in Lesbos.[62] We may safely assume this is deliberate: self-referentially Lucan has changed one of the *minora fata* in order to tell us about the possibility of changing *minora fata*; has set an exposition of the rules of historical fiction inside a historical fiction.

So Erictho is a *vates*, she sings *carmina*, and like a historical poet she can only change the course of events in minor ways. We cannot stop there; it must be shown how such metapoetic symbolism affects our reading of the poem, for the 'poetic programme', whatever form it takes, is not an inert thing, a more or less clever trope to throw into the melting-pot of overdetermination; it is, or should be, a dynamic, provocative voice in the dialectic between poem and reader. What we must ask is not only what Erictho tells us about the *Bellum Civile*, but also how her opposition to the Delphic episode complicates the 'message'.

If Erictho and Sextus can replay the roles that Phemonoe and Appius played, how does it affect our understanding of

---

[62] App. *BCiv* 2.83, Dio 42.2.3. See various reactions to this in Bourgery 1928B p. 299, Dick 1963 p. 43, Morford 1967 p. 66 n. 2; Ahl (1976 p. 134) points to *BC* 8.204–5 to show that Lucan himself was perfectly aware that Sextus was in Lesbos. The choice of Sextus as protagonist (rather than any other character in the poem) has provoked some comment. Dick (loc. cit.) surprisingly claims that it was less of a historical distortion to move Sextus from Lesbos than to have made Pompey (the more obvious choice) participate in a necromancy. How so? Surely it is precisely the reverse – Sextus has been chosen because he cannot be there. For other discussions, see the commentators already cited, and Paoletti 1963 p. 14 n. 8.

the poem, the poet, the composition myth, that they are so emphatically *evil*? Erictho's *carmina* are her *crimina*, according to the Ovidian pun;[63] hence the scribal confusion in the line

> hos scelerum ritus, haec dirae *crimina* gentis (507)

Housman, faced with a split in the manuscripts between *carmina* and *crimina* here, rightly opts for *crimina*, suggesting that the variant might have arisen from a reminiscence of line 444. Indeed!

> caelicolum *dirae* convertunt *carmina gentis* (444)

That is no accident, surely: the scribes are responding to an effect inherent in the text, a near precise reminiscence which substitutes one word for the other and thus proposes their basic equivalence. A wicked *vates*, then, a punily evil enquirer, songs that are crimes, a polluted art (509) – what have these to do with the virtuous, indignant Lucan? Can he really be talking about himself, about his poem?

Of course, partly. How Lucan's 'evil' might manifest itself has been one of the many threads I have been investigating in this book; but let us approach the question slowly, and on a local level. Concerning ourselves for the moment only with the necromancy, we must respond to the authorial condemnation of these nefarious rites. One of the main reasons that we know necromancy to be evil is that Lucan tells us so; to be sure, we can find evidence in other authors that such practices were 'generally' thought to be abhorrent, impious, un-Roman, but none the less in this poem the wickedness is hardly ever allowed to speak for itself: at every turn the author is there to bulldoze us with his sense of outrage. That said, Lucan's episode is 'a careful account of the practice of necromancy, the fullest in Latin literature';[64] so full, in fact, that we are faced with the urgent question of where Lucan got his information from, and some scholars have suggested that he might have taken part in

---

[63] Ov. *Ars* 134: 'inque meo nullum carmine crimen erit'; literally speaking, of course, the word *crimen* is contained in the word *carmine*: so Hinds apud Sharrock 1988 p. 12.

[64] Morford 1967 p. 67.

a necromancy himself.[65] Others have rejected this explanation,[66] I suppose dimly sensing the contradiction that is surely the nub of the whole problem: how can Lucan on the one hand vigorously decry the *nefas* of necromancy, and simultaneously offer us an account of it so detailed that it sounds like the report of an eyewitness, a scholar in magical lore, or an expert in magical practice? The important thing about this paradox is that it would remain a paradox even if it were discovered by some means that the rites described by Lucan bore very little resemblance to any such practices in 'real life'. As a starting-point it is amusing to think that Lucan the man might have taken part in just those practices which condemn Sextus in the work of Lucan the poet, but the paradox's kernel is more simple than that, and less dependent on our notion of a real world beyond the poetic world and a real man beyond the poetic persona (important though such notions are):[67] the point is that there is a basic difficulty in resolving Lucan's professed

[65] Bourgery 1928ʙ p. 304–5; Eitrem 1941 p. 70 n. 3; MacMullen 1967 p. 120; so Morford 1967 p. 68, 'It will become evident later that Lucan's knowledge of the ritual goes far beyond that of Ovid and that he must either have attended magical séances or have consulted handbooks on the subject'; similarly Baldini Moscadi 1976 esp. pp. 189–90. For Nero's interest in magic, and for the suggestion that Sextus may be intended as an allegorical Nero figure, see Morford 1967 p. 70, Le Bonniec 1970 p. 189, Fauth 1975 p. 332, Martindale 1980 p. 371.

[66] Most strenuously, Paoletti 1963 p. 18.

[67] One has sympathy with Johnson (1987 p. 21 n. 21), who allows the possibility that Lucan may have practised magic 'out of curiosity', but denies its importance for the interpretation of the poem: 'Lucan the magician may unnerve us (because we keep trying to make our poets "sane"), but Lucan the man is not very available to us, so I don't bother with him'. This may be false innocence, however: in many ways, it is entirely natural that we should deduce 'facts' about the poet's life from his works; it is, after all, what the ancients themselves did in their biographies (see Fairweather 1974 pp. 232ff; Lefkowitz 1981 passim), and therefore must have formed an important part of the way they (some of them, at least) read. Needless to say, one must abandon any hope of these deductions having much bearing on the real life of the man behind the poems. We are told, for instance, by Vacca (his *Life* of Lucan) that Lucan served a term as augur. This might be true, but it is just the sort of detail that might have been invented by an ancient biographer on the basis of Lucan's apparent interest in divination in his poems. True or not, it is part of my reading.

horror with his apparent willingness to continue writing, in such detail, in such depth. Luck is speaking for a generation of critics when he says: 'The rites involved are presented as monstrous and disgusting, but the poet goes on and on, as if he enjoys all the gruesome details. It is a neat literary trick: Lucan professes to be shocked by the magical practices he describes, and yet they seem to give him a certain thrill.'[68]

A literary trick indeed; it is a pity that Luck is content to leave it, unexplored, as 'neat'. Put simply, Lucan is tarring himself with his own brush; by denouncing the necromancy and at the same time displaying such obvious, (pseudo-) knowledgeable relish in his treatment, he is in effect denouncing himself. More profoundly, the author of the necromancy will inevitably be tainted by the evil he describes, for as author he is *creator* of that evil, which is, simply by virtue of its existence in the poem, celebrated in the poem. The only virtuous response to evil is silence – euphemy – for evil is *nefas, nefandum*, that which cannot be spoken of;[69] hence to speak of evil and (what is worse) to make it the subject of one's poem is to speak the unspeakable, perpetrate and perpetuate the impiety, no matter how much the poet may protest his innocence.[70]

---

[68] Luck 1985 p. 194. Cf Le Bonniec 1970 p. 186: 'Sans doute faut-il faire à la rhetorique sa part, mais quelques amplifications ne sauraient dissimuler le fait essential, c'est que le poète croit à la magie et même ressent pour cet art maudit une secrète attirance'. The reader is tainted too; as Gordon rightly says (1985 p. 236 – speaking specifically with regard to Theocritus *Id.* 2 and Virg. *Ecl.* 8.64–109): 'Inevitably, the most lurid details are at a premium, since the very function of literary magic of this type is to play on the disjuncture between the reader's supposed superiority to such beliefs and an implied fascination with them'.

[69] On *fas, nefas* and *fari* see O'Higgins 1988 p. 217 n. 28. *Fatum* is another member of the set; so cf. the *vates* Arruns (a precursor of Phemonoe in his fear of speaking):

> his ubi concepit magnorum *fata* malorum
> exclamat 'vix *fas*, superi, quaecumque movetis
> prodere me populis . . .
> . . . *non fanda* timemus . . .'   (1.630–2, 634)

[70] Compare Walsh 1984 on Pindar (a poet writing in another genre that is normally concerned with encomium) and the problem of silence and

We are now back on familiar ground, for it is clear that these observations about the gusto with which the necromancy is treated (and the fact that it is treated at all) apply in exactly the same way to the whole poem whose subject is the *nefas* of civil war; as a poet who has chosen *that subject*, no matter how much he may stress his allegiance to *fas, ius* and the side that might be thought to have struggled to preserve the good (though everything in that brief formulation must be, as we have seen, open to radical questioning), no matter how much he may appear to represent himself as an impotent moral authority in a world where madness and crime have taken hold, he is still inevitably implicated in that madness and crime, and Caesar, not even in spite of but because of his wickedness, is as much the 'hero' of the poem as Pompey;[71] the poem is, remains, cannot be other than, a celebration of evil.

Erictho 'speaks', Phemonoe is 'silent'; and in that ground opposition, in the oxymoron of *tacitum sed fas,* heaped over to the point of collapse with the crushing weight of ironies, lies the difference between good and evil. More than that, though. It has already been suggested that there is something Pompeian about Appius, something Caesarian about Sextus, and a further opposition springs to mind which confirms an

speech about criminal matters: 'More specifically, a song about crime and danger becomes dangerous and criminal ...' (p. 41) so that '... the inward-turning, private knowledge of the dark intervals that separate moments of brilliance, lies concealed behind the encomiast's celebration of *areta*, although it emerges occasionally, half-acknowledged, in the ambiguous form of half-silent reproach' (p. 61). See also his explication of Aristophanes' apparent critique of Euripides: 'Since men will tend to take on the qualities of whatever they see around them in the city or on the stage, a poet teaches evil simply by representing it or describing it, *his judgements about what he presents notwithstanding*' (p. 90; my italics). In the realm of history, Dionysius of Halicarnassus found fault with Thucydides for recounting a war that had better be left to disappear from memory: ὁ δὲ Θουκυδίδης πόλεμον ἕνα γράφει, καὶ τοῦτον οὔτε καλὸν οὔτε εὐτυχῆ. ὃς μάλιστα μὲν ὤφειλε μὴ γενέσθαι, εἰ δὲ μή, σιωπῆι καὶ λήθηι παραδοθεὶς ὑπὸ τῶν ἐπιγιγνομένων ἠγνοῆσθαι (*Letter to Pompeius* 3).

71 I use the term 'hero' loosely. Cautionary remarks in Feeney 1986B.

impression that the Pompeian and Caesarian is at the heart of the difference between Phemonoe and Erictho. The Delphic oracle is the *traditional* form of prophecy, resting on its laurels, its reputation, but now inert and useless; contrast the highly effective, destructive art of Erictho, whose violence and wickedness so clearly parallels that of Caesar. Contrast too the fact that although her art is as ancient as oracular prophecy, none the less this is a tradition she rejects, improves, innovates on:

> hos scelerum ritus, haec dirae crimina gentis
> effera damnarat nimiae pietatis Erictho
> inque novos ritus pollutam duxerat artem.   (6.507–9)

And Erictho's innovativeness continues: at the beginning of the episode proper, Sextus discovers her even now making unheard-of *carmina*:

> illa magis magicisque deis incognita verba
> temptabat carmenque novos fingebat in usus.   (6.577–8)

The novelty is pointed[72] and programmatic.[73] In the contrast between archaic inertia and restlessly innovative efficacy, we cannot but see the shadow of the Pompeian oak, the violence of Caesarian lightning. We should view these as different forces at work in the poem. On the one hand, the 'virtuous' Pompeian side: unprovocative, respectful towards the huge weight of tradition which makes up the history of epic, but stunningly impotent, gagged and bound, unable to rise to the heights of its past glory; and on the other hand the 'nefarious' Caesarian side: disrespectful, iconoclastic, violent, but because of that, effective. Each is important; each undercuts the other. In spite of the fact that Lucan's violence, his perversity, his savage manipulation of the epic genre marks him clearly as a 'Caesarian' type of poet, in spite of the fact that in the reading-order Erictho climactically caps everything that Phemonoe stands for, none the less we must take seriously, in part, Lucan's claim to be a Pompeian, one who deplores Caesar's viciousness and laments the fall of the great old order. And so

[72] Gordon 1987 p. 239.   [73] Martindale 1980 pp. 374–5.

Lucan is at war with himself, torn between a tradition his *pietas* demands that he respect, and the requirement of innovation, whose price is the *nefas* of parricide, of destroying what gave him birth.

7

THE ENDLESSNESS OF THE CIVIL WAR

The best evidence for the intended ending of a poem is the place where it does, in fact, end. Poets lie; biographers distort; readers misread. Not always, but enough times to warn us to be on our guard. In Lucan's case, as I shall show, the external evidence for the incompleteness of the *Bellum Civile* is so extraordinarily flimsy that it can sometimes be adduced as evidence for *completeness*; the arguments from supposed structure of the poem are vacuous, arbitrary, and in some cases verging on the dishonest; and the arguments from supposed aesthetic or political purpose are circular in the most viciously partisan sense. In the absence of any compelling case for the incompleteness hypothesis, I repeat: the best evidence for the intended ending of the poem is the place where it does, in fact, end.

The external evidence

Lucan died young. Suddenly, unexpectedly, by his own hand.[1] Tacitus tells the story of his involvement in the Pisonian conspiracy, and his death, mentioning the suppression of his poetry as a reason for his hatred of Nero, but saying nothing about the state of his poems at the time of his death; and for that reason he will not figure largely in my discussion.[2]

---

[1] See, however, Tucker's (1987) fascinating suggestion that Tacitus records Lucan's *execution*, and that Lucan's suicide in the later biographies is a myth; presumably invented to align Lucan with the *amor mortis* of his poem.

[2] Tac. *Ann.* 15.49, 56–7, 70. On Nero's jealousy of Lucan's poetry cited as a cause of the ban, see also Dio Cassius 62.29.4. There is a problem about the date implied by Dio, since he lists the ban at the end of his account of AD 65, without mentioning the fact that Lucan died in that year.

Suetonius' *Life* of Lucan[3] tells a similar story. Lucan became embittered with Nero because of an incident in which
Nero showed his contempt for Lucan's poems by walking out
in the middle of a recitation. His initial pique grew into overt
malice against the emperor, and finally bore fruit in his involvement in the conspiracy, which led to his death. Concerning the state of his poems, Suetonius gives us two clues. First,
he says that Lucan gave a recitation of his *Bellum Civile*, at
some point after Nero's Quinquennium and before Nero's ban
on Lucan's poems:

[Lucanus] prima ingenii experimenta in Neronis laudibus dedit quinquen-
nali certamine, dein civile bellum quod a Pompeio et Caesare gestum est
recitavit. (332.1–4)

Taken literally, the words imply that Lucan recited the
whole of his epic. We do not have to believe that; we may
insist, on the basis of other evidence, that Lucan recited only a
part,[4] but that is not what Suetonius says. He gives no indication that the poem was incomplete; indeed his anecdote that
Lucan introduced his recitation with the proud boast 'et quantum mihi restat ad Culicem?' (332.4–6) might have less point if
the whole of the *Bellum Civile* did not exist to stand comparison with Virgil's *Aeneid*.[5] Secondly:

impetrato autem mortis arbitrio libero codicillos ad patrem *corrigendis*
quibusdam versibus suis exaravit. (333.15–17)

Before his death, Lucan made some corrections to some of his
lines. Which poem or poems these involved is not made clear.

---

[3] Printed in Hosius 1905; numerical references to the Suetonian *Vita*, as
to all the Lucanian *Vitae* discussed in this chapter, are to page and line
numbers of Hosius' edition. I have not always preserved his punctuation.

[4] Or even, with Rostagni 1944 p. 144, a mere preliminary sketch.

[5] The point of the boast must be that Lucan is still younger than Virgil was
when he wrote the *Culex*. The Suetonian life of Virgil gives 15, 16 or 17 as
the age at which the *Culex* was written – depending on which manuscript
reading we choose. So unless we wish to believe that Lucan had started
the *Bellum Civile* (not an entirely impossible position) while still in his
mid-teens, this particular fragment of evidence is of little use.

Perhaps the *Bellum Civile*;[6] but if so, no mention from Suetonius of the epic's incompleteness. A brief coda on the fate of
Lucan's poems similarly fails to comment on the problem.

So far, then, the combined witness of Tacitus and Suetonius, if no other evidence existed, would give us no reason
to believe that the *Bellum Civile* was not completed some
time before Lucan's suicide; possibly, indeed, before Nero's
suppression of Lucan's poems, if we take Suetonius' statement
about the recitation literally. Let us turn now to Vacca, an
unknown commentator on Lucan supposed by Rostagni to
have been Lucan's near contemporary,[7] but more plausibly
dated by Ahl to the fifth century AD.[8] His *Life* of Lucan is full
and rich with detail; while much of this detail seems convinc-
ing in its precision,[9] it is clear that the tendency to mythologise
and romanticise the poet's life has already taken hold. The
standard elements of the biographies of poets re-emerge: the
miraculous portent of the bees playing around the infant
Lucan's mouth;[10] the education by *praeceptoribus tunc emi-
nentissimis* (though mercifully Vacca refrains from telling us
their names); Lucan's astonishing talent displayed at an early
age. Given the fecund inventiveness of the biographical tradition, we should be grateful that Vacca seems to exercise so
much restraint: witness the irony with which he introduces the
story of the bees:

> ac ne dispar eventus in eo narraretur eius, qui in Hesiodo refertur, cum
> opinio tunc non dissimilis maneret ...   (335.1–3)

In the part of Lucan's story we are interested in, Vacca
fleshes out the bare bones of the Suetonian account with new
amplification. The young and talented Lucan comes to the
notice of the emperor, quickly and precociously enters upon a
political career, a quaestorship, an augurate;[11] but then comes

---

[6] So Rostagni 1944 p. 148.
[7] Rostagni 1944 pp. 176–8 (some time after Nero's death).
[8] Ahl 1976 pp. 333–4.
[9] For instance, the exact date of Lucan's birth and death; Lucan's age
  when he left Spain; the name of Lucan's maternal grandfather.
[10] See Rostagni 1944 pp. 180–1.
[11] But on the augurate, see chapter 6 n. 67.

the turning-point in Lucan's fortunes: Nero becomes jealous of Lucan's poetic successes; with surpassing vanity and arrogance Nero bans Lucan's poems, and forbids him to be heard in the lawcourts. Lucan is enflamed, joins the conspiracy, but thereby tragically rushes to his doom.

In these essentials, then, Vacca does not depart radically from Suetonius; at most we can detect the emphasising of a tendency, already apparent in the Suetonian biography, to make the life fit into a familiar pattern: young precocious genius, malignant potentate; admiration at first, then the clash, and finally, tragedy. But on the subject of Lucan's poems, Vacca offers us some interesting scraps of information that are unavailable from any other source. First, concerning recitations of Lucan's poetry (which are cited as a reason for Nero's jealousy):

> quippe et certamine pentaeterico acto in Pompei theatro laudibus recitatis in Neronem fuerat coronatus et ex tempore Orphea scriptum in experimentum adversum complures ediderat poetas *et tres libros, quales videmus.* (335.21–5)

The recitation of the *laudes Neronis* at the Quinquennium we know of through Suetonius; the Orpheus is new;[12] what of the 'three books', which were published presumably some time after the Quinquennium? We would have little reason to suppose that they were three of the books from the *Bellum Civile*, were it not for a passage a little further on in the Life, after the description of Lucan's death.

> reliqui enim VII belli civilis libri locum calumniantibus tamquam mendosi non darent, qui tametsi sub vero crimine non egent patrocinio: in isdem dici, quod in Ovidii libris praescribitur, potest: 'emendaturus, si licuisset, erat'. (336.12–17)

---

[12] The *Orpheus* is attested in Statius *Silv.* 2.7.59 and Serv. ad Virg. *Georg.* 4.492, who preserves one of the fragments. Other lost works attributed to Lucan by Vacca in 336.17–22 are also found in Statius (see infra); fragments survive of his *Iliacon, Catacthonion* and *Epigrams.* Given the accuracy of those parts of Vacca's list that we can check, we should not doubt the remainder – the *Saturnalia, Silvae, Medea, Salticae fabulae* (though this may be a corrupt reading), the double oration for and against Octavius Sagitta, and the *Epistulae ex Campania.*

This is something new, then. Before Nero's ban (Vacca 336.1), Lucan publishes three books; the remaining seven seem to have been published after his death. How do we square this with the information given by Suetonius? Simply enough: we assert that Suetonius was speaking equivocally, and that Lucan's recitation of the 'bellum civile quod a Pompeio et Caesare gestum est' should not be understood as referring to the whole poem, only a part of it. *If* we believe Vacca.

Vacca also gives us an opinion about the state of the *Bellum Civile* after Lucan's death. The poem may have its blemishes, but essentially stands on its feet; the most you can say about it is that Lucan would have emended it if he could.[13] How trustworthy is Vacca here? There are two factors to take into consideration. First, Vacca's use of the Ovidian tag, taken from *Tristia* 1.7.40. Ovid is referring to his own *Metamorphoses*, and, with some facetiousness I think, is moulding the composition myth of his poem to that of Virgil's *Aeneid*, which we know through the Virgilian *vitae*. Just as Virgil on his deathbed is supposed to have wished to burn the *Aeneid* because he had not been able to work on his proposed three-year revision of the poem,[14] so too Ovid makes out that he had burnt his *Metamorphoses* at the time of his exile – his living death – for two reasons, of which the second is 'quod adhuc crescens et rude carmen erat' (Ov. *Trist.* 1.7.22).[15] Given that one poet was interested in reforming his own life-story to accord with the Virgilian prototype – for whatever reason – we may well suspect that Vacca is similarly distorting Lucan's story to fit the same model. The case is, indeed, similar to that of the Hesiodic tag about the bee prodigy earlier in the *Vita*. So, secondly, the information that Lucan would have emended his verses if he had been able may be a mythic amplification of the

---

[13] Rose 1966 p. 391, rightly: 'That is not how one describes a poem lacking several books'.

[14] Suetonius/Donatus *Vit. Virg.* 35–42; Servius *Vita* 27–42; *Vita Probiana* 22–28; references are to Hardie's OCT *Vitae Vergilianae* (1966).

[15] Cf. Ov. *Trist.* 2.555; the 'ultima manus' topos recurs, probably with an implicit reference to Lucan, in the introduction to Eumolpus' *Bellum Civile* (Petr. *Sat.* 118).

simpler statement made by Suetonius, that Lucan wrote a letter to his father containing 'corrigendis quibusdam versibus'.

Once this door has been opened, suspicion may fall on two other elements in the biography. First that Lucan's poems caused his downfall: we should wonder if Nero's jealousy of Lucan's poetry was a fiction concocted to make Lucan's life fit the Ovidian pattern – the poem that caused Ovid's exile, referred to obliquely as the first reason for Ovid's wishing to destroy the *Metamorphoses*.[16] It is a possibility, but since both Tacitus and Suetonius make Lucan's poetry the cause of the split,[17] we should perhaps give Vacca the benefit of the doubt, and note merely that, if true, the downfall of Lucan is a convenient coincidence which could be emphasised by a biographer who wished to make his biography conform to a pattern. Secondly, the publication of the three books. This fits the Virgilian pattern; from the Suetonian life of Virgil we learn that during the period of the composition of the *Aeneid*, Augustus repeatedly requested of Virgil

> ... ut sibi de Aeneide, ut ipsius verba sunt, vel prima carminis ὑπογραφή vel quodlibet κῶλον mitteretur. cui tamen multo post perfectaque demum materia *tres omnino libros recitavit, secundum quartum et sextum* ... (Suet. Vit. Virg. 31–2)

It is, then, within the bounds of possibility that the story of the publication of Lucan's 'three books' is Vacca's fiction, brought into the biography on the basis of the story in the Virgilian myth. For various reasons, though, I think it unlikely that it is totally fictitious. If we presume that Vacca's information about the three books corresponds to Suetonius' account of the public recitation of the *Bellum Civile*,[18] then Vacca, whose fictions thankfully do not seem to be as bold as they could be, would be unlikely to speak of a three-book publication unless, at least, he had some information that the

---

[16] *Trist.* 1.7.21, 'vel quod eram Musas, ut crimina nostra, perosus'.

[17] Though Suetonius may be distorting the story along Ovidian lines when he refers to a specific *famosum carmen* (333.5).

[18] The dividing line between 'publication' and 'recitation' is not always clear; Due (1962 p. 91) separates them.

early publication of the poem mentioned in Suetonius was only *partial*. In other words, Vacca might have made three advance books out of four or five, but not three advance books out of a complete recitation. But there is another important possibility to take into consideration. Lucan may indeed have published or recited three books in advance of the rest, precisely *because* he was conscious of the fact that Virgil had done similarly with the *Aeneid*. Certainly, Lucan was conscious of his emulation of the Virgilian 'myth', as he indicated in the preamble to his recitation: 'et quantum mihi restat ad Culicem?' now is just as pointed, even if only three books of the *Bellum Civile* were offered.[19]

And finally, the negative evidence. At no point does Vacca give so much as a hint that the *Bellum Civile* was 'unfinished' in the sense that its endpoint had not been reached. Vacca does tell us that Lucan's tragedy, the *Medea*, was 'imperfecta', but no such adjective is applied to the epic. When Vacca tells of Lucan's death, we might expect to hear something about a poem cut off in its prime. What we get is this:

> nam sua sponte coactus vita excedere venas sibi praecidit periitque ... XXVI aetatis annum agens, non sine iactura utilitatis cum patriae, quae tantam immature amisit indolem, tum studiorum quoque. reliqui enim VII belli civilis libri ... [needed revision – see supra]   (336.7–13)

Lucan goes down boasting; a talent cut off in its prime, and a poem never to receive its final revision.

From our examination of Suetonius and Vacca, we have managed to work up two hypotheses, depending on whether we believe Vacca to be a reliable source. The first hypothesis, based only on Suetonius, is that the *Bellum Civile* might have been complete (or complete enough to read in public) before Nero's ban. The second hypothesis, based on Vacca in conjunction with Suetonius, is that part of the poem (perhaps

---

[19] Which three books were published? Rose 1966 p. 384 says that 'it is out of the question that Vacca refers to books other than the first three; no-one would publish individual books of a historical epic out of chronological sequence'. But why not, given the Virgilian precedent? See also Due 1962 p. 92.

222

three books) was published before the ban, and that the remainder, which (perhaps) had not received the poet's *ultima
manus*, was published after his death. It does not matter yet
which of these hypotheses is more likely. What is important is
that in the sources presented so far, there is not a scrap of
evidence to support a hypothesis that the poem failed to reach
its planned conclusion.

The omission is thought by some scholars, notably
Buchheit,[20] to have been filled by Statius' *Genethliacon Lucani*
(= *Silv.* 2.7), a poem whose core consists of a prophecy given
by the muse Calliope as she nestles the infant Lucan in her
bosom. As a source for Lucan's life and works, this prophecy
is important because Statius was a close contemporary of
Lucan, and a frequent guest at the house of his widow Polla.
We cannot doubt, then, that Statius had access to the truth
(such truth as was available); but to derive from that, as
Buchheit tries to do (p. 365), the implication that everything
Statius says in his poem must be true, or even entirely free
from unintended error, is more than we can do. We are, let it
be said, dealing with a poem, not a document, and we are
dealing with a birthday eulogy which is an early attempt at
making Lucan's life into a myth; this being the case, we cannot
base our reading of the poem on the assumption that Statius is
entirely innocent of the sort of tricks familiar to us from the
biographers. All we can assume is that Statius would have
been more fully aware (than a later writer) of the difference
between his own account and the 'way things really happened'; hence it seems plausible to expect any distortions to be
relatively minor.

In spite of my cautioning, I do not in fact wish to challenge
substantially the reliability of Statius' testimony; I wish only
to retain a sense of perspective. Let us now look at the prophetic part of the poem in some detail. Lines 41–53 deal with
the quality of Lucan's poetic talent. In language which, in spite
of the poem's late date, still unmistakably recalls the conceits
of Augustan (or Callimachean) literary polemic, Calliope pre-

---

[20] Buchheit 1961; cf. Marti 1970 p. 18 n. 2.

dicts a poetic career whose crowning achievement will be Roman political epic. Then (54–63) we are given a rapid synopsis of some of those early Lucanian works which are now lost to us:[21] more or less oblique references to his *Iliacon, Catacthonion, Laudes Neronis, Orpheus, De incendio urbis*, and the otherwise unattested *Adlocutio ad Pollam*. This leads to a longer section in which the muse outlines the contents of the *Bellum Civile* (64–72) and compares it favourably with the other masterpieces of Roman epic (73–80), briefly alluding to Lucan's boast about the Culex (74) which we know from Suetonius. In addition to these poetic gifts, Lucan will be endowed with a wonderful wife (81–88).

So far, nothing crucial has been revealed about the composition of the *Bellum Civile* or the state of the poem at the time of Lucan's death. All we can tell is that, according to the scheme, the epic is the product of Lucan's maturer years. Scholarly consensus has rightly condemned the supposition that Statius' reference to the poem as 'Philippos et Pharsalica bella' points to a planned conclusion with the battle of Philippi.[22] But now we come to a passage which does seem to offer us what we are after. The climax of the muse's prophecy laments the savagery of fate which too quickly destroys the best things; three exempla are offered of figures cut off in their prime: Alexander, Achilles and Orpheus. To these, now add Lucan:

> sic et tu – rabidi nefas tyranni!
> iussus praecipitem subire Lethen,
> dum pugnas canis arduaque voce
> das solatia grandibus sepulcris,
> o dirum scelus! o scelus! tacebis.   (Stat. *Silv*. 2.7.100–4)

Buchheit's comments are short and to the point:

Theoretisch ist zu erwägen, ob das entscheidende dum ... canis statt temporal nicht eher kausal ist. Aber der Zusammenhang, in dem diese Verse stehen, lehrt, dass dum hier nur temporal gebraucht sein kann. Lucan wird als viertes Glied in die Reihe bedeutender historischer und mythischer

[21] Well discussed by Ahl 1976 pp. 336–43.
[22] Haffter 1957 p. 119 n. 4; Buchheit 1961 p. 363; Grenade 1950 p. 48 n. 1.

Gestalten eingefügt, die alle zum Beweise der in der Antike oft geäusserten Auffassung dienen:

o numquam data longa fata summis   (v. 90)

Demnach sagt hier Statius, Lucan sei durch die grausame Tat Neros *mitten aus seinem Dichten an der Pharsalia abberufen worden.*   (p. 364, my emphasis)

Clearly *dum* is temporal, not causal, as Buchheit says;[23] clearly, too, *pugnas* can only refer to the *Bellum Civile.* But where the crucial point of slippage occurs is, of course, in Buchheit's gloss 'mitten' for *dum.* To make the interpretative slide from 'while singing' to 'while in the midst of singing' precisely begs the question Buchheit is trying to prove. We can show, in fact, how wide and vague is the range of meanings that can be attached to the word *dum* by a simple experiment: what if Statius had written 'postquam cecinisti pugnas. . .'? In other words, at what stage can a poem be thought of as finished? When the last line has been written, and the plan essentially fulfilled? Of course not: that is only the first objective of a series. After revision – a long process to which Virgil, as we know, was to have dedicated a further three years?[24] But when does the revision stop? With publication? Here I think is a stage for which Statius might have written *postquam* rather than *dum.* But we know of second thoughts, second editions . . . when does work on a poem ever really stop, and at what point is it *impossible* to write *dum canis*?

Dum canis therefore proves nothing about the incomplete-

---

[23] Buchheit is presumably alluding to the school of thought which would make the insulting and dangerously subversive nature of the *Bellum Civile* the prime reason for Nero's ban. Against this view, see Ahl 1976 pp. 346–8. In particular, the Vaccan *Vita* is cited as evidence that Nero banned Lucan's poems because of the publication of the three books. This evidence is presented with an injudicious use of dots, thus: '. . . ediderat . . . tres libros quales videmus. Quare inimicum sibi fecit imperatorem'. (So Due 1962 p. 91 n. 128). This truncation destroys the sense of the passage; a full quotation would reveal that the publication of three books is just one of a number of examples of a career made conspicuous by continual poetic success, which resulted in the jealousy of the emperor.

[24] Suet. *Vit. Virg.* 35.

ness of the poem, the unfulfilled plan. At most it proves that no authorised edition was published during Lucan's lifetime. The next stage of my argument is anticipated by Buchheit, and I quote him again:

> Zwar kann man daran denken, dass diese Angabe einem heroisierenden Familienbedürfnis entsprungen ist. Auch könnte erwogen werden, ob nicht die Möglichkeit, dass das Werk der letzten Feile des Dichters ermangelt (vgl. Haffter selbst S. 119), die Feststellung des Statius bewirkt hat. Sind diese Verse, so könnte man weiter fragen, nicht überhaupt als blosse rhetorisch-konsolatorische Floskel zu verstehen, weil es Statius in jedem Falle auf die Einreihung unter die vorgeführten Beispiele angekommen sei? (p. 365)

Without wishing to condemn Statius' verses as 'mere rhetorical, consolatory verbiage', I believe that this is quite close to what was in fact the case. As I suggested earlier, Statius was probably under an obligation to stick as closely as possible to the realities of Lucan's life; but the very fact that Lucan is aligned with such exempla as Alexander, Achilles, Orpheus; the fact that all of this information appears in a prophecy spoken by a muse; that the muse's prophecy is set inside a poem which accords nearly divine honours to Lucan on his birthday; that the prophecy is followed by a description of Lucan's rise to heaven which is clearly designed to recall Lucan's own description of Pompey's apotheosis; and that in the afterlife Lucan is imagined to have his poem's protagonists Cato and Pompey for company – all of this precisely indicates the tendency to glorify, heroicise, mythologise the figure of Lucan in this, his first literary biography. And so, if (as I suggest) Lucan died before he had a chance to publish his poem complete, we cannot expect anything less of Statius than that he should allow the equivocality of his verses to suggest, however subtly, that Lucan too was victim to that cruel law of fate which calls the great to their deaths while they are in full flow. The particular case of Orpheus is most revealing: obviously Statius had a lot to gain by showing a parallel between Lucan and the archetypal poetic genius of myth. Luckily, they both died early deaths, and one of the most striking features of Orpheus' death is that his head continued singing even after it had been torn off (hence *non mutum caput* 99); of Orpheus it was literally true that he died *dum canit*. Given that Lucan's poem had not been given its final imprimatur, how could Statius refrain from exploiting a parallel that required little, if any, amplification?

Because Buchheit (strangely, in spite of the remarks cited above about the poem lacking final polish) does not allow for ambiguity in Statius' *dum canis*, which as far as he is concerned can only mean that Lucan was in the middle of composing his poem, he believes there are only two alternatives: either Statius is correctly asserting that Lucan's epic is incomplete, or Statius is lying. To counter his own objections he therefore argues for the reliability of Statius' testimony: that all of the other facts in the poem tally with what we know from other sources; that Statius was intimate with Lucan's widow. Since I am arguing not that Statius is telling an out-and-out lie, but that he is allowing the truth to speak in such a way as to give a pleasingly misleading impression – abiding by the letter rather than the spirit of the facts – these counterarguments have no force. We conclude, then, that Statius' *Genethliacon Lucani* cannot substantiate the claim that Lucan's poem failed to achieve its planned endpoint. It is not the incontrovertible evidence we are looking for.[25]

We have now examined four important sources for Lucan's life and career. The first three give us no reason at all to think the poem incomplete, and in fact may be evidence to the contrary. The fourth is, it would appear, purposefully vague, and, on its own, proves nothing. Taken together with the information provided by Suetonius and Vacca, however, Statius' poem, if anything, enables us to let go of our first hypothesis (that the poem was complete and published before Nero's ban) and concentrate on our second hypothesis (that the poem was unpublished at the time of Lucan's death). Unless some positive evidence is found to contradict it, this second hypothesis must stand.

---

[25] Rose 1966 p. 391, 'It must have been obvious to everybody that the *De Bello Civili* was not complete to the final touch – which is all that can be safely deduced from Statius' words'. See also Brisset's (1964 p. 166 n. 2) refutation of Buchheit.

We turn, at last, to the positive evidence, our fifth and final major source for Lucan's life: the anonymous *Vita* attached to the Codex Vossianus II, which is datable to the tenth century AD. Here is the relevant passage:

> unde morte praeoccupatus quaedam, quae inchoaverat, inperfecta reliquit. Nam mortem Pompei atque Catonis descripsit. (337.13–16)

In one stroke, the biographer (hereafter referred to as 'X')[26] destroys our second hypothesis and gives us a *terminus post quem* for the intended scope of the unfinished epic. But considering the lateness of his testimony, and considering too that he includes matter that is mentioned by no other source in antiquity, the legitimate – urgent – question is, how reliable is this witness? And from where does his information derive?

Reading the *Vita* of the second Vossian codex one receives a strong impression that its author has read Suetonius (or a source in the Suetonian tradition) but has ignored, or is unfamiliar with, Vacca. For instance, when X writes (of Lucan's disgraceful behaviour after the detection of the conspiracy)

> cumque non inveniretur in eo talis constantia, qualis putabatur ... (337. 7–8)

he seems to be echoing this phrase from Suetonius' *Vita*:

> verum detecta coniuratione nequaquam parem animi constantiam praestitit. (333.10–11)

In both cases, the moral judgement on Lucan's fickleness is explained by the story that Lucan betrayed his innocent mother – a detail which appears in Suetonius (333.13–15), though not in Vacca.[27] Similarly, the description of his death in X:

---

[26] A convenient designation which should be taken to mean 'the biographer of the second Vossian codex *or his source*'.

[27] Our other source on the incident, Tacitus *Ann.* 15.56 and 71, does not raise the question of Acilia's complicity. At most we are told of the reaction to Lucan's betrayal: she was ignored ('sine absolutione, sine supplicio dissimulata'). Why *shouldn't* Acilia have been involved?

Critics favourable to Lucan have tended to treat the story as a malicious rumour; see Getty 1940 pp. xviii–xxi; and Ahl 1976: 'The rumour that Lucan had incriminated his mother, Acilia, in a vain effort to save his own life, would have made any pretense of high principle on his part shabby and hypocritical in the eyes of a judge as harsh as Tacitus ...

qui largiter epulatus iussit sibi archiatrum accessiri et incisis omnibus venis corporis periit. (337.12–13)

appears to derive from the Suetonian account:

epulatusque largiter bracchia ad secandas venas praebuit medico. (333.17–18)

The two details – the big dinner and the doctor who cuts the veins (though how many veins?) – are unique to these two accounts. Vacca, who mentions no dinner, has it that Lucan cut his own veins (336.8). Tacitus is unspecific (but see n. 1).

Up to this point, then, our anonymous biographer seems to offer nothing more than a shortened, though slightly intensified, version of Suetonius' *Vita*. After the account of the suicide, however, we are offered a coda in which we are presented with a number of pieces of information for which there is no authority before the tenth century. Two of them – the incompleteness of the *Bellum Civile* and the planned inclusion of the death of Cato – we have seen already. Here is what remains:[28]

Whether the rumour is true or not is, at this stage, irrelevant. That Tacitus thought it was true meant that he could not take Lucan's political ideals seriously' (pp. 343–4). So because Ahl needs to rescue a politically idealistic Lucan for his overall theory, Tacitus, and later Suetonius, are dismissed as hostile witnesses. Since, as I have shown, Lucan the idealist is a myth, I think we should be more faithful to the external evidence we have. The bare facts seem repulsive; but we are denied the chance to examine Lucan's motives, his plans (perhaps he knew that Acilia would have a good chance of escaping punishment), which must have been, in a circumstance such as this, complicated to say the least. In any case this hardly affects our estimation of Lucan as a poet: as Johnson wisely remarks: 'The slender information we have about [Lucan] depicts the sort of unstable compound of high spirits, raw nerves, and gross vanity which is not uncommon in poets. I am sorry he ratted on his mother, if he did, but if he did that does nothing to diminish the genius of his poem. I am looking for poetry to give me sensuous and intellectual pleasure, not role models' (1987 p. 21 n. 21). Even the 'hostile witness' Tacitus apparently felt the same: elsewhere he lists Lucan with Virgil and Horace as three of the all-time greats (Tac. *Dial.* 20.5).

[28] The Comm. Bern. (ad 1.1), also of the tenth century, tells the same story: 'hos vii versus primos dicitur Seneca ex suo addidisse, ut quidam volunt avunculus Lucani, ut quidam volunt frater, ne videretur liber ex abrupto inchoare dicendo, Quis furor'. Cf. the *Adnotationes* ad loc.

> libellos etiam suos inemendatos avunculo suo Senecae, ut eos emendaret, tradidit. sciendum, quia primo iste liber a Lucano non ita est inchoatus, sed taliter: Quis furor, o cives, quae tanta licentia ferri. Seneca autem, qui fuit avunculus eius, quia ex abrupto inchoabat, hos VII versus addidit: Bella per Emathios, usque, Et pila minantia pilis. (337.16–22)

The first part of this passage makes no sense unless we understand that Lucan is giving his unemended verses to Seneca just before he is to die; similarly, Seneca's addition of the first seven lines of the poem must be supposed to have taken place after Lucan's death. In any case the context, in which the death of Lucan and the unfinished state of his poem are the matter under discussion, makes this assumption unavoidable. Perhaps, after all, X has read Vacca, or has heard from another source of the tradition that Lucan's poem was *inemendatum*; though in view of what has gone before it is perhaps more likely that he has taken the germ of this story from the Suetonian *Vita*, which tells of Lucan's instructions to his father concerning *corrigendis quibusdam versibus* in a letter written just before his death. In that case, the emendation of a few verses has been exaggerated into a request for a posthumous edition; and the more famous Seneca has been put in the place of Lucan's father – who better than a poet to complete the work of a poet? But we know X's version cannot be true for the simple reason that Seneca was dead;[29] he had committed suicide a short time before, similarly because of his alleged involvement in the Pisonian conspiracy.[30]

What then of this mythical edition that Seneca is supposed to have produced after Lucan's death? More specifically, how seriously do we take X's assertion that the first seven lines of the poem are Seneca's own composition, or, broadly, not by Lucan?[31] We do have an independent witness to the fact that

---

[29] The absurdity is noted by Rose 1966 p. 391, and implied by Bruère 1950 p. 225; see most fully Getty 1940 pp. xxi–iv.

[30] Tac. *Ann.* 15.60–3.

[31] For instance, it has been suggested on the grounds of the scholion in the *Comm. Bern.* (if *frater* is a corruption of *pater*) that Lucan's father was responsible for the lines. This theory, advanced by Weber and Plessis, is discussed and rejected by Getty 1940 pp. xxii–iv.

these lines were, in the second century at least, considered to be genuine. The orator Fronto complains of the vices of rhetorical overkill in a letter to Marcus Aurelius which discusses these very seven lines of Lucan. His opinion is hardly favourable, but there can be no doubt that he regards Lucan's proem as the genuine article. After discussing Seneca, he goes on:

unum exempli causa poetae prohoemium commemorabo, poetae eiusdem temporis eiusdemque nominis; fuit aeque Annaeus. is initio carminis sui septem primis versibus nihil aliud quam bella plus quam civilia interpretatus est. nunc hoc replicet quot sententiis? iusque datum sceleri: una sententia est. in sua victrici conversum viscera: iam haec altera est ... (Front. *Epist. ad Ant. Imp. de Or.*)[32]

Did X know this passage? Is his invention of Seneca's interpolation of the lines designed to save Lucan from Fronto's censure? I think it unlikely. The *Vita* does not display any propensity towards showing Lucan in a favourable light; and besides, it is not certain that this source would have been available to him. But it is equally unlikely that the story was made up out of thin air, even though it is untrue. The clue, I think, lies in the canonical version of Virgil's biography. There too we find a premature death; an unemended poem; a posthumous edition published by close friends; there too, notoriously, a detachable prologue. I quote from the Suetonian *Vita Vergili*:

Nisus grammaticus audisse se a senioribus aiebat, Varium duorum librorum ordinem commutasse, et qui tunc secundus esset in tertium locum transtulisse, etiam primi libri correxisse principium, his versibus demptis
ille ego qui quondam gracili modulatus avena [etc.]
(Suet. *Vit. Verg.* 42)

The claim being made here is of course that Virgil *did* write the lines in question; the claim of X that Lucan did not. But I think the parallel stands: since in Lucan there is no tradition of an extra group of lines that may or may not be spurious, X had

---

[32] Van den Hout's edition p. 155 (but reading *nunc* for *num*); also available in Heitland pp. xix–xx. Other attestations to the early date of the lines are: Serv. ad Virg. *Aen.* 1.1; Aug. *Civ. Dei* 3.13; Priscianus in *Gramm. Lat.* (ed. Keil) II.348; Isid. *Orig.* 18.3.2.

to work with what he had, and thus cast aspersions on lines that are undoubtedly genuine, neatly depriving the *Bellum Civile* of a beginning (so 'ex abrupto inchoabat') in the same movement with which he deprived it of an end. And so it seems that X too, in the best tradition of biography, has fallen into the vice of preferring an archetypal pattern to the historical 'truth', of forcing Lucan's life into a Virgilian mould at whatever cost.

For these reasons we should be equipped with a healthy scepticism when we approach the other assertion, for which X is our only witness: that the *Bellum Civile* is incomplete, and that it should have included the death of Cato. Since this information contradicts the hypothesis we have derived from an examination of four much earlier sources, and since the *Vita* is demonstrably unreliable in the other case where it ventures a previously unattested opinion, I do not see why we should treat its testimony with anything more gracious than contempt. That said, it is again pertinent to ask how X came to make his assertion. The answer is, presumably, in much the same way as modern scholarship has all but unanimously arrived at the same conclusion, and certainly with no greater justification. Statius' *dum canis*, as we have seen, seems actively to encourage a blurring of the distinction between a *carmen imperfectum* and a *carmen inemendatum*. It is quite possible that X knew of the *Genethliacon Lucani*; if so, this suggests one reason why X may have proposed the death of Cato for inclusion in the epic. In the first place, Statius' poem gives more emphasis to the figure of Cato than is justified by his importance in the *Bellum Civile*: when describing the contents of the poem he gives one line each to Caesar, Cato and Pompey, in that order (67–9). Consequently, when we read the passage which deals with the 'incompleteness' of the poem

> dum pugnas canis arduaque voce
> *das solatia grandibus sepulcris* (102–3)

the vague plural for singular could mislead the clue-hunter into imagining that more than one funeral sequence was in the process of being depicted in the poem, all the more so since

Pompey's tomb does not appear to merit the qualifier *grandi-bus*. Of course, it *is* Pompey's tomb that is being referred to here, Statius knowing full well that Lucan's point was to provide in words the spectacular funeral that was denied in history (and besides, the whole world is Pompey's tomb). A combination of these elements – the missing tomb, and the undeserved emphasis on the figure of Cato – accounts very nicely for the deduction that Lucan intended to include the death of Cato in his poem. Interestingly, too, it suggests an explanation for X's bad Latin: 'nam mortem Pompeii atque Catonis *descripsit*'. Why not *descripsisset*? Because a naïve implication of X's misreading of Statius would be that Lucan was already in the process of describing Cato's funeral when he met his own death; a part of the poem which, according to X's scheme, must not have come down to us, presumably because of its fragmentary state.

So much for X and Statius. Other factors make such a misreading all but inevitable. Such internal evidence as there is (the surprise ending – which I will discuss in its place), combined with a few facts about Lucan's life culled from an earlier biographical tradition (the poem unpublished and perhaps unrevised at the time of Lucan's tragic early death), can, in the hands of a biographer as irresponsible as X, be brewed into a lethal concoction, all the more lethal because it is more attractive to the taste. How great a leap is it from the poet cut off in his prime to the poet cut off in the middle of his masterpiece? And which makes the better story?

In favour of the incompleteness hypothesis, there is an ambiguous passage in Statius (first century), and the testimony of a convicted liar of the tenth century. On the other side, for the completeness hypothesis, the same passage in Statius, which is equally at home in both camps, and the testimony of Suetonius in the first century and Vacca, possibly in the fifth. Ultimately the moral is that we know frighteningly little about Lucan's life or about the chronology of his career, but if we are content with hypotheses based on the argument from probability, I see no way of escaping the fact that probabilities are heavily in favour of the following hypothesis, its details still unrefined, but essentially consistent with the best and most evidence. A part of the poem was made public before Nero's ban; we do not know when the remaining books were composed (indeed they may have been essentially composed by the time of the publication of the others), but they were substantially complete at some time before Lucan's death; for whatever reason, either because of Nero's ban or because of the process of revision (or both), they were withheld from publication during Lucan's lifetime; after Lucan's death, which would have interrupted the revision if nothing else, the whole poem was published posthumously, in spite of its being regarded (perhaps) as lacking in polish.

This hypothesis fits the best external evidence; it is now time to turn inward.

The internal evidence and contemporary scholarship

The question that immediately confronts us is: what exactly *counts* as internal evidence for the completeness or incompleteness of this poem? What do we expect a completed poem to look like? What do we expect an incomplete poem to look like? What kind of signals can a poet give of his intended scope? What is illusory in structural terms, what is real? What is intended, and what is coincidence? Does the poet ever intend to deceive? And so on. In the scholarly controversy that has raged over this problem, particularly in the fifties and sixties, commentators have argued for their individual positions not, generally, by pointing out faulty reasoning or adducing new evidence, but precisely by disputing the *validity* of what their predecessors had cited as evidence; in other words, we seem to have moved away from the domain of rational argument-from-probability into a battleground where attractive theory rivals attractive theory in a war that can never end because the very terms of the conflict are in dispute. It is obvious that the problem cannot be dealt with as a purely philological concern; it is a problem that has been shown to be inseparable from that awesome, tremendous question: 'What is Lucan's poem *about*?' But there's the rub: without an ending, we cannot

234

know what Lucan's poem is about, for the end is one of the single most important constituents of a poem's 'meaning'. As Pompey by dying is turned from weak and would-be tyrant into beloved republican martyr, so the possible endings of the poem might have made Lucan anything from a Stoic asserting the glory of suicide, to a revolutionary preaching the glory of tyrannicide, to an imperial mole celebrating the glories of a world pacified. From there, it is one step into the abyss. The incompleteness of the *Bellum Civile* is its Achilles' heel, is the handle by which scholarship has tried to control the poem's message,[33] to turn dissatisfaction with the end as we have it into a means by which to force Lucan to be what the various global visions have needed him to be: a Stoic, a revolutionary, a hypocrite. It is only rarely that the important question is asked: 'What does the poem mean with the ending it actually has?' That was the question asked by Heinz Haffter in a magnificent article in 1957; and that is the question to which we will return in the next section.

But in the meantime, I want to look a little more closely at the various arguments for continuations of the epic that have been made with such ferocious fecundity in the scholarship of the past. The literature on the subject is vast, and the survey I offer is of necessity brief and selective; it is to be hoped that such a lightning tour may none the less give a flavour of the kind of issues regularly raised, if only to give some substance to my assertion that the basis on which the various end-points have been proposed is far from satisfactory.[34]

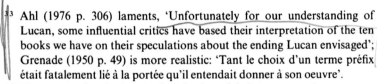

[33] Ahl (1976 p. 306) laments, 'Unfortunately for our understanding of Lucan, some influential critics have based their interpretation of the ten books we have on their speculations about the ending Lucan envisaged'; Grenade (1950 p. 49) is more realistic: 'Tant le choix d'un terme préfix était fatalement lié à la portée qu'il entendait donner à son oeuvre'.

[34] The proposed endpoints (and a selection of their proponents) are:

(1) The death of Cato: Pichon 1912 p. 270 (strictly, just after the African campaign); Pfligersdorffer 1959 pp. 359ff; Rutz 1965 pp. 262–71; Frank 1970; Due 1970 (his revised opinion: see the discussion of Marti's paper in Marti 1970 pp. 41–2); Ahl 1976 pp. 306–26; Häussler 1978 pp. 257–8.

The Bellum Civile is unfinished, therefore it is unfinished

This is not a parody. I quote Rose:[35] 'For the purposes of the present enquiry, question 5 [What signs are there of incompleteness?] will assume that the text of Lucan, as we have it, is incomplete; that is, that Lucan did intend to write more.' Why *is* it necessary to make that assumption? Because the evidence would otherwise be inconclusive. Which of course it is. It is rare for the scholarship to be so open about its circularity; this particular logical fallacy is more often left hidden. The poem is unfinished – that is obvious, proven, hardly worth discussing, can be assumed on the basis of past work on the problem.[36] Past work on the problem of course proceeded from the same assumptions, and so backwards ... each new theory leaning on an old theory leaning on an older theory, like the soldiers on the hillock at Ilerda. It is high time the assumption was questioned; high time, indeed, considering that the external evidence points to a different conclusion, that the assumption was *reversed*, and that we attached some importance to the poem actually before us rather than to a hypothetical, manipulable fantasy. For the purposes of *this* enquiry, then, it will be assumed that the text of Lucan is complete, that is, that Lucan did *not* intend to write more; the task will now be to see how seriously this assumption can be challenged by the evidence usually adduced in support of the incompleteness hypothesis.

(2) The death of Caesar: Heitland p. xxxiv n. 1; Grenade 1950 pp. 48–50 (one option); Syndikus 1958 pp. 118–21; Marti 1970.
(3) Philippi: Weber 1829 pp. 569–82; Grenade 1950 pp. 48–50 (the other option); Due 1962 pp. 106ff (his early opinion).
(4) Actium: Bruère 1950; Thompson 1964.
(5) The epic is complete: Kaestner (cited by Haffter, but unavailable to me); Haffter 1957; Schrempp 1964; Brisset 1964 esp. p. 164 n. 2.

[35] Rose 1966 p. 389.
[36] Bruère 1950 p. 217, 'That Lucan's poem is incomplete, breaking off as it does in the midst of a sentence with Caesar in mortal peril on the Alexandrian mole, is too evident to require proof'.

Anticipation

It is prophesied that Sextus will see his father in Sicily; therefore Lucan's epic would have gone at least so far.[37] Civilwar battles fought after Pharsalus are mentioned or alluded to in the prologue, in prophecies, in Lucan's impassioned asides: Thapsus, Munda, Philippi, Mutina, Perusia, the Bellum Siculum, Actium. Therefore Lucan must have intended to include all, must have intended to include some, of these.[38] The assassination of Caesar is one of the most frequently anticipated events not yet in the poem. Of course, Lucan was to have treated the episode in full. And so on. Every prophetic anticipation of an event has been adduced to prove one ending or another. But we cannot proceed in this way. By the same sort of argument, the *Iliad* must end with the death of Achilles, the fall of Troy. Our experience of epic is that prophecy as often as not *forestalls* the need for later, fuller treatment; for prophecy and anticipation, like retrospect and precedent, all serve the end of contracting into a single, limited period the vaster scope, the wider implications. Not that the scholarship has been unaware of this delicate point; on the contrary, everyone but the hard-line proponents of the Actium end-point has allowed for the fact that there is a difference between anticipation which prepares us for later episodes, and anticipation which merely extends the implications of action within a more limited scope.[39] The problem arises when one tries to distinguish between the two, for the only real test is retrospective –

[37] Bruère 1950 pp. 228–9; Due 1962 p. 127; Thompson 1964 p. 147. On this particular problem, see chapter 6 pp. 201–4.

[38] Bruère 1950 p. 225ff; Dick 1963 p. 40 (on the Roman matron); Due 1962 pp. 129–30. Ahl (1976 pp. 311–16), discussing the matron's prophecy (1.678–95), rightly shows how the references to battles after Munda in fact preclude the possibility of their being dealt with in the poem.

[39] Grenade 1950 p. 48; Haffter 1957 p. 119; Syndikus 1958 pp. 118–19; Due 1962 p. 127; Brisset 1964 p. 142; Schrempp 1964 p. 3 and 91ff (on the epic tradition); Rutz 1965 p. 267; Albrecht 1970 p. 275 n. 6; Häussler 1978 p. 257.

that is, foretold events are indications of intended scope only if it in fact turns out that these events *were* dealt with in the poem. Scholarship has usually tried to draw the line somewhere;[40] but if one admits that one foreshadowed event may be beyond the scope of the poem, there is no compelling reason why all foreshadowed events should not be equally questionable as evidence for scope.

Preparation for significant characters

Characters are prepared in advance for important roles they will play later in the poem; meaning that characters who play important roles appear briefly in earlier parts of the poem. Thus Curio appears in book 1, preparing for his moment of glory and defeat in book 4; so too Cato's appearance in book 2 prepares for his lengthy march across Libya in book 9,[41] which in turn prepares for his suicide in an unwritten part of the poem;[42] so too Brutus' appearance in book 2 prepares for the Ides of March and Philippi;[43] and Sextus' appearance in book 6 implies a continuation at least as far as the Bellum Siculum.[44]

---

[40] Marti, for instance, quite arbitrarily uses frequency as the criterion: 'En général, quand une bataille est simplement mentionée, surtout si c'est dans une liste ou un catalogue, à l'intérieur d'une prophétie, cette mention ne représente pas nécessairement, à mon avis, un premier jalon signalant une scène à venir. Elle peut avoir cette fonction, mais peut aussi simplement avoir celle d'établir des rapports entre la guerre de César et certains événements ultérieurs ou passés, ou à en relier d'autres entre eux. Au contraire, les allusions à la mort de César sont aussi explicites qu'elles sont fréquentes' (1970 p. 28). Similarly, but obscurely, Heitland p. xxxiv n. 1.

[41] Syndikus 1958 p. 114.   [42] Rutz 1965 p. 268.

[43] Syndikus 1958 p. 119; Marti 1970 pp. 20–1: 'Lucain ne met jamais tant de soins à caractériser un personnage s'il n'a pas l'intention de lui faire jouer un rôle. La conversation [between Cato and Brutus in book 2] sert non seulement à préparer la tétrade-Caton; elle prépare également, à mon avis, la fonction vengeresse que Brutus remplira dans les scènes ultimes du poème'.

[44] Bruère 1950 pp. 228–9: 'The poet emphasises the role of Sextus to a degree quite unjustified by his actions at the time; the violence done in

Again, this is open to the objection that if *some* of these preparations are discounted, they can all be discounted. We cannot use this argument to prove an ending at Utica, since we have failed to account for Brutus, Sextus and others. Secondly, if this argument rests on an analysis of 'normal Lucanian practice', we must explain away all those characters who are not prepared for, and whose appearance manifestly does not prepare for any greater role later in the poem: Domitius, Afranius, Petreius, Appius, Cicero, Lentulus, Antony, Juba, Cleopatra, Pothinus, and, of lesser historicity, Scaeva, Vulteius, Amyclas, Cordus, Erictho. According to the unfalsifiable terms of the argument, these may indeed be explained away: some of these characters *would* have played a major role later, others historically had no role available to them, others were not important enough. But what positive evidence is there for character preparation? Curio is introduced in book 1 to reappear in book 4; and Cato is introduced in book 2 to reappear in book 9. This seems a slender basis on which to dismiss the rather more obvious deduction, founded on the poem as we have it, that *there is no rule about preparation*. Sometimes characters appear out of the blue and disappear back; sometimes they appear more than once in roles of approximately equal importance; and sometimes they have short preliminary roles followed by long important ones.

There is a moral to this confusion: again it is a problem of circularity. Preparation of characters for important roles is only 'normal Lucanian practice' *if* the poem is incomplete, for it is only then that we can explain why most of the evidence contradicts that analysis; and if preparation is normal Lucanian practice, then the poem may be incomplete.

this episode to historical fact, together with the allusions, fictional and otherwise, to Sextus' later career, can only be explained by the assumption that the civil warfare waged by Sextus after the death of his father and elder brother was to form an integral part of the poem'. But Lucan emphasises the role of (e.g.) Appius too, who is irrelevant to the poem.

Models

One can adduce ancient accounts of the civil-war period to show that, for instance, the civil wars from the crossing of the Rubicon until the battle of Actium were thought of as comprising a unity, or from the Rubicon until the Ides of March, or indeed any number of sequences longer than the one actually covered by Lucan. Since the poem promises to recount civil wars, one should expect more of civil-war history than Lucan gives us;[45] or since Lucan based his poem on the historiographers (particularly Livy), we should expect him to be working with the same conceptual unities that inform the work of his sources.[46] Choose your conceptual unity, and you have found the intended scope of the poem.

There are two main weaknesses in this argument. First, Lucan is not a historiographer; and while history is quite comfortable with the idea of treating a whole series of events from beginning to end, this is a technique that is basically foreign to epic poetry, which, as we have noted, prefers to compress the larger story into a single, limited, representative period;[47] and

---

[45] Bruère 1950 pp. 225ff.

[46] *Ibid.* p. 221, 'In view of Lucan's dependence upon Livy for his historical material, how the historian defined the period of civil strife is of particular significance, since it is probable that the poet would conceive the conflict, at least in its grand outlines, as did the historian he chose for his guide' – that is, that 'civil war' should embrace the twenty years from 49 to 30. Similarly Marti 1970 p. 7, arguing for a shorter period: 'Nous savons que Lucain a emprunté à l'historien [Livy] les lignes directrices, le mouvement, la substance historique de son poème. La confrontation des deux textes est donc justifiée lorsque nous cherchons à établir les limites chronologiques que le poète avait fixées à son récit. La distribution des épisodes chez Tite-Live, le schéma qu'il avait adopté pour son exposé, peuvent nous fournir sinon des arguments probants, du moins quelques analogies frappantes'.

[47] Bruère does cite poetic sources (Virgil, Horace, Ovid) for his thesis that the twenty years from the Rubicon to Actium were conceived as a unit; but of course it is one thing for a poet to *allude* to this concept in passing (as Lucan himself does), and quite another for a poet to base an entire poem on it. Bruère's citation of Petronius' *Bellum Civile* as evidence for this all-embracing view of the civil-war period (pp. 223–4) is perplexing;

besides, an epic which treated the whole civil-war period would be gargantuan.[48] Second, such arguments deny the possibility of innovation. There is, I think, no justification for assuming that Lucan *must* have worked in the same way as his sources, and every reason to believe that he would want to invent his own conceptual unities;[49] rather than rewriting the poem to fit these preconceived patterns, we should examine the poem as it is to see how it manipulates historiographical conceits and techniques for its own ends.

There is, in fact, a historiographical model to which the poem does fit very closely: Caesar's commentary on the civil war, which ends, abruptly enough, at the start of Caesar's war against the Alexandrians.[50] On the relevance of Caesar's work to Lucan's I have had much to say in the preceding chapters; and although it has been held in the past that Livy was far more important to Lucan as a source, I think nothing short of blindness can have allowed critics to ignore the Caesarian model, and make the most violent changes to Lucan's poem in order to fit it to a Livian model of which we know far too little and whose relevance should still be considered moot.[51] The

for although it is quite probable that Petronius' poem was written with Lucan's in mind (see e.g. Rose 1971 pp. 60– 8; the opposite case, however, is made by Grimal 1977 esp. pp. 239ff), it is precisely evidence for the opposite of the general point Bruère is making. That is, Petronius certainly does regard the civil-war period as continuing up to Actium; but this certainly does not imply anything about the scope of his poem, which actually ends before civil war has properly got going. This may seem a banal observation; but none the less Petronius is the counterexample to the (already absurd) rule that if an event is 'adumbrated' (Bruère's word) it must be within the poem's intended scope.

[48] Grenade 1950 p. 48; Marti 1970 p. 27; Ahl 1976 p. 308, 'In the first place, the sheer massiveness of the resultant opus is more suggestive of history than an epic; even as history it would probably have been longer than Livy ... It is hard to imagine that Lucan would have covered the remaining events in less than fifty additional books'.

[49] Due 1962 p. 126.

[50] The crucial point made by Haffter 1957 p. 121; on which see further below. Lucan's poem similarly *begins* in much the same place as Caesar's commentary.

[51] On this issue, see chapter 2 pp. 15–19.

poem as we have it fits Caesar and not Livy; and since we have yet to find any positive evidence for supposing the poem incomplete, there can be no basis on which to assert that the Livian model should predominate.

Tetrads

A useful observation is made: books 4 and 8 both end with a death which is fêted with something like a funerary eulogy. It is further argued that the ends of these books mark a definite pause in the poem's structure (a claim for which I can find no basis).[52] The argument continues: the poem is therefore structured in blocks of four books ending with the death of a major character. And so, book 12 would have ended with the death of Cato, and perhaps book 16 with the death of Caesar.[53]

The poem is not made up (exclusively) of tetrads, since it is ten books long.[54] Once again the critics are inventing a new poem to provide them with the evidence to back up their claims. Curio is hardly as 'important' a character as Pompey; and though in the suggested scheme this is forgivable, since the deaths of Cato and Caesar would allow Curio to fit in as a lesser example in a greater pattern,[55] it is not possible to argue from Curio and Pompey alone that such a scheme exists. But

[52] Syndikus, who proposes a tetradic structure on thematic grounds (books 1–4 are introductory, while 5–8 are concerned with the build-up to Pharsalus and its aftermath: pp. 109ff), none the less argues, more convincingly in my opinion, that nearly all Lucan's books have a definite beginning and end (pp. 108–9). More specific thematic arguments are put forward by Rutz (1965 pp. 262–3) and Frank 1970.

[53] Schönberger 1961 p. 69 and Rutz 1965 p. 268 for the death of Cato; Marti 1970 pp. 10–15, for the death of Caesar.

[54] Consider, too, that if it was the first three books that Lucan published in advance of the rest, it is unlikely that he considered the first four books an indissoluble unity; so Ahl 1976 p. 318. Tetrads may, however, be one of many helpful ways of viewing the poem's structure (at least in the first eight books): see below.

[55] Thus Schönberger 1957 p. 254, and Marti 1970 p. 32: 'Chaque mort qui sert de conclusion à l'une des tétrades dépasse celle qui la précède en puissance dramatique et symbolique. Celle de César devait fournir le point culminant ...', though one is left wondering how Lucan would have managed to outdo the death of Pompey to the same degree by which the death of Pompey outdoes the death of Curio.

let us go on. The Livian model is again adduced by Marti, in a manner which sets a standard for muddiness of logic. Lucan's first two books correspond to Livy's book 109; Lucan's third and fourth book to Livy 110.[56] Not quite: Lucan has made some changes in order to give the death of Curio pride of place at the end of the first tetrad.[57] We are told that this is a striking similarity. But the further we go, the less striking it becomes. Lucan's second tetrad ends somewhere in the middle of Livy 112; the final two books of Lucan fill out the rest of Livy 112.[58] On this basis Marti is willing to deduce further correspondences between later Livian books and intended but unwritten books by Lucan: the death of Cato, the end of the hypothetical third tetrad, would bring us to the middle of book 114; the death of Caesar at the end of the fourth tetrad would coincide with the end of the last of Livy's books on the Caesarian civil war.[59] She concludes: 'Malgré ces légères divergences, ces différences d'accentuation et d'articulation, la correspondance entre les deux textes est frappante' (p. 13). Considering that Lucan is treating the same historical period as Livy, the difference between the two texts, it seems to me, could not be more complete. As Marti's argument goes on, the 'légères différences' receive less and less notice: 'Nous avons vu que deux livres, plus ou moins, de Tite-Live, c'est-à-dire un quart de son Bellum Civile, correspondent a une tétrade de Lucain' (p. 114). No: what we have seen is that the first tetrad covers nearly the same material as Livy 109–10, that books 5–7 correspond to 111, and that books 8–10 correspond to 112; implying, if anything, a structure of one tetrad and two triads. The rest is pure hypothesis; and when we are told that Lucan would have had to *alter his pace* in order to fit later events into the Livian, tetradic pattern,[60] we must know for certain that Marti has pulled the rug from under her own feet,

---

[56] *Ibid.* p. 10.   [57] *Ibid.* pp. 10–11.

[58] *Ibid* p. 11; Lucan's new expansiveness in comparison with his Livian 'model' is, revealingly, explained by rhetoric or padding.

[59] *Ibid.* pp. 11–13.

[60] *Ibid.* p. 12, '... ce qui laisse à penser qu'il aurait abrégé un peu plus rigoureusement le récit de la campagne en Espagne que celui des récits précédents'.

since she bases everything on the premise that Lucan would have continued composing in the same way as he had begun.

Against Haffter

Haffter's article of 1957, in which he argued for completeness, partly on the grounds that the *Bellum Civile* ends in the same place as Caesar's commentary, and partly with the help of a keen aesthetic perception of what actually seemed to be going on in the poem, is one of the great moments of Lucanian scholarship. The colossal indecency of his position and his argumentative technique sparked a reaction which has meant that he has since been universally dismissed as an aberration. But while Haffter made the strategic error of choosing an unpopular point of view, and the tactical error of using some arguments which were definitely implausible, his fundamental thesis was based on an enthusiasm for the poem and a healthy scorn for the affectations of contemporary criticism that gave him the vision to see what no-one – not even Kaestner, I think – had seen before him, and what very few have seen since. The proponents of the incompleteness hypothesis were compelled for the first time to consider the possibility that the critical tradition might be wrong, and although their first line of defence tended to be unscholarly, Haffter's article became the peg on which to hang a few refutations of the completeness of the poem that at least went through the motions of serious discussion. Many of these refutations consisted in emphatic reiteration of arguments I have already discussed, and therefore were not refutations at all; but what is new deserves some notice.

Haffter, I think rather crudely, proclaimed that the *Bellum Civile* should be divided into two halves of five books each, and that these pentads correspond to hexads in Virgil's *Aeneid*.[61] The evidence he cited was very weak, and was rightly attacked: most notoriously, he wished to see a parallel between Caesar's crossing of the Adriatic (*BC* 5) and Aeneas' journey through the underworld (*Aen.* 6; both feature the

---

[61] Haffter 1957 pp. 124–5.

hero's *Alleingang*), whereas, it was objected, the real parallel
lay between Virgil's underworld episode and Lucan's Erictho
episode.[62] None the less, though wrong in detail, there is much
to be said for Haffter's division into pentads, not least because
Virgil's sixth book is mirrored in *both* Lucan's fifth book (the
Delphic oracle) *and* sixth book (Erictho). Ultimately I think
that arguments about structure get us nowhere, because structure is more profound and complicated a thing than any mere
division and subdivision into equal parts: structure is made
strong by the fact that there will always be competing ways of
viewing it, so that it should not so much surprise us as delight
us to find triads and tetrads and pentads working across each
other as the poem proceeds.[63] Hence it is hardly an objection
to Haffter's theory when Marti complains: 'La division en pen-
tades ne tient pas compte des coupures très distinctes après les
livres quatre et huit' (*ibid.* p. 18),[64] even if we believe that
tetrads exist.[65]

Haffter had claimed that it is too much of a coincidence that
Lucan's poem was cut off at the very point where it coincided
with the ending of Caesar's commentary;[66] Rutz counters
that it is too much of a coincidence that Lucan should have
died immediately after completing his masterpiece.[67] This
would be a fair point, save for the fact that it is not necessary
to claim that Lucan's death occurred immediately after (Rutz:
'unmittelbar nach') completion of the poem. We do not know

---

[62] Rutz 1965 p. 269; Marti 1970 p. 18. Not that Haffter was unaware of this
parallel (1957 p. 120).

[63] Multiple structural systems are proposed by Schönberger 1957 pp. 253–
4, Frank 1970, and Häussler 1978 p. 257.

[64] Similarly Rutz 1965 pp. 263–4. To which we reply, in the same vein: the
division into tetrads does not take account of the very distinct ending of
the poem, at book 10 ... The pot is calling the kettle black when Rutz
later complains (pp. 268–9), 'Haffters Meinung, die *Pharsalia* sei in
Pentaden komponiert, ist nicht Grundlage, sondern Konsequenz [seiner]
Hypothese'.

[65] Marti's only two other objections are: first that book 10 is much shorter
than the others, on which see my n. 74; and second, that Statius considered the poem incomplete, which is a false deduction.

[66] Haffter 1957 p. 122.   [67] Rutz 1965 p. 269.

for certain when Lucan did reach the planned conclusion of his epic, for the external evidence we have will only allow us to deduce that the poem was never published during his lifetime – not that he was writing up to the very last minute; it is quite possible that the end was reached many months before the suicide. And even if we cannot accept this view of the poem's chronology, we are only left with a choice of coincidences: both would be remarkable, but one of them must be only coincidence.[68]

Rutz's second objection is that the poem as it stands is not Catonian enough;[69] that is an objection which is, as I have argued before now, based on a prejudice. There is little reason to suppose that Lucan is pro-Cato any more than he is pro-Pompey,[70] but scholarship has regarded Lucan's decision not to emphasise the figure of Cato as a mistake or a failure. Rutz's third objection – in many ways the most interesting – is that the ending as we have it is anticlimactic, and that the poem lacks a proper τέλος; I will deal with this in the next section.

Pfligersdorffer, countering Haffter's appeal to the Caesarian model for Lucan's ending, maintains that Caesar's commentary is itself 'incomplete', in that Caesar was forced to stop where he did by circumstance; and that Lucan would hardly have based his ending on a model that he knew lacked a proper conclusion.[71] We may object: first, it is not clear that

---

[68] It may interest the reader to know that this, my final chapter, was composed when I was one month before the age (25 years and nearly 6 months) at which Lucan killed himself. Coincidence?

[69] Rutz 1965 p. 269; see too Pfligersdorffer 1959 p. 359.

[70] Haffter's view of Cato as a figure of less prominence than Caesar or Pompey is entirely just (1957 p. 125).

[71] Pfligersdorffer 1959 p. 360. It seems to have been well known from an early date that Caesar left off writing at the beginning of the *Bellum Alexandrinum*; Hirtius, in *Bell. Gall.* 8 *pref.*, claims to have completed Caesar's unfinished work from that point; and Suetonius later provides different suggestions for the authorship of the non-Caesarian books following the *Bellum Civile* (Suet. *Jul.* 56). For the controversy over whether Caesar intended to write more, but was prevented, see on the one side Barwick 1938 pp. 132ff, and on the other, Abel 1958 p. 61.

Caesar's commentary is incomplete, and on the contrary it is
suggested that Caesar stopped abruptly where he did with deliberate intent: in Ahl's words, 'Caesar concludes where he
does so that he can represent the wars after Pompey's death as
foreign rather than civil'.[72] Second, even if Caesar's commentary is, accidentally, incomplete, and Lucan knew it to be so,
why should he *not* have wished to base his ending on Caesar's
non-ending?[73] In the following section I shall suggest some
reasons why a non-ending would be a very appropriate model
for the conclusion of Lucan's epic.

Endlessness

We can now turn to what must be regarded as the principal
objection to believing the *Bellum Civile* complete as it stands. I
quote Rutz:

[Haffter] glaubt, so ein einheitliches, in sich geschlossenes Gedicht vor sich
zu haben. Aber welches soll das τέλος dieses Gedichtes sein? Und nicht auf
die ὅλη, sondern auf die ὅλη καὶ τελεία πρᾶξις kommt es doch der
peripatetischen Lehre an, der Lucan im Aufbau der Werkteile wie des
Ganzen folgt. (Rutz 1965 p. 269)

And indeed Rutz seems to have a point. When all is said and
done, the poem does have a very peculiar shape: book 9 is
absurdly long, book 10 absurdly short;[74] the poem ends sud-

---

[72] Ahl 1976 p. 307. Further: 'Lucan would hardly want to concede this
view'; but Lucan has taken great pains to ensure that this view is *not*
conceded, by insisting that the civil war will carry on and on far past the
end of the poem: see below. If Lucan chose to end in the same place as
Caesar, that does not imply that he did so *for the same reason as* Caesar.

[73] Dionysius of Halicarnassus (*Imit.* 6.3.2) cites the case of the historian
Philistos, who imitated the broken-off ending of Thucydides' history
(ἐζήλωκεν δὲ πρῶτον μὲν τὸ τὴν ὑπόθεσιν ἀτελῆ καταλιπεῖν τὸν αὐτὸν
τρόπον). I cannot, finally, agree with Brisset (1964 p. 165 n. 2) when she
says that Lucan's continuation as far as the battle on the Alexandrian
mole is a 'completion' of Caesar's rather abrupt ending, though she is not
far from the truth. I prefer to *stress* the abruptness of Lucan's ending; see
infra.

[74] Syndikus 1958 p. 107 and n. 26; Rose 1966 p. 387; Marti 1970 p. 18. The
short length of book 10 need not imply anything missing from the end;
for the excessive length of book 9 is equally striking, and must be taken

denly, anticlimactically, and apparently in the middle of an episode, after having dragged on with no apparent purpose for two books after the high points of Pharsalus and the assassination of Pompey. If one works from the assumption that everything that is not climax must be preparation for a climax, it is hardly surprising that it has been felt that the final two books must have been intended as a slow build-up to an episode which Lucan never managed to write; without such a climactic episode, the poem does seem to have no τέλος.[75]

But let us be precise. Bruère's statement that the poem breaks off in mid-sentence is outrageous, and without the shadow of basis in the text.[76] More than that, the last twelve lines of book 10 constitute what is quite recognisable as an epilogue (see below). So what is at issue here is not the question of whether or not the text literally 'breaks off', which it clearly does not, but whether the poem is felt to have an ending that is, in a broader aesthetic sense, smooth, rounded, satis-

as part of the same problem. Both sides of the dispute have noted that the last 150 lines of book 9 (the part dealing with Caesar's journey from Pharsalus to Egypt) would be more at home as an introduction to book 10 (see Haffter 1957 p. 119 and n. 5; and Syndikus 1958 p. 107: 'Im 9. Buch ist auffallend, dass die Caesarhandlung des 10. Buches bereits hier beginnt. Stoffmangel in der Handlung des 9. Buches kann nicht der Grund sein: das 9. Buch wäre auch ohne die Caesarszenen das längste Lucans'). Re-dividing the books accordingly would leave book 10 quite long enough to pass muster; but that is a drastic solution. If the books have been transmitted as Lucan left them, the peculiar distribution of the lines gives us no basis on which to argue that Lucan failed to complete his poem; merely that, at worst, he did not manage to arrange it properly before he died (though it is hard to imagine how the problem could have arisen); or, at best, that he felt there was something to gain from arranging it so provocatively – for instance, the effect of surprise at the brevity of the final book.

[75] Bruère 1950 p. 230, '... the circumstance that Lucan did not bring his narrative to a close with the aftermath of Pharsalia. On the contrary, after the death of Pompey the story continues with renewed vigour; the end is nowhere in sight'. See also Syndikus 1958 pp. 115–16 (the new beginning in books 9 and 10), and p. 120 (thematic threads that should be continued after book 10); Marti 1970 p. 31; and Ahl 1976 p. 308.

[76] Bruère 1950 p. 217; echoed by Ahl 1976 p. 307.

fying; whether, to use Rutz's terms, the poem fits into the Aristotelian mould of the ὅλη καὶ τελεία πρᾶξις. But this, exactly this, should sound the warning note. *Is* the Aristotelian ideal relevant here at all?[77] No doubt Lucan was aware of such Aristotelian formulations, if only indirectly; now on what grounds can we agree with Rutz that 'Lucan followed Aristotle as much in the structure of the parts as of the whole'? Ancient theory, that is prescriptive 'how-to' theoretical writing on poetry, is largely a red herring if it is ever supposed that the poets used it as the basis for the proper composition of their works; and indeed we have no evidence at all for the assumption, commonly made these days, that after Aristotle there was any major tradition of *detailed* theoretical material on epic or even, more widely, on genre.[78] Of course what the epic poets did was derive whatever idea they had of what epic was from the sum of the epic tradition that preceded them;[79] and if we want to know on what basis Lucan wrote his poem, we must look not to the formulations of Aristotle, but to the examples of Homer, who founded the tradition, and of

---

[77] Häussler's caution (1978 p. 258) unfortunately proves to be a feint.

[78] *Pace* Hinds 1987 p. 116: 'The Augustans are heirs to a tradition of Alexandrian learning one of whose specialities is εἰδογραφία, research on poetic genres. The well-known passage on genres defined by metre and subject in the *Ars Poetica* (Horace *A.P.* 73–85) ... shows the influence of this tradition; and, whilst Horace's words may be no literal guide to the practice of Augustan poetry, they are a very important witness to the theory which lies behind the practice'. In the first place, the word εἰδογραφία is attested only once, very late, with the meaning 'putting on make-up'. The librarian Apollonius was called εἰδογράφος not because he was noted for his work on genres (Brink 1971 ad *A.P.* 73–85), but because he classified lyric poems according to their musical types (Pfeiffer 1968 p. 184). There is no other Greek evidence. The Roman evidence is confined to three passages, of which two (Hor. *A.P.* 73–85 and Ov. *Rem.* 371–82) deal with each genre, superficially, in a line or two, while the remaining one (Accius *Didascalica* fr. 13 Morel), in its fragmentary state, need imply nothing more detailed than what we find in Horace and Ovid. The most likely deduction is that all three are playing with a traditional topos of rapid listing of genre-characteristics; and there is nothing to suggest an Alexandrian tradition of detailed genre-theory.

[79] Albrecht 1970 p. 271.

the later epicists, each one expanding and subverting the example of the last, until Virgil, Ovid, and (if only they were extant) the epics of Lucan's own time.

Genre is nothing more nor less than *imitatio* on a grand scale; and this has some profound implications. For built into the practice of *imitatio* is the requirement of deviation, subversion, change. In other words, genre is not prescriptive; it is a challenge. And for this reason, even if (as is probably the case) there existed an intuitive perception of the structure of epic as a unity with beginning, middle and end, a perception which coincided with Aristotle's formulation of a ὅλη καὶ τελεία πρᾶξις, it is entirely illegitimate to foist this perception on Lucan as if it were a rule from which he could not possibly deviate. Quite the contrary, it is in the field of narrative technique, as much as in every other aspect of epic composition, that Lucan shows himself to be the perverse, destructive iconoclast to whom nothing, absolutely nothing, is sacred. If we have learned anything from Lucan's obsession with delay and postponement, and his exaltation of anticlimax into the ruling narratological principle,[80] then a neat, rounded, climactic τέλος for the poem is absolutely the last thing we should expect.

Virgil made the τέλος of the epic poem a live issue; the astonishingly abrupt ending of his *Aeneid* may, indeed, be

---

[80] Rutz (1965 p. 262) finds the Aristotelian ideal of build-up to climactic telos at work even on the microscopic level of the *scene*; our examination of, for instance, the Delphic episode, will have shown this to be an illusion. Salutary remarks on Lucan's narrative technique from Johnson 1987 p. 110: '... with the single exception of book 8, where the pathos of Pompey ironically takes on something like Aristotelian tragic unity, this epic consistently saps the comforting logic of chronology by obscuring transitions from one event to another, by expanding various kinds of digressions and by vividly dramatizing the irrelevant and the unreal. Even after allowing for the complexity of the historical materials ... we may argue that Lucan deliberately complicates and further disorders the complex untidiness of the story he has chosen to tell ... the very concept of unity of action is useless to him except insofar as it represents a false and dangerous myth (disorder masquerading as order) that satire may demolish in order to let its poet approach the truth of chaos'.

squared with an Aristotelian idea of how epic should be constructed,[81] but this is to elide the sense of unexpectedness which is surely its most striking feature. With no epilogue, with no funeral rites, no marriage and no resolution of differences between Trojans and Latins to follow it, the death of Turnus constitutes a classic 'surprise ending'.[82] But while Virgil's epic can be thought to have reached at least the beginning of a τέλος – though much remains unsatisfactory, unresolved – Lucan has out-Virgiled Virgil in presenting us with an ending which shows us no death of a principal character, no resolution of a crisis, an ending which in fact at the very last moment points explicitly to its own inconclusiveness. Rather than using this remarkable finale as evidence that Lucan really intended to go on further, can we not see that the lack of a 'proper' conclusion is in fact *the* great strength of the poem's ending, stimulated not only by the exigencies of genre and creative, innovative *imitatio*, but by the nature of the subject-matter itself?

For the civil war can have no ending. Everything about the war and the poem is boundless, illimitable, infinite. Caesar's ambition, *nil actum credens cum quid superesset agendum*; Pompey's tomb, which spatially confines him to a few feet of earth, but by a trick of rhetoric expands over the whole world; the enormity of the *nefas* in which the whole universe participates; the grotesque repetitiveness of the series of civil wars which go on and on over the same ground *ad nauseam*. To treat all of this in its entirety – in any case an impossible task – to gather everything into the form of completeness, would be to contain and limit what must, in Lucan's terms, be uncontainable. These are general points; more specifically we see shot through the poem a concern with the question of what is

---

[81] Rutz 1965 p. 268.

[82] See Farron 1982, contrasting the Aeneid's end with the 'normal' practice of slow wind-down; though I wonder if he is not overstating the case. Either by coincidence or design, incompleteness (and its symptom, the sudden end) is almost a characteristic of the genre; and it is hard not to believe that Virgil and Lucan were conscious of this when they came to write their own endings.

the *finis* – what is the *finis* of this civil war, of this story, of this poem. It is this very question that Appius and Sextus pose to their respective prophetesses; but earlier than that the problem is raised by the astrologer Nigidius Figulus:

> et superos quid prodest poscere finem?
> cum domino pax ista venit.   (1.669–70)

A fascinating passage which, so far from proving that the poem must end with the coming of the *dominus* (be he Caesar or Octavian),[83] suggests precisely the opposite, that since the only possible resolution of the civil war is the advent of a *dominus*, the poem must have no resolution. Later, in book 5, the war-weary soldiers in Caesar's legions complain:

> finis quis quaeritur armis?
> quid satis est, si Roma parum est?   (5.273–4)

A question that at this early point in the story may seem little more than rhetorical: what is there left to achieve, if Caesar has conquered Rome? Pharsalus, of course, and the death of Pompey. But compare this later passage from book 9, from another mutiny which is clearly parallel to the Caesarian mutiny in book 5, where, this time, it is the republican soldiers who complain:

> nam quis erit finis si nec Pharsalia pugnae
> nec Pompeius erit?   (9.232–3)

That is exactly our question. We have seen Caesar victorious,[84] we have seen Pompey murdered; where now? Thapsus, of course, and the death of Cato, events that we will not see represented in the poem. But if they *were* represented, there would always remain that question, *where will it end*? What will the *finis* be, if Thapsus and Cato's suicide are not enough? Munda, Philippi.... But at every stage we will already have had too much, and what is to come is always more than too much. At every stage we will have to ask *quis finis*? because

---

[83] Bruère 1950 p. 227.

[84] Pharsalus *is* the *finis* promised by Pompey, win or lose: 'finis civilibus armis / quem quaesistis, adest' (7.343–4).

history, relentlessly, continues to heap more and more onto the bulk of the *nefas* that has already been enacted. And this ultimate outrage, that the outrages never end, this grinding *ennui*, this satiety to the point of sickness as we find that nothing ever gets better, it only gets worse, more enormous, and beyond[85] – this, if anything, is central to Lucan's extraordinary vision.

A poem must stop somewhere; it is rhetorically, poetically, aesthetically inefficient to represent superfluity by being superfluous. For a poem whose premise is the endlessness of its material the only possible ending is one which proclaims in its last throes how much more there is yet to come. In addition, the civil war is a dilemma without a solution; it is a war where no one side is right, where merely to take sides – or to take the side of impartiality – is wrong. For a poem whose premise is the impossibility of its resolution, the only possible ending is one which cuts us off at that moment where nothing is resolved; which freezes for us the *par quod semper habemus* locked forever, exemplarily, in bitter, precarious balance. It is with these two points in mind – endlessness and unresolvability – that we should now turn to the last twelve lines of Lucan's epic.

Although Lucan's end-point clearly parallels the end of Caesar's commentary, the parallel is not exact, since Lucan actually ends at a point which is treated a little way into the pseudo-Caesarian *Bellum Alexandrinum* – a fact which has been used insensitively as evidence against the belief that the parallel exists at all.[86] But we should allow Lucan some leeway; and the fact that Lucan has chosen to carry on the story

---

[85] On Pharsalus as the first phase of a struggle that will get much worse, see the discussion by Marti 1970 pp. 24–5, and in Lucan's epic such passages as 7.871–2: 'Hesperiae clades et flebilis unda Pachyni / et Mutina et Leucas puros fecere Philippos'. I am not convinced by Ahl's attempt to show that Lucan tones down the importance of these later conflicts (1976 pp. 312–13).

[86] Notice the emphasis on the 'almost' in Pfligersdorffer 1959 p. 360, 'beide Werke reichen ungefähr (aber nur ungefähr!) gleich weit'; and in Rutz 1965 p. 268, 'den (fast!) gleichen Schlusspunkt'.

slightly further than Caesar suggests that he was not content
with merely repeating the Caesarian ending, but was actually
concerned to finish his poem at a point which allowed for
some overdetermination. And the point he has chosen to end
on represents quite an extraordinary moment. Caesar is belea-
guered on Pharos, attacked from all sides, while he murders
Pothinus (the last event reported in Caesar's *Bellum Civile*),
and sees Achillas murdered by Arsinoe. Ganymede rouses up
the Alexandrians against Caesar again, with some success;
such success, indeed, that the battle can be referred to as a
summum discrimen which might have been the end of Caesar.
The extra events covered by Lucan take place, it is true, over a
period of several months; but are rapidly skimmed over in a
précis of barely fifteen lines. With the battle hardly begun, the
narrative stops. Lucan concludes his poem with twelve lines of
reflection on the dangers of Caesar's position and his state of
mind. It is instructive at this point to compare what the author
of the *Bellum Alexandrinum* has to say on this same moment:

quo facto dubitatione sublata tantus incessit timor ut ad extremum casum
periculi omnes deducti viderentur atque alii morari Caesarem dicerent quin
navis conscendere iuberet, alii multo gravius extimescerent, quod neque
celari Alexandrini possent in apparanda fuga, cum tam parvo spatio dis-
tarent ab ipsis, neque illis imminentibus atque insequentibus ullus in navis
receptus daretur ... Caesar suorum timorem consolatione et ratione
minuebat. (*Bell. Alex.* 7.1 and 8.1)

Not such an extraordinary moment according to the historian:
Caesar's troops are in a state of panic, occasioned, as it happens, by a contamination of water-sources with seawater (*Bell.
Alex.* 6). Caesar reacts to this predicament by delivering a
speech of encouragement with a precise plan of action for ob-
taining fresh water. And so history continues as it has always
done: Caesar fights his way through every difficulty, and is
eventually victorious.

In Lucan, however, the episode has been given a remarkable new bent. Caesar is suddenly (*subitus*) – astonishingly –
terrified, trapped, caught in a tangle from which no escape is
possible:

molis in exiguae spatio stipantibus armis
dum parat in vacuas Martem transferre carinas,
dux Latius tota subitus formidine belli
cingitur: hinc densae praetexunt litora classes,
hinc tergo insultant pedites. via nulla salutis,
non fuga, non virtus; vix spes quoque mortis honestae.
non acie fusa nec magnae stragis acervis
vincendus tum Caesar erat sed sanguine nullo.
captus sorte loci pendet; dubiusque timeret
optaretne mori... (10.534–43)

Lucan has taken his cue from the report of the historian that Caesar's troops were afraid, and transferred this fear to Caesar himself. What we must emphasise is that this terror and helplessness on Caesar's part are uncharacteristic:[87] Caesar often comes close to disaster, but his standard reaction is to plunge headlong into peril with an arrogant confidence that Fortune will see him through. And this fear that descends so suddenly on him now is more than the local fear of a perilous situation – no mention here of undrinkable water: it is the *tota ... formidine belli*, 'the whole fear of war', as if all the horror recounted in the course of the poem grips him now, here, at this last moment, in retrospect.

Here too, briefly, as the poem ebbs away in its last four lines, we have what is literally a retrospect:

dubiusque timeret
optaretne mori respexit in agmine denso
Scaevam perpetuae meritum iam nomina famae
ad campos, Epidamne tuos, ubi solus apertis
obsedit muris calcantem moenia Magnum. (10.542–6)

Caesar sees Scaeva among his soldiers at Pharos; the historical Scaeva did not die at Dyrrachium, and there is some grotesque humour to be got out of Lucan's version in which a soldier

[87] This I take to be the drift of Ahl's comment (1976 p. 306): 'Yet book 10 shows [Lucan] in a mood of greater confidence. Caesar suddenly becomes more vulnerable, and Caesarism less monolithic'. For Gagliardi (1978 p. 249) the effect is to give Caesar a certain humanity. On Caesar's fearlessness, see Marti 1945 p. 365, Syndikus 1958 p. 96.

who receives so many wounds that there is no room left for more should be allowed to survive a combat which would have killed any ordinary mortal. But in *respexit* there is also the metaphorical sense of looking back in time,[88] as Caesar (or Lucan) recalls Scaeva's moment of glory on the plains of Dyrrachium. It is a moment of retrospect that is, for Caesar, utterly unprecedented in the poem. Pompey is the man in love with his past; but Caesar never looks at anything but the future – except in these final lines.

Scaeva's appearance at this point is not fortuitous, for Dyrrachium was the other place where Caesar narrowly escaped defeat. So this reminiscence underlines, or undermines, a curious effect which has received little notice from the commentators: Alexandria *appears* to be the scene of Caesar's final defeat. There is, simply, no way out; Caesar is trapped. It is Dyrrachium all over again, except that this time we are not to be shown how Caesar lived to fight another day (nor can we guess!). If we did not know anything about the history of the civil war, we should have every right to imagine that Caesar did not escape. If we did not know ... but of course we do know; and Lucan has taken care to remind us, only five lines before our epilogue:

> dum patrii veniant in viscera Caesaris enses
> Magnus inultus erit. (10.528–9)

If the project of the poem is to see Pompey avenged, then this last-minute anticipation has told us that the poem, ending where it does, has failed to tell the whole story. And of course, Alexandria cannot be Caesar's place of doom if he must face the Ides of March in Rome. What is happening should be clear: with one gesture Lucan is building up the battle on the mole (out of nothing) into a crisis which has all the trappings

---

[88] So Pompey recalls his past happiness in 7.688 (the same verb); the symbolism of 'looking back' is obvious, and surfaces most strikingly (in this poem) at the beginning of book 3, where Pompey watches the shores of Italy recede into the distance (Hübner 1984 pp. 229–30). Among the commentaries, Bourgery/Ponchont ad loc. insist on the literal sense here; Haskins and Griffa are less certain; Weise sees a metaphor.

of a final, climactic, moment, in which the protagonist meets his end; and with another gesture he is insisting that the end is still a long way off, that Caesar will escape even from here, as he did from Dyrrachium.[89]

Fear and retrospect, then, mark out this final passage as significantly at variance with the characterisation of Caesar in the body of the poem; and together with this defeat-no-defeat mark the epilogue as an 'extraordinary moment' on which to end. What is most extraordinary about it is brought out by Haffter's stirring rhetoric:

> Cäsar am Anfang und am Ende! Was uns die stoffliche Abgrenzung des Werkes, der Anschluss an Cäsars eigene Schrift, zu glauben nahelegt und was anzunehmen uns der Inhalt vielfach im einzelnen veranlasst ... dahin weist uns auch der Aufbau der Dichtung: Lucans Epos ist ein Cäsar-Epos; dem Cäsar als dem gigantischen Täter des Bösen im Bürgerkrieg, ihm gilt das Interesse, ihm die künstlerische Sympathie des Dichters. (p. 126).

Haffter is of course going too far; but his comment does have the virtue of emphasising for us one crucial aspect of the poem's conclusion: that Caesar has pride of place, a position of honour, and that by implication the poem is a glorification of Caesar. But running counter to this pseudo-encomiastic function are a number of factors of which Haffter has failed to take account. Caesar is suffering a *defeat* – is terrified, helpless – so that the epilogue presents us with a tension between Caesar's implicit prominence and his explicit vulnerability. Furthermore, it is not strictly true to say that Caesar is 'at the end'; obviously he is the central character of the final episode, but in the very last three lines the attention veers away from him, and pride of place is granted, first, to one of Lucan's minor characters, and then to Caesar's arch-enemy. Scaeva is, perplexingly, congratulated as having earned *perpetuae ... nomina famae*; in

---

[89] According to Haffter 1957 p. 124, Pfligersdorffer 1959 p. 361, Schrempp 1964 p. 129, and Gagliardi 1978 p. 246, Scaeva is there to assure us that Caesar will escape; and certainly, Lucan's insistence on using the name 'Caesar' for Caesar's troops (see esp. 10488–9 'adest defensor ubique / Caesar et hos aditus gladiis, hos ignibus arcet'; also 10.507) implies a one-man-against-an-army scenario which parallels the Scaeva story; hence, if Scaeva escaped, Caesar will escape. Or perhaps not ...

other words, the claim that *should* have been made for Cae-sar[90] is made instead for one of his insignificant underlings, as if to displace Caesar from the *fama* of which this poem is apparently the celebration.[91]

And finally, to Pompey is given, literally, the last word. Pompey's name (specifically 'Magnus') is also the final word of book 2, and appears in the final line of books 5 and 8; so that book 10's ending conforms to Lucanian precedent,[92] and suggests that whatever may be the true state of the poem, complete or incomplete, we cannot suppose that composition was broken off suddenly at line 546, mid-sentence or mid-book: there *is* an epilogue. Further, if the poem is complete, then it is clear that Pompey's name in the last place gestures towards the Homeric model of Ἕκτορος ἱπποδάμοιο at the end of the Iliad: ending, that is, with the name of the antagonist.[93] Gestures only; for the Iliad ends at a point (Hector's funeral rites) where Hector's name is a natural enough thing to mention, whereas Lucan seems to make a point of picking Pompey's name out of the blue, and making it the climactic point of an episode to which it has no special relevance. And it is, of course, the very irrelevance of Pompey in this context that makes the Iliadic allusion so striking, and again urges us to see Caesar's absence from the last lines of 'his' poem as a deliberate displacement, a poetic slight contrived by the creator against his creation.

The epilogue *is* perplexing: it presents us, as we have seen, with a central character at his moment of final defeat which is

---

[90] And nearly was, ten lines earlier: 'potuit discrimine summo / Caesaris una dies in famam et saecula mitti' (10.532–3). Lucan also promises fame to Caesar in the apostrophe 9.980–6. Scaeva has his fame already (*iam* 544); Caesar will have to wait for his till kingdom come.

[91] Cf. the end of Ovid's *Metamorphoses*, which similarly raises the issue of *fama* in its last lines; and which similarly seems to displace Augustus from the position of honour, to favour the poet himself.

[92] Haffter 1957 p. 124.

[93] In a less obvious way, the Aeneid too ends with the antagonist, Turnus: even if his name is not mentioned, the last line is all his. The last word of the *Aeneid* is 'umbras'; perhaps Lucan had in mind his own 'magni nominis umbra'.

not his final defeat, and gives him pride of place only to displace him at the last moment. For those who wish to make the arbitrary assumption that the poem is incomplete, these contradictions will seem to be nothing more than natural confusions resulting from an unplanned and sudden stop. But the contradictions are more organised than such an assumption would allow; the uniqueness of the moment and the manipulation of other classic epic endings tend rather to confirm what the external evidence suggests and what no internal evidence can contradict, that the poem does have an end, and that it is the end Lucan intended it to have. A strange, unconventional end, to be sure, pointing as it does to its own inconclusiveness, avoiding as it does any kind of resolution, but one which in being so preserves the unconventional premises of its subject-matter: evil without alternative, contradiction without compromise, civil war without end.

BIBLIOGRAPHY

Abel, K. (1958) 'Zur Datierung von Cäsars Bellum Civile', *MH* 15: 56–74

Ahl, F.M. (1976) *Lucan: an introduction.* Cornell Studies in Classical Philology 39, Ithaca
  (1984) 'The art of safe criticism in Greece and Rome', *AJPh* 105: 174–208
  (1985) *Metaformations: soundplay and wordplay in Ovid and other classical poets.* Ithaca

Albrecht, M. von (1970) 'Der Dichter Lucan und die epische Tradition'. In *Entretiens Hardt* 15 (Lucain). Geneva: 267–308

Amandry, P. (1950) *La Mantique apollinienne à Delphes.* Paris

Aumont, J. (1968) 'Caton en Libye (Lucain Pharsale IX 294–949)', *REA* 70: 304–20

Austin, R.G. ed. (1977) *P. Vergili Maronis Aeneidos Liber Sextus.* Oxford

Bachofen, A. (1972) *Cäsars und Lucans Bellum Civile: ein Inhaltsvergleich.* Diss. Zürich

Baldini Moscadi, L. (1976) 'Osservazioni sull' episodio magico del VI libro della "Farsaglia" di Lucano', *Stud. It. Fil. Class.* 48: 140–99.

Barratt, P. ed. (1979) *M. Annaei Lucani Belli Civilis liber V.* Amsterdam

Barwick, K. (1938) 'Caesars Commentarii und das Corpus Caesarianum', *Philologus suppl.* 31/2

Bayet, J. (1946) 'La Morte de la Pythie'. In *Mélanges dédiés à la mémoire de Félix Grat* Vol. I, 53–76.

Benario, H.W. (1983) 'The carmen De Bello Actiaco and early imperial epic', *ANRW* II 30.3: 1656–62

Berthold, H. (1977) 'Beobachtungen zu den Epilogen Lucans', *Helikon* 17: 218–25

Bloom, H. (1973) *The anxiety of influence.* Oxford

Bohnenkamp, K.E. (1977) 'Zum Nero-Elogium in Lucans Bellum Civile', *MH* 34: 235–48
  (1979) 'Zu Lucan 1.674–95', *Gymnasium* 86: 171–7

Bourgery, A. 'La Géographie dans Lucain', *Rev. de Phil.* series 3, vol. 2 (1928A) 25–40
  (1928B) 'Lucain et la magie', *REL* 6: 299–313

Bramble, J.C. (1982) 'Lucan'. In *The Cambridge history of classical literature*, vol. 2: 533–57

Brink, C.O. (1971) *Horace on Poetry: the Ars Poetica*. Cambridge

Brisset, J. (1964) *Les Idées politiques de Lucain*. Paris

Bruère, R.T. (1950) 'The scope of Lucan's historical epic', *CPh* 45: 217–35

(1951) 'Palaepharsalus, Pharsalus, Pharsalia', *CPh* 46: 111–15

Buchheit, V. (1961) 'Lucan's Pharsalia und die Frage der Nichtvollendung', *RhM* 104: 362–5

Cairns, F. (1972) *Generic composition in Greek and Roman poetry*. Edinburgh

Casson, L. (1971) *Ships and seamanship in the ancient world*. Princeton

Cattin, A. (1963) 'La Géographie dans les tragédies de Sénèque'. *Latomus* 22: 685–703

Conte, G.B. (1966) 'Il proemio della Pharsalia'. *Maia* 18: 42–53

(1970) 'Ennio e Lucano', *Maia* 22: 132–8

(1974) *Saggio di commento a Lucano. Pharsalia 6.118–260. L'aristia di Sceva*. Pisa

D'Alton, J.F. (1931) *Roman literary theory and criticism*. New York

De Romilly, J. (1975) *Magic and rhetoric in ancient Greece*. Harvard

Dick, B.F. (1963) 'The technique of prophecy in Lucan', *TAPhA* 94: 37–49

(1965) 'The role of the oracle in Lucan's Bellum Civile', *Hermes* 93: 460–6

(1967) 'Fatum and Fortuna in Lucan's Bellum Civile', *CPh* 62: 235–42

Due, O.S. (1962) 'An essay on Lucan', *Class. & Med.* 22: 68–132

Duff, J.D. (trans.) (1928) *Lucan: the civil war*. Loeb Classical Library, Harvard

Dyson, S.L. (1970) 'Caepio, Tacitus, and Lucan's sacred grove', *CPh* 65: 36–8

Eitrem, S. (1941) 'La Magie comme motif littéraire chez les Grecs et les Romains', *SO* 21: 39–83

Esposito, P. (1987) 'Tra una battaglia e l'altra: tracce ovidiane nella Pharsalia', *Vichiana* 16: 48–70.

(1988) *Il racconto della strage: le battaglie nella Pharsalia*. Naples

Fahz, L. (1904) *De poetarum Romanorum doctrina magica quaestiones selectae*. Giessen

Fairweather, J.A. (1974) 'Fiction in the biographies of ancient writers', *Ancient Society* 5: 231–75

Fantham, E. (1985) 'Caesar and the mutiny: Lucan's reshaping of the historical tradition in De Bello Civili 5.237–373', *CPh* 80: 119–31

Farron, S. (1982) 'The abruptness of the end of the *Aeneid*', *Acta Classica* 25: 136–141

Fauth, W. (1975) 'Die Bedeutung der Nekromantie-Szene in Lucans Pharsalia', *RhM* 118: 325–44.

Feeney, D.C. (1986A) ' "Stat magni nominis umbra": Lucan on the greatness of Pompeius Magnus', *CQ* 36: 239–43.

(1986B) 'Epic hero and epic fable', *Comp. Lit.* 38: 137–158

(1986C) 'History and revelation in Vergil's underworld', *PCPhS* 212: 1–24

Fish, S. (1980) *Is there a text in this class?* Harvard

Fontenrose, J. (1959) *Python: a study of Delphic myth and its origins.* California

(1978) *The Delphic oracle.* California

Frank, E. (1970) 'The structure and scope of Lucan's De Bello Civili', *CB* 46: 59–61

Gabba, E. (1971) 'The Perusine war and triumviral Italy', *HSCPh* 75: 139–60

Gagliardi, D. (1974) 'Lucano e Sallustio', *Boll. Stud. Lat.* 4: 16–21

(1978) 'Osservazioni sul libro X della Pharsalia', *Boll. Stud. Lat.* 8: 245–51

Galinsky, G.K. (1975) *Ovid's Metamorphoses: an introduction to the basic aspects.* Los Angeles

Gassner, J. (1972) *Kataloge im römischen Epos: Vergil – Ovid – Lucan.* Diss. Augsberg

Getty, R.J. ed. (1940) *M. Annaei Lucani De Bello Civili liber I.* Cambridge

(1951) 'East and West in Lucan 1.15 and elsewhere', *CPh* 46: 25–9

Goebel, G.H. (1981) 'Rhetorical and poetical thinking in Lucan's harangues', *TAPhA* 111: 79–94

Goerler, W. (1976) 'Caesars Rubicon-übergang in der Darstellung Lucans'. In *Studien zum antiken Epos, Franz Dirlmeier und Victor Poeschl gewidmet*, ed. H. Goergemanns and E.A. Schmidt, *Beitr. zur klass. Philol.* 72 Meisenheim Hain: 291–308

Goold, G.P. ed. (1977) *Manilius: Astronomica.* Loeb Classical Library, Harvard

Gordon, R. (1987) 'Lucan's Erictho'. In *Homo Viator: classical essays for John Bramble*, ed. M. Whitby and P.R. Hardie, Bristol: 231–41.

Grenade, P. (1950) 'Le Mythe de Pompée et les Pompéiens sous les Césars', *REA* 52: 28–63

Griffin, M.T. (1984) *Nero: the end of a dynasty.* London

Grimal, P. (1960) 'L'Éloge de Néron au début de la Pharsale est-il ironique?' *REL* 38: 296–305

(1970) 'Le Poète et l'histoire'. In *Entretiens Hardt* 15 (Lucain). Geneva: 51–117

(1977) *La Guerre civile de Pétrone dans ces rapports avec la Pharsale.* Paris

Griset, E. (1954) 'Lucanea I: Le due Farsaglie', *Riv. di Stud. Class.* 2: 109–13

(1955) 'Lucanea IV: L'Elogio Neroniano', *Riv. di Stud. Class.* 3: 134–8

Guillemin, A. (1951) 'L'Inspiration Virgilienne dans la Pharsale', *REL* 29: 214–27

Haffter, H. (1957) 'Dem schwanken Zünglein lauschend wachte Cäsar dort', *MH* 14: 118–26

Hardie, P.R. (1985) 'Cosmological patterns in the *Aeneid*', *PLLS* 5: 85–97

(1986) *Vergil's Aeneid: Cosmos and Imperium.* Oxford

Harrison, G.W.M. (1979) 'Lucan *Bellum Civile* 5.27–29: a reply', *CB* 55: 77–8

Haskins, C.E. (1887) *M. Annaei Lucani Pharsalia* (with introduction by W.E. Heitland). London

Häussler, R. (1978) *Studien zum historischen Epos der Antike II: Das historische Epos von Lucan bis Silius und seine Theorie.* Heidelberg

Heitland, *see* Haskins.

Henderson, J.G.W. (1976) *Anecdote and Satire in Phaedrus: commentary and discussion.* Diss. Oxford

(1988) 'Lucan / The word at war'. In *The Imperial Muse: Ramus essays on Roman literature of the empire* ed. A.J. Boyle, Victoria: 122–64

Henry, J. (1889) *Aeneidea* (Vol. III). Dublin

Heyke, W. (1970) *Zur Rolle der Pietas bei Lucan.* Diss. Heidelberg

Hinds, S.E. (1987) *The metamorphosis of Persephone.* Cambridge

Hofmann, H. (1986) 'Ovid's *Metamorphoses: carmen perpetuum, carmen deductum*', *PLLS* 5: 223–41

Hope Simpson, R. and Lazenby, J.F. (1970) *The catalogue of ships in Homer's Iliad.* Oxford

Hosius, C. ed. (1905) *M. Annaei Lucani De Bello Civili libri decem* (2nd edn.). Leipzig

Housman, A.E. ed. (1970) *M. Annaei Lucani Belli Civilis libri decem.* Reprint of 2nd edn., 1927. Oxford

Hübner, U. (1975) 'Studien zur Pointentechnik in Lucans Pharsalia', *Hermes* 103: 200–11

(1984) 'Episches und Elegisches am Anfang des dritten Buches der "Pharsalia"', *Hermes* 112: 227–39

Jal, P. (1965) 'Nature et signification politique de l'oeuvre de Florus', *REL* 43: 358–83

Jenkinson, J.R. (1974) 'Sarcasm in Lucan 1.33–66', *CR* 24: 8–9

Johnson, W.R. (1987) *Momentary monsters: Lucan and his heroes.* Cornell Studies in Classical Philology 47, Ithaca

Kenney, E.J. (1958) 'Nequitiae poeta'. In *Ovidiana*, ed. N.I. Herescu. Paris: 201–9

(1973) 'The style of the *Metamorphoses*'. In *Ovid*, ed. J.W. Binns., London: 116–53

Kirk, G.S. (1985) *The Iliad: a commentary*, Vol. I. Cambridge

Knauer, G.N. (1964) *Die Aeneis und Homer*. Göttingen

Kraner, F. and Hofmann, F. ed. (1906) *C. Iulii Caesaris commentarii de bello civili*. Berlin

Kromayer, J. and Veith, G. (1924) *Schlachten-Atlas zur antiken Kriegsgeschichte*. Leipzig

Kühner, R. and Stegmann, C. (1912–1914) *Ausführliche Grammatik der lateinischen Sprache*. Hanover

Lapidge, M. (1979) 'Lucan's imagery of cosmic dissolution', *Hermes* 107: 344–70

Lausberg, M. (1985) 'Lucan und Homer', *ANRW* II 32.3: 1565–1622

Lebek, W.D. (1976) *Lucans Pharsalia: Dichtungsstruktur und Zeitbezug*. Göttingen

Le Bonniec, H. (1970) 'Lucain et la religion'. In *Entretiens Hardt* 15 (Lucain). Geneva: 161–95

Lefkowitz, M.R. (1981) *The lives of the Greek poets*. London

Levi, M. (1949) 'Il proemio della "Pharsalia"', *RFC* n.s. 27: 71–8

Lieberg, G. (1982) *Poeta Creator*. Amsterdam

Linn, H.-W. (1971) *Studien zur Aemulatio des Lucan*. Diss. Heidelberg

Lintott, A.W. (1971) 'Lucan and the history of the civil war', *CQ* 21: 480–505

Longi, E. (1955) 'Tre episodi del poema di Lucano'. In *Studi in onore di Gino Funaioli*. Rome: 181–8

Luck, G. (1985) *Arcana mundi*. Baltimore

Lyne, R.O.A.M. (1987) *Further voices in Vergil's* Aeneid. Oxford

MacMullen, R. (1967) *Enemies of the Roman Order*. Harvard

Marti, B.M. (1945) 'The meaning of the Pharsalia', *AJP* 66: 352–76

(1958) *Arnulfi Aurelianensis glosule super Lucanum*, Papers and Monographs of the American Academy in Rome XVIII

(1970) 'La structure de la *Pharsale*'. In *Entretiens Hardt* 15 (Lucain). Geneva: 3–38

Martindale, C.A. (1980) 'Lucan's Nekuia'. In *Stud. Lat. Lit. II* (ed. C. Deroux), *Coll. Latomus* 168: 367–77

(1981) 'Lucan's Hercules: padding or paradigm? A note on De Bello Civili 4.589–660', *SO* 56: 71–80.

(1984) 'The politician Lucan', *G&R* 31: 64–79

Mayer, R. ed. (1981) *Lucan Civil War VIII*. Warminster

(1986) 'Geography and Roman poets', *G&R* 33: 47–54

Mendell, C.W. (1942) 'Lucan's rivers', *YCS* 8: 3–22

Momigliano, A. (1942) 'Camillus and Concord', *CQ* 36: 111–20

Morford, M.P.O. (1967) *The poet Lucan*. Oxford

Morrison, J.S. and Coates, J.F. (1986) *The Athenian trireme.* Cambridge

Narducci, E. (1973) 'Il tronco di Pompeo (Troia e Roma nella Pharsalia)', *Maia* 25: 317–25

(1974) 'Sconvolgimenti naturali e profezia delle guerre civili: Phars. 1.522–695', *Maia* 26: 97–110

(1980) 'Cesare e la Patria (ipotesi su *Phars.* 1.185–92)', *Maia* 32: 175–8

(1985) 'Ideologia e tecnica allusiva nella "Pharsalia"', *ANRW* II 32.3: 1538–64

Newman, J.K. (1967) 'The concept of *vates* in Augustan poetry', *Coll. Latomus* 59:

Newmyer, S. (1983) 'Imagery as a means of character portrayal in Lucan'. In *Stud. Lat. Lit. III* (ed. C. Deroux), *Coll. Latomus* 180: 226–52

Nisbet, R.G.M. 'The oak and the axe: Symbolism in Seneca *Hercules Oetaeus* 1618ff'. In *Homo Viator: classical essays for John Bramble*, ed. M. Whitby and P.R. Hardie., Bristol 1987, 243–51

Nisbet, R.G.M. and Hubbard, M. (1970) *A commentary on Horace: Odes book I.* Oxford

(1978) *A commentary on Horace: Odes book II.* Oxford

Nock, A.D. (1926) 'The proem of Lucan', *CR* 40: 17–18

O'Higgins, D. (1988) 'Lucan as *vates*', *Class. Ant.* 7: 208–26

Oliver, R.P. (1972) 'Lucan's naval battle'. In *Homenaje a Antonio Tovar*, Madrid: 323–34

Opelt, I. (1957) 'Die Seeschlacht vor Massilia bei Lucan', *Hermes* 85: 435–45

Paoletti, L. (1963) 'Lucano magico e Virgilio', *Atene e Roma* 8: 11–26

Parke, H.W. (1967) *Greek oracles.* London

Parke, H.W. and Wormell, D.E.W. (1956) *The Delphic oracle.* Oxford

Parke, H.W. (1988), ed. B.C. McGing, *Sibyls and Sibylline prophecy in classical antiquity.* London

Paschalis, M. (1986) 'Virgil and the Delphic oracle'. *Philologus* 130: 44–68

Pfeiffer, R. (1968) *A history of classical scholarship from the beginnings to the end of the Hellenistic age.* Oxford

Pfligersdorffer, G. (1959) 'Lucan als Dichter des geistigen Widerstandes', *Hermes* 87: 344–77

Phillips, O.C. (1968) 'Lucan's grove', *CPh* 63: 296–300

Pichon, R. (1912) *Les sources de Lucain.* Paris

Rambaud, M. (1960) 'L'opposition de Lucain au Bellum Civile de César', *Inf. Lit.* 12: 155–62

(1970) ed. *C. Iulius Caesar, de bello civili, liber primus.* Paris

Reitzenstein, E. (1935) 'Das neue Kunstwollen in den Amores Ovids', *RhM* 84: 62–88

Rose, H.J. (1913) 'The witch scene in Lucan', *TAPhA* 44 Proceedings l–lii

Rose, K.F.C. (1966) 'Problems of chronology in Lucan's career', *TAPhA* 97: 379–96

(1971) *The date and author of the Satyricon.* Leiden

Rosner-Siegel, J.A. (1983) 'The oak and the lightning: Lucan B.C. 1.135–57', *Athenaeum* n.s. 61: 165–77

Rostagni, A. (1944) *Svetonio: de Poetis e biografi minori.* Turin

Rowland, R.J. (1969) 'The significance of Massilia in Lucan', *Hermes* 97: 204–8

Rutz, W. (1960) 'Amor mortis bei Lucan', *Hermes* 88: 462–75

(1963) 'Die Träume des Pompeius in Lucans Pharsalia', *Hermes* 91: 334–45

(1965) 'Lucan 1943–1963', *Lustrum* 9: 234–340

(1985) 'Lucans Pharsalia im Lichte der neuesten Forschung', *ANRW* II 32.3: 1457–1537

Samse R. (1942) 'Lukans Exkurs über Thessalien VI 333–412', *RhM* 91: 250–68

Sandbach, F.H. (1975) *The Stoics.* London

Saylor, C.F. (1978) '*Belli spes improba*: the theme of walls in Lucan, Pharsalia VI', *TAPhA* 108: 243–57

(1982) 'Curio and Antaeus: the African episode of Lucan Pharsalia 4', *TAPhA* 112: 169–77

(1986) 'Wine, blood, and water: the imagery of Lucan Pharsalia IV. 148–401', *Eranos* 84: 149–56

Schönberger, O. (1957) 'Zur Komposition des Lucan', *Hermes* 85: 251–4

(1960) 'Leitmotivische wiederholte Bilder bei Lucan', *RhM* 103: 81–90

(1961) *Untersuchungen zur Wiederholungstechnik Lucans.* Diss. Heidelberg

Schrempp, O. (1964) *Prophezeiung und Rückschau in Lucans Bellum Civile.* Diss. Winterthur

Schwemmler, F. (1916) *De Lucano Manilii imitatore.* Diss. Leipzig

Shackleton Bailey, D.R. (1987) 'Lucan revisited', *PCPhS* 33: 74–91

Sharrock, A.R. (1988) *Reading Ovid's* Ars Amatoria: *selected passages from book II.* Diss. Cambridge

Shoaf, R.A. (1978) ' "Certius exemplar sapientis viri": rhetorical subversion and subversive rhetoric in Pharsalia 9', *PhQ* 57: 143–54

Skutsch, O. ed. (1985) *The Annals of Quintus Ennius.* Oxford

Spoerri, W. (1959) *Späthellenistische Berichte über Welt, Kultur, und Götter.* Basel

Sullivan, J.P. (1985) *Literature and politics in the age of Nero.* Ithaca

Syme, R. (1987) 'Exotic names, notably in Seneca's tragedies', *Acta Classica* 30: 49–64

Syndikus, H.P. (1958) *Lucans Gedicht vom Bürgerkrieg*. Diss. Munich

Tartari Chersoni, M. (1979) 'Lucano e la tradizione epica Virgiliana: ripresa e contrapposizione nel libro VI del Bellum Civile'. *Boll. Stud. Lat.* 9: 25–39

Thomas, R.F. (1983) 'Callimachus, the *Victoria Berenices*, and Roman poetry', *CQ* 33: 92–113

Thompson, L. (1964) 'Lucan's apotheosis of Nero', *CPh* 59: 147–53

Thompson, L. and Bruère, R.T. (1968) 'Lucan's use of Vergilian reminiscence', *CPh* 63: 1–21

(1970) 'The Virgilian background of Lucan's fourth book', *CPh* 65: 152–72

Thomson, J.O. (1951) 'Place names in Latin poetry', *Latomus* 10: 433–8

Tucker, R.A. (1987) 'Tacitus and the death of Lucan', *Latomus* 46: 330–7

Volphilac, J. (1978) 'Lucain et l'Égypte dans la scène de nécromancie de la Pharsale VI 413–80 à la lumière des papyri grecs magiques', *REL* 56: 272–88

Walsh, G.B. (1984) *The varieties of enchantment*. North Carolina

Weber, C.F. (1828–9) 'Dissertatio editoris de eo quod summum est in Pharsalia'. In his edition of Lucan, Leipzig vol. 2: 569–90

Westerburg, E. (1882) 'Lucan, Florus und Pseudo-Victor', *RhM* 37: 35–49

Williams, G. (1968) *Tradition and originality in Roman poetry*. Oxford

(1978) *Change and Decline*. California

Wilson, A.M. (1985) 'The prologue to Manilius 1', *PLLS* 5: 283–98

Wimmel, W. (1960) *Kallimachos in Rom. Hermes Einzelschriften* 16

Wünsch, M. (1930) *Lucan-Interpretationen*. Leipzig

INDEX